INTRODUCTION TO COMPUTER GRAPHICS DESIGN PROFESSIONAL

By Daniel Bouweraerts

Introduction to Computer Graphics—Design Professional

by Daniel Bouweraerts

Executive Editor:
Nicole Jones Pinard

Production Editor:
Pamela Elizian

Marketing Manager:
Joy Stark

Senior Product Manager:
Christina Kling Garrett

Developmental Editor:
Barbara Clemens

Text Designer:
Ann Small

Associate Product Manager:
Emilie Perreault

Composition House:
GEX Publishing Services

Illustrator:
Philip Brooker

Editorial Assistant:
Shana Rosenthal

QA Manuscript Reviewers:
Jeff Schwartz, Ashlee Welz, Susan Whalen

Cover Design:
Philip Brooker

Summing It Up, pg. 118 Left, © Courtesy of Jeffrey Hogan

Summing It Up, pg. 118 Right, © Courtesy of Michael Ganschow-Green

Design Project, pg. 124 Top, © Courtesy of Michael Ganschow-Green

Design Project, pg. 124 Middle, © Courtesy of Jeffrey Hogan

Design Project, pg. 124 Bottom, © Courtesy of Honor West

3-45, pg. 125, © Courtesy of Amy Guip/www.amyguip.com

Chapter 4, Page Layout Software

4-1, pg. 129, © Cary Graphic Arts Collection/Rochester Institute of Technology

4-2, pg. 129 Top, © Tony Leone/www.leone-design.com

4-2, pg. 129 Bottom, © Courtesy of Judy Walker Design & Illustration, www.theequestriannews.com

4-3, pg. 129 Top, © Courtesy of Quark Incorporated

4-3, pg. 129 Bottom, © Courtesy of Adobe Systems Incorporated

Summing It Up, pg. 170 Left, © Courtesy of Michael Ganschow-Green

Summing It Up, pg. 170 Right, The Equestrian News, © Courtesy of Judy Walker Design & Illustration, www.theequestriannews.com

4-57, pg. 176 Left, © Courtesy of Honor West

4-57, pg. 176 Right, © Courtesy of Micheline Crawford

4-58, pg. 177 Left, © Courtesy of Hirshorn Zuckerman Design Group/www.hzdg.com

4-58, pg. 177 Center, © Courtesy of Hirshorn Zuckerman Design Group/www.hzdg.com

4-58, pg. 177 Bottom Right, © Courtesy of designer James Evelock/HZDG and the Mills Corporation

Chapter 5, Electronic Publishing and Proofing

5-1, pg. 181, © Hemera Photo Objects

5-2, pg. 181, © Hemera Photo Objects

5-3, pg. 181, © Courtesy of John Warnock

5-5, pg. 185, © Courtesy of Christina Micek

5-15, pg. 195, © Courtesy of Epson Worldwide

5-16, pg. 197, © Courtesy of Xerox Corporation

5-17, pg. 204, © Courtesy of Xerox Corporation

Chapter 6, Production and Reproduction Technologies for Print Media

6-1, pg. 209, © Courtesy of Dan Bouweraerts

6-9, pg. 219, Left, © Heidelberg USA, Incorporated

6-9, pg. 219, Right, © Heidelberg USA, Incorporated

6-12, pg. 223, © Heidelberg USA, Incorporated

6-13, pg. 223, © Heidelberg USA, Incorporated

6-14, pg. 223, © Heidelberg USA, Incorporated

6-16, pg. 225, © Heidelberg USA, Incorporated

6-18, pg. 226, © Heidelberg USA, Incorporated

6-20, pg. 227, © Heidelberg USA, Incorporated

6-22, pg. 228, © Heidelberg USA, Incorporated

6-24, pg. 229, © Courtesy of Xerox Corporation

6-25, pg. 230, © Courtesy of Hewlett Packard 2004 Hewlett-Packard Development Company, L.P.

6-27, pg. 231, © Courtesy of Hewlett Packard 2004 Hewlett-Packard Development Company, L.P.

Summing It Up, pg. 232, © Heidelberg USA, Incorporated

Design Project, pg. 238 Left and Right, © Heidelberg USA, Incorporated

6-28, pg. 239, © Courtesy of Dan Bouweraerts

Chapter 7, Electronic Design for Digital Media

7-1, pg. 243, Courtesy of Cold North Wind's Paper of Record Web site of historical newspapers (www.paperofrecord.com)

7-2, pg. 244, © Courtesy of Alias/ Created by Vector Zero

7-3, pg. 245, © Courtesy of Jason Allen Bronson

7-8, pg. 252, © Courtesy of Don Gerds

7-10, pg. 252, © Courtesy of Kirk Treakle/Alamy

7-11, pg. 253, © Courtesy of Alias/ Created by ARTVPS, LTD.

7-12, pg. 253, © Courtesy of Jason Allen Bronson

7-15, pg. 259, © Courtesy of Omnica

Summing It Up, pg. 260 Left, © Courtesy of Jason Allen Bronson

Summing It Up, pg. 260 Right, © Courtesy of CLM Design

7-16, pg. 266, © Courtesy of Jason Allen Bronson

7-17, pg. 267 Left, © Courtesy of Jason Allen Bronson

7-17, pg. 267 Right, © Courtesy of CLM Design

Design Professional Series Vision

The Design Professional Series is your guide to today's hottest multimedia applications. These comprehensive books teach the concepts and skills behind the application, showing you how to apply smart design principles to multimedia products, such as dynamic graphics, animation, Web sites, and video.

A team of design professionals including multimedia instructors, students, authors, and editors worked together to create this series. We recognized the unique learning environment of the digital media or multimedia classroom and have created a series that:

- Gives you comprehensive explanations
- Offers in-depth explanation of the "why" behind a skill
- Includes creative projects for additional practice
- Explains concepts clearly using full-color visuals

It was our goal to create a book that speaks directly to the multimedia and design community—one of the most rapidly growing computer fields today.

This series was designed to appeal to the creative spirit. We would like to thank Philip Brooker for developing the inspirational artwork found on each chapter opener and book cover. We would also like to give special thanks to Ann Small of A Small Design Studio for developing a sophisticated and instructive book design.

—The Design Professional Series

Author's Vision

In writing this book, my goal has been to create a unique book that would help to give the firm foundation necessary to becoming successful in graphic design. I have tried to strike a balance between design theory and technology. With the incredible technology growth over the years, it has been an increasing challenge to keep students focused in both areas. Although learning the technology is necessary, it must be within the context of good graphic design principles.

Yet, there are many levels of technology to learn. Many step-by-step books exist that go into depth on individual applications, but I have felt the need for a text that presents an overview of the available applications for both print and digital media. Once students understand the context of each application and have learned the basic skills presented here, they can move on to more in-depth application study.

This is my first book and I've learned a lot — especially that this is hard work! Luckily, I had a strong support team. There are so many people to thank. First to Nicole Pinard, the first person to believe that this book was necessary and that I could write it; I also thank her for giving me the dream editorial team to put it together: Thanks to my Developmental Editor Barbara Clemens, the true author behind the author, the one who kept me organized and kept me moving forward when the words sometimes weren't there. To Senior Project Manager Christina Kling Garrett, for always having words of encouragement to help me keep going. To Technical Editors Jeff Schwartz, Ashlee Welz, and Susan Whalen, whose knowledge and expertise helped to direct so many areas of this book. To Production Editor Pam Elizian and the entire GEX production team; as a fellow designer who's worked in the trenches for many years, I want you to know you are the true artists of our industry! And to Christina Micek, our diligent and creative photo researcher, who helped us find the beautiful images in this book. And many thanks to the talented artists whose work appears in every chapter and who kindly granted us permission to use their works.

Our two manuscript reviewers, Susan Oakes, Briarcliffe College, and John Sledd, New River Community College, get extra-large thanks; their insights and support helped to shape the content of this book and helped me to expand my own knowledge in areas where I needed help. Thanks also to Diane Lee at Maxon USA for her able assistance. Another big thanks goes to the teachers who shaped my career, Don Gerds, my true mentor from Santa Monica College; and Pierre Rademaker, Chuck Jennings, and Bob Desham and all of the amazing instructors in the Graphic Communications department at Cal Poly San Luis Obispo.

Which leads me to my regular day job at Truckee Meadows Community College (TMCC). I am so lucky to be able to work at something I love, and that's teaching. TMCC is an incredible institution for learning, and everyone who works at TMCC gives it their very best, every day. Thank you to fellow professor Ron Marston, a true friend who inspired many of the projects in this book. To Grace Kendall, our new addition and an incredibly creative and talented designer. To my hallmates and friends Ellis, Ric, Dennis, and Brian, for always having a smile and words of encouragement. And to all of the graphic communications students past, present, and future, my goal will always be your success.

And finally I would like to dedicate this book to my two daughters, Andrea and Erica. No matter what happens or where life takes us, you are both the true shining lights in my universe.

SERIES & AUTHOR VISION

Introduction

Welcome to *Introduction to Computer Graphics—Design Professional*. This book builds a foundation in design theories and concepts to foster student creativity. This text is organized into two sections — one dedicated to print media and the other to digital media. Within these sections, the chapters introduce the tools that have revolutionized computer graphics, including software, production and reproduction technologies, and electronic publishing and proofing. Design tips and sidebars address topics related to chapter content.

What You'll Learn

The beginning of every concept features a What You'll Learn bullet and graphic. The bullet gives you an at-a-glance look at the concept covered in the chapter so that before you start each concept, you will know what "territory" it will cover. Above the bullet is a "sneak preview" of part of a screen or a piece of artwork from the concept.

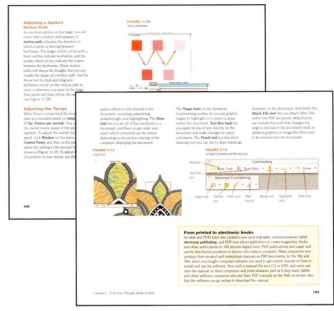

Chapter Introduction

Before the first concept in each chapter, a chapter introduction lays the groundwork for the concepts that follow. These introductory pages give a brief historical perspective on the chapter topic, leading up to the present time, and/or explain relevant terminology and processes that help you understand the context of the concepts that follow.

Software Overview

The majority of the chapters describe the leading software packages in a given area; in these chapters, the first concept always features a software overview. It explains the uses of each package, briefly compares their major features, and displays a screen of each one. This way you learn what the major industry players are in each software category and why a firm with particular needs might select one over another.

Software Discussion and Instructions

Almost all chapters that describe software packages contain commands, within the text, for completing some basic software procedures using some typical tools. These steps are generic, not tied to any particular Data File. Combined with explanations of selected tools and other interface elements, these instructions give you brief, hands-on experience that lets you view the software package's basic capabilities, helps you appreciate a program's strengths, and prepares you for a more comprehensive course in the application.

Summing It Up

At the end of the last concept in each chapter, a Summing It Up page provides a short summary of the major points covered in the chapter. Each Summing It Up page also contains design samples by professional and student designers that illustrate the concepts and skills covered.

Projects

This book contains a variety of end-of-chapter material for additional practice and reinforcement. The **Key Terms** list includes all boldfaced terms and concepts covered in the chapter, letting you review the terms to check your mastery of the chapter material. The **Chapter Review** contains questions about chapter content that you can use as a self-test.

The chapter concludes with four projects: two Project Builders, one Design Project, and one Gallery. The **Project Builders** require you to apply the concepts and software skills you've learned in the chapter to create a project. The One Step Beyond and Two Steps Beyond features let you extend your knowledge further into the concepts. In the **Design Project**, you create a project from scratch, with less guidance. The **Gallery** features real-world work by professional designers and asks you to evaluate the works based on how they illustrate the concepts discussed in the chapter.

What Instructor Resources Are Available with This Book?

The Instructor Resources CD-ROM is Course Technology's way of putting the resources and information needed to teach and learn effectively into your hands. All the resources are available for both Macintosh and Windows operating systems, and many of the resources can be downloaded from *www.course.com*.

Instructor's Manual

Available as an electronic file, the Instructor's Manual is quality-assurance tested and includes chapter overviews and detailed lecture topics for each chapter, with teaching tips. The Instructor's Manual is available on the Instructor Resources CD-ROM, or you can download it from *www.course.com*.

Syllabus

Prepare and customize your course easily using this sample course outline (available on the Instructor Resources CD-ROM).

PowerPoint Presentations

Each chapter has a corresponding PowerPoint presentation that you can use in lectures, distribute to your students, or customize to suit your course.

Figure Files

Figure Files contain all the figures from the book in bitmap format. Use the figure files to create transparency masters or include them in a PowerPoint presentation.

Data Files for Students

To complete most of the chapters in this book, your students will need Data Files. Put them on a file server for students to copy. The Data Files are available on the Instructor Resources CD-ROM and the Review Pack, and can also be downloaded from *www.course.com*.

Solutions to Exercises

Solution Files are Data Files completed with comprehensive sample answers. Use these files to evaluate your students' work. Or, distribute them electronically or in hard copy so students can verify their work. Sample solutions to all lessons and end-of-chapter material are also provided.

Test Bank and Test Engine

ExamView is a powerful testing software package that allows instructors to create and administer printed, computer (LAN-based), and Internet exams. ExamView includes hundreds of questions that correspond to the topics covered in this text, enabling students to generate detailed study guides that include page references for further review. The computer-based and Internet testing components allow students to take exams at their computers, and also save the instructor time by grading each exam automatically.

CHAPTER 1   ELECTRONIC DESIGN FOR PRINT MEDIA

CONTENTS

CHAPTER 2 | **VECTOR-DRAW SOFTWARE**

CHAPTER 3 — RASTER/PAINT SOFTWARE

CONTENTS

CHAPTER 6 — PRODUCTION AND REPRODUCTION TECHNOLOGIES FOR PRINT MEDIA

CHAPTER 7 — ELECTRONIC DESIGN FOR DIGITAL MEDIA

CONTENTS

CHAPTER 12 **CONCEPTS OF 3-D DESIGN AND ANIMATION**

Intended Audience

This text is designed for beginning graphic design students who want an overview of graphics concepts as well as the most widely used software packages in both print and electronic media. It is also intended for students who want a thorough look at production and reproduction technologies used in today's print and electronic publishing businesses, and the role of the graphic designer throughout the design and production process.

Approach

This text is unique in its approach: It is a conceptual presentation of design principles, software applications, and production technologies, combined with brief steps that allow students to get a hands-on introduction to most of the applications. It assumes that after this introductory presentation, students will proceed to more specific texts and courses for each application to learn details.

The software sections are intended to give an overview of the major packages in each area, and in many cases give steps on how to complete basic tasks. Where possible, the available packages are compared and contrasted so that students will feel comfortable discussing the benefits and features of each one in a work environment.

The end-of-chapter material contains:

- **Chapter Review questions** to help students check their understanding of major chapter concepts;
- **Project Builders** that use the skills taught in the chapters, sometimes modifying supplied Data Files. These exercises assume that students will have access to a more detailed application text, if they want to take their projects further. Project Builders also feature One Step Beyond and Two Steps Beyond, which allow students to extend their knowledge and experience.
- **Design Projects** are open-ended tasks that allow students to integrate all of the software and design skills to create a project from scratch.
- The **Gallery** at the end of each chapter shows professionally designed works and asks students to critique them, using the design principles and software knowledge they have gained.

Figures

The screen shots in this text were taken on a Macintosh computer; for applications that are also on the PC platform, screens will vary slightly. Students using a Macintosh computer may see differences in dialog boxes, depending on whether they have expanded particular sections.

Conceptual art includes diagrams to help students understand processes as well as print technologies. The text shows numerous design examples throughout that illustrate the principles discussed. Examples on the Summing It Up and Design Project sections are by both professional and student designers.

Data Files

Selected Project Builders and Design Projects ask students to open files supplied in the Data Files for this text. See the inside back cover of this book for information on how to obtain Data Files. Students then download the files to a location they select, such as a hard drive, a network server, or a Zip drive. The instructions in the lessons refer to "the location where you store your Data Files" when referring to the Data Files for this book. The Data Files also include animation files for selected chapters, for cases where a screen shot cannot adequately represent the concepts.

Student Online Companion

The Student Online Companion is a Web page containing links to Web sites discussed in the chapters. Because the Web is such a dynamic environment and URLs change frequently, when students are sent to a Web site, the text tells student to "Connect to the Internet, go to www.course.com, navigate to the page for this book, click the Student Online Companion link, then click the link for this chapter." The site also contains references to supplementary resources the author feels will assist students who want to learn more on a particular area, and selected additional materials.

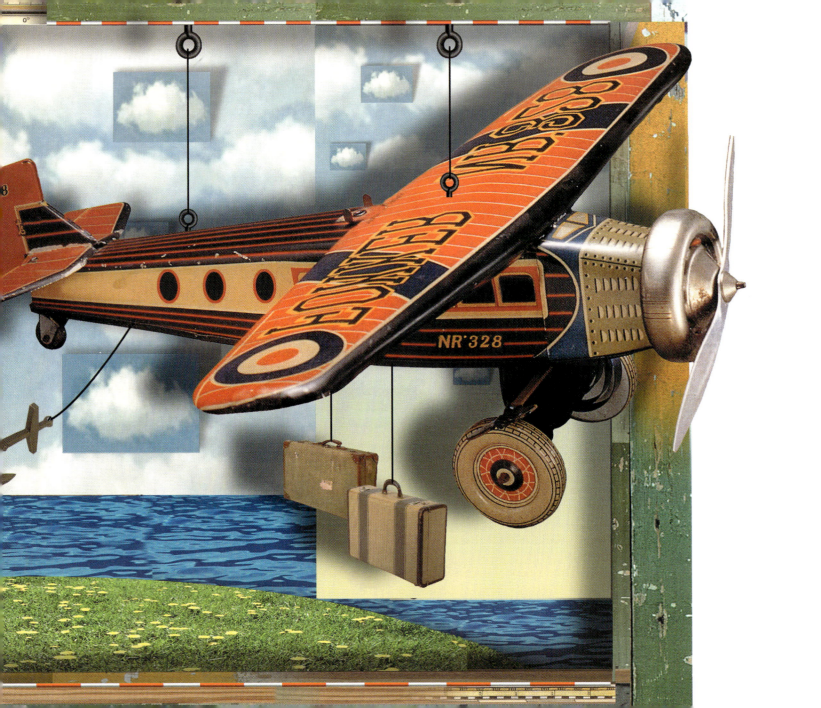

CHAPTER 1

ELECTRONIC DESIGN FOR PRINT MEDIA

3

ELECTRONIC DESIGN FOR PRINT MEDIA

Introduction

Computer graphics is a relatively new industry. It began with three major product introductions in 1984 and 1985. The Apple Macintosh was the first desktop computer that was easy to use and that had enough graphics power to let users command the computer using a mouse. The second product was the Apple LaserWriter laser printer, which offered enough speed and resolution to print graphics-quality images. The LaserWriter used the Postscript page description language to process graphics files at higher resolutions than was possible with previous desktop printers. The third product was electronic page layout software called Aldus PageMaker, invented by Aldus owner Paul Brainard. PageMaker initially ran exclusively on the Macintosh using the Apple operating system, which made the Macintosh computer very popular in the graphics industry.

Macintosh—the first successful GUI computer

Back in 1979, computers were large machines that required users to know hundreds of typed codes to operate them. But a team at the Xerox Palo Alto Research Center (PARC) developed a new approach to running a computer. The PARC team created an operating system that used a WIMP (windows, icons, menus, and pointers) process to control the computer. This new system was demonstrated to a group of computer engineers from a small, upstart company called Apple Computer. One of the engineers was Steve Jobs, the eventual leader of a development team creating a new desktop-based computer for Apple. Released in 1984, the Macintosh computer was the first to use file and folder icons, drop-down menus, and a mouse to perform actions with the computer. This method of controlling a computer is known as a graphical user interface (or GUI, pronounced "gooey"), and the Macintosh was the first to use it successfully in the commercial marketplace. And the rest, as they say, is history.

FIGURE 1-1

Original Macintosh computer

FIGURE 1-3

First version of Aldus PageMaker

FIGURE 1-2

Original Apple LaserWriter

The Birth of Desktop Publishing

Aldus and Apple were eager to promote their new products, so Brainard coined the term "desktop publishing." Prior to desktop publishing, designers and art directors created hand-drawn presentations using felt-tip markers to show clients their creative ideas. They decided the type style and layout, and had a type house create the type on white photographic paper using a Linotronics photocomposition typesetting machine. Production artists shot logos and photographs on small **process cameras** (specialized cameras that shoot artwork for reproduction on a printing press) and printed them on photographic paper. The production artist then cut out the type and graphic elements and pasted them on a piece of illustration board. Once approved by the client, these **pasteups** (also called **mechanicals** and **camera-ready art**) were sent to a printer, who would shoot them on a larger, highly accurate process camera and reproduce them on graphic arts film. The printer would use this film to produce the aluminum printing plates that would be mounted on a printing press to reproduce the job. See Figure 1-4 for an overview of a designer's traditional workflow.

FIGURE 1-4
Traditional design workflow

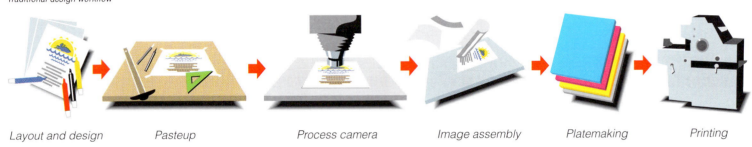

Layout and design   Pasteup   Process camera   Image assembly   Platemaking   Printing

The Design Revolution

Desktop publishing forever changed the way designers created and produced their work. By 1990, many graphics studios and advertising agencies had purchased Macintosh computers, laser printers, and PageMaker software as their primary design tools. With the addition of other software applications like QuarkXPress, Illustrator, FreeHand, and Photoshop, designers could develop all manner of print graphics completely within the electronic environment. Printers and other equipment were also becoming part of the digital revolution: Designers used high-resolution scanners and imagesetters to input images and output film, replacing photocompositors, pasteup boards, and process cameras.

As the 1990s progressed, graphics software and computer systems (both Apple and Windows) became more powerful, and higher quality scanners, imagesetters, platesetters, and digital printers appeared in the industry. The workflow, shown in Figure 1-5, became faster and more efficient, helping designers to create projects that could be produced in less time and with professional quality.

Today "desktop publishing" is considered a dated term. Whether it's called computer graphics, digital design, or electronic design, with all the digital power available at a designer's fingertips, the computer revolution has completely changed the visual communications industry over the last 20 years.

FIGURE 1-5

Today's electronic workflow

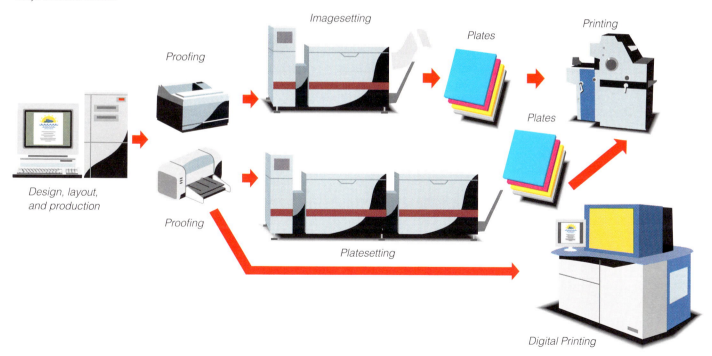

Design, layout, and production

Proofing

Proofing

Imagesetting

Platesetting

Plates

Plates

Printing

Digital Printing

IT STARTS WITH CREATIVITY

What You'll Learn

▶ *In this lesson you will learn about the importance of creativity in visual commu-nications. You will also become familiar with the steps that are part of a designer's creative process.*

About Creativity

Are people born with artistic talent? This is a difficult question to answer, because everyone is born with certain innate skills. Some people are born to be doctors; others are born to be lawyers; some people are born to fix transmissions; and some have the right combination of creative talents to be designers. Artists from Leonardo da Vinci to Paul Rand just seemed to have a natural ability to create great design.

But can **creativity** be learned? Yes and no. The creative process can be learned, as can the theories of design. But the tricky part is putting together creative ability with the processes and theories; not everyone can be taught to make it all work together. But a book, a class, or a workshop on creativity and design can certainly help most people expand the creative abilities they already have. Is understanding how to use design software important? Yes! But no one can create good design without understanding certain basic processes, theories, and concepts.

Do you have to be creative to get a job?

One misconception that people have about the visual communications industry is that you must be highly creative and artistic to get a job. In fact, there are many jobs that require little if any creative skill. Production jobs actually outnumber creative jobs, so don't become frustrated if you discover you aren't the most creative individual. Most of the concepts taught in this book are production-oriented, so if you discover that you work well with the technology, there is a job out there for you!

Meeting Client Needs

Unlike fine artists who often create artwork for themselves, designers and others who work in a visual communications environment, such as filmmakers, Web designers, and commercial photographers, create artwork for someone else: the client. The designer/client relationship governs the entire design process. Successful designers understand this. Other talented designers may not understand the importance of addressing the client's wants and needs. If a client rejects their designs, they may blame the client for not understanding their artistic vision.

The Design Process

As part of the creative process, designers follow a fairly structured methodology, or set of procedures, to come up with creative solutions to clients' design problems. Although individual designers have their own ways of doing the same tasks, you should learn the basic steps in the **design process**. These steps are:

Define the Problem

Research the Project

Create Thumbnails and Roughs

Prepare Comprehensives

Review and Refine the Design

FIGURE 1-6

Leonardo da Vinci drawing

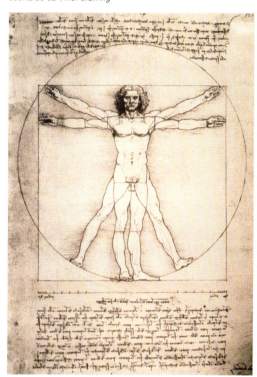

FIGURE 1-7

Paul Rand logo

Each of these steps lets the designer move through a series of **alternative solutions** until the best possible solution comes to the surface. This final alternative will be the one that best solves the client's problem.

Defining the Problem

When you get a job from a client, you first need to **define the problem**. Does the client want an ad or a mailer, a brochure or a poster, a Web site or a multimedia presentation? Sometimes clients don't really know what they want, so it's up to you, the designer, to ask the correct questions to determine what the client's needs are. What budget and time frame are required? Many larger agencies and studios have account executives that deal directly with the client. But in smaller companies it's often the designer who meets with the client and gets the necessary information. Once the problem has been defined, it then moves into the studio or agency as a project.

Researching the Project

It's now time to begin the **research** stage to understand the client and the project. Good research can focus and speed up the design process; poor research can limit the number of successful designs you can produce. It's easy to tell when designers haven't taken the time to research a project properly: Their designs have little relationship to the client's needs and generally don't advance the project very well.

Here's one example of project research: A client wants a designer to create a logo for

FIGURE 1-8
Researching personal watercraft

Visit the company showroom

Look at product brochures

Read magazines and articles about the product

Search the Web

a personal watercraft company. The designer has never used a personal watercraft and doesn't hang out with people that use them. How can the designer possibly create a successful logo if he or she doesn't know anything about the company, its product, or the people who use the product? The designer must research the company, personal watercrafts, and competitive watercraft ads before creating concepts for the logo.

Research today is so much easier than it was 20 years ago. The Internet can provide information on personal watercrafts and your client's competition. But don't rely exclusively on the Internet; you need to do some footwork, too. You could start by visiting the company's showroom and talking to their salespeople and customers. Visit the company's competitors and compare products and services. Find magazines and articles on personal watercraft at the library.

In addition, go to places where personal watercraft are used, talk with the people who own them, get an understanding of the audience that would be viewing the logo. Always do this type of research before you lift a pencil or touch a mouse (see Figure 1-8).

Creating Thumbnails and Roughs

Once you have completed your research, it's time to come up with ideas for the logo. As you get ideas, create thumbnails, which are the way designers "think with their pencils." **Thumbnails** are small, fast sketches that the designer uses to explore many potential solutions. They're simple, with little detail, and rarely use color (see Figure 1-9). Produce thumbnails quickly and in large quantities. You don't need to spend too much time creating small masterpieces. The idea is what's important at this point, and the more ideas the better.

It's also important that you not even consider using a computer during the thumbnail stage. The computer is a powerful tool that can help you develop great design. But creative ideas come from the designer (you), not the computer (a machine). Don't spend time worrying about whether an idea can be done on the computer. Be creative, come up with imaginative concepts. And whatever you come up with, it will eventually work on the computer.

Once you have produced enough thumbnails, review what you have created. You will probably be able to throw out some ideas almost immediately. This is part of the process. As you review each idea, keep asking yourself "Does it solve the client's problem?" Keep reviewing, analyzing, and discarding until you have a manageable number of thumbnails. Somewhere between three and eight usually works, but every project is different.

DESIGNTIP **Make a list**

Another technique that helps designers develop multiple ideas is creating a list. Just start writing anything that pops into your head about the subject; for the personal watercraft, you might jot down "cool, racy, blue." Then review the list and start drawing forms that relate to the words. If you get stuck, walk away from the project, do something else for a while, then come back to it with a fresh mind.

Now it's time for the rough stage, where you begin to develop each idea. A **rough** is a tighter, more visually refined representation of a thumbnail concept. Either manually or on the computer, start to work on required or potential formats, layouts, typography, and color for each idea. Will the design include photographs or illustrations? What will the copy (words) say? How is the finished piece going to be produced? What type of paper will be used? Will there be bindery or other specialty processes? All of these questions affect not only the final look of the piece but also the cost and the production timeframe. The answers to these questions may limit what you can include in your design solution, but creative solutions can always be found.

Preparing Comprehensives

Eventually you will take two to four of the strongest ideas (the number will vary depending on the job and the client) the next step to the comprehensive stage. A

FIGURE 1-9

Thumbnails for personal watercraft logo

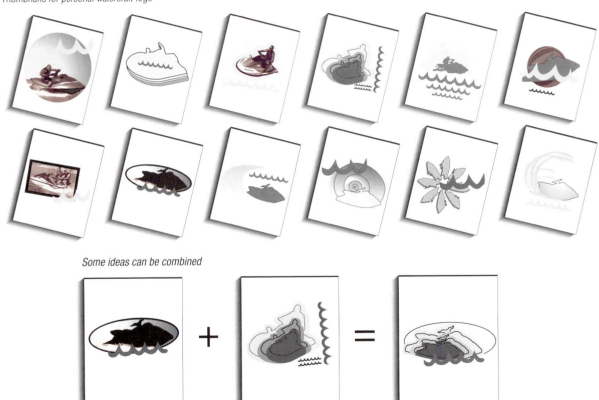

Some ideas can be combined

comprehensive is an accurate (or as accurate as possible) reproduction of potential solutions to the client's problem. Designers almost always create comprehensives (often called "comps") on the computer, with type, photography, and illustrations laid out to show the client what each idea looks like (see Figure 1-10).

Reviewing and Refining the Design

After creating comps, the designer presents them to the client. The client and designer work together to choose which idea will work best. Sometimes they combine different ideas. Sometimes the client doesn't like any of the potential solutions, and the designer has to go back (hopefully with strong client input) and produce more ideas. The process continues until the client is satisfied and agrees to move the project forward into the production phase.

As designers move through the process of creating thumbnails, roughs, and comps, they are constantly using basic elements and principles of design that form the foundation of their visual solutions. The next section covers the elements and principles of good design.

FIGURE 1-10
Producing comprehensives on the computer

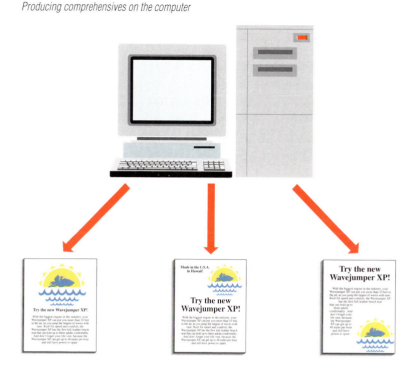

Keeping your creative muscles in shape

Graphic design is like any other skill; you have to keep practicing to get better at it. Gather as much information as you can about design. There are dozens of great design books, as well as books that show work being done by top designers from around the world. Subscribe to an industry magazine. Check out the hundreds of Web sites related to the visual communications industry. Go to museums and galleries. Join a graphics industry club or users group. And drive your family and friends crazy by critiquing every menu and billboard you see.

LEARN THE FUNDAMENTALS OF DESIGN

What You'll Learn

▶ *In this lesson you will learn about important design elements and principles you should keep in mind as you create solutions for creative projects.*

Introducing Design Fundamentals

Like many other disciplines, design has basic principles that all new graphic designers must learn in order to create effective visual communication. These elements and principles are called the **fundamentals of design** and apply to almost every area of a designer's work.

Design elements are the building blocks of design, just as electrons, protons, and neutrons are the building blocks of matter. These elements include:

Line

Any artist's tool or computer software can produce the most basic of elements, a **line**. Children learn that lines can be used to create almost any image they want. A line at its most fundamental level has four properties: length, width, style, and color. Lines can be geometric or expressive.

They can create images or define positions in space. You can use lines to organize a design and to move the viewer's eye into and out of the design. See Figures 1-11, 1-12, and 1-13 for graphics created with lines.

Shape

Lines can be used to create shapes. **Shapes** are the various visual forms that designers use to build designs. Shapes have height and width. The three most fundamental shapes are the circle, the square, and the triangle. From these three shapes all other shapes and forms can be produced. Like lines, shapes have various properties; they can be geometric or expressive. They can be representational (that is, they may look like something you recognize) or they can be abstract. Shapes can appear to be dimensional and can have various colors and textures. In Figure 1-14, shape functions as the predominant design element.

FIGURE 1-11

Lines used to emphasize form and direction

FIGURE 1-12

Lines used to create forms

FIGURE 1-13

Lines as the predominant design element

FIGURE 1-14

Shapes used in graphics

 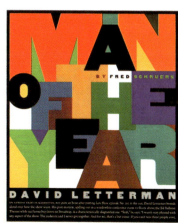

Understanding shapes is a basic skill all designers should have; logo and icon design, for example, require the designer to have strong skills with using and manipulating shapes. Figures 1-15, 1-16, and 1-17 show the use of simple shapes in effective and well-known logos.

Value and Color

Much can be accomplished in black and white design using only lines and shapes. Once you move beyond black and white, you can start to add value and color to a design. **Value** is the use of various shades of gray, also called **grayscale**. Adding value can make a shape more recognizable; it can also add dimension and depth to a form or composition (see Figure 1-18). The use of **color** can expand design concepts even further. Now a banana can be yellow, the sky can be blue, and the grass green.

FIGURE 1-15
Apple Computer logo

FIGURE 1-16
Nike logo

FIGURE 1-17
McDonald's logo

The use of color in a design can depend not only on the creative effect the designer or artist wants to portray but also on the overall budget for a job. Color has become less expensive over the last several years, thanks to digital printing technologies, so more designers are creating full-color projects than ever before. In Figures 1-19 and 1-20, color becomes one of the prominent design elements.

Texture

Texture is a surface pattern that gives the impression of a tactile surface. People associate many types of materials with their textures, such as metal, wood, or glass. In design, you can use texture to create interesting-looking forms or backgrounds (see Figure 1-21). Many traditional art tools such as pastels or charcoal create a distinct texture. Software has attempted to recreate these tools, some more successfully than others. Figure 1-21 uses texture to communicate roughness.

Space

Space is the area or void into which designers place forms. The forms then become **positive images**, and the space where no forms exist becomes **negative space**. Figure 1-22 shows negative space in black and the positive image in blue, white, and yellow. Placing forms into space creates a **composition**. The boundaries of the composition are the **format** of the design.

FIGURE 1-18
Use of value

FIGURE 1-19
Use of color

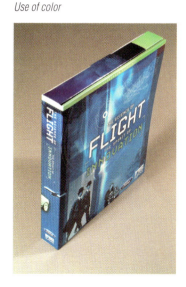

FIGURE 1-20
Use of color

Format is very important for designers to understand, because many jobs require the use of standardized formats, such as an envelope or billboard.

Design principles are the rules designers use to organize elements in space. A designer's ability to apply these principles determines how well he or she can organize elements into an effective, coherent design. These design principles include balance, proximity, alignment, unity, emphasis, and rhythm.

Balance

When images are distributed somewhat equally throughout a design, they create **balance**. There are two types of balance: symmetrical and asymmetrical. **Symmetrical balance** is a very formal structure where the position of forms on one side of a composition matches the position of forms on the other side. This type of balance leads to highly organized designs that are easy to read and visually move through, but these designs can also be stagnant and lack visual interest. **Asymmetrical balance** is a looser, less formal structure in which forms on one part of a design are not repeated in another, corresponding part of the design. In Figure 1-23, the woman on the left side creates a feeling of asymmetrical balace. Asymmetrical balance can make designs harder to read or understand. But this type of balance can also create more exciting, dynamic designs that have more visual movement.

FIGURE 1-21
Use of texture

FIGURE 1-22
Use of space

Proximity and Alignment

Designers must create a visual organization within a design project so the viewer can understand the message or messages being communicated. They achieve this communication by grouping elements that work together, known as **proximity**. You can achieve proximity in many ways, including grouping by content, shape, and color. You can also create proximity by lining up elements to create columns or visual (not actual) lines to move the eye through the design. This practice, called **alignment**, can help organize and present information more effectively. The magazine cover in Figure 1-24 uses the alignment of text and graphics to organize the visual space.

An element that relates to proximity and alignment is the grid. **Grids** are a formalized division of a page into a set pattern of square and rectangular spaces. Grids can help organize visual information on a page, creating hierarchies of reading order that present information so the audience can more effectively read and understand it.

Unity

Designers achieve **unity** when they use similar elements in a design so they will "work together" visually. This creates a design that communicates the message more effectively. To create unity, designers can use similar shapes, colors, or typography, or they can group similar elements

FIGURE 1-23
Use of asymmetrical balance

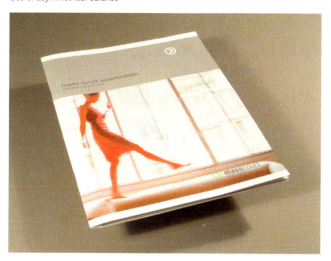

FIGURE 1-24
Use of alignment

together. A non-unified design will cause the viewing audience to skim over or totally ignore the design. Figure 1-25 uses color (as well as shape) to achieve unity among the various pieces of a job.

Emphasis

As designers work through concepts, they will evaluate the different elements within the design and decide on the relative importance of each one. Through the use of **emphasis**, a designer can make parts of a design more important than others. Often a designer will emphasize a particular element to draw the viewer's eye to that place in the design first; this element is called a **focal point**. Another element of emphasis is **contrast**, which is making one element different from the others. The more contrast you add to an element in a design, the more it stands out, and the more emphasis it has. In Figure 1-26, the use of furniture creates emphasis within the design.

Rhythm

There are many ways designers can create interesting, exciting designs. One common technique is to create visual movement by repeating elements. This is known as **rhythm**. There are many different types of visual rhythm, just as there are many

FIGURE 1-25
Use of unity

FIGURE 1-26
Use of emphasis

musical rhythms. In Figure 1-27, the repetition of square elements throughout the design pages creates rhythm. The two most common types of visual rhythm are progressive and alternating. **Progressive rhythm** moves through a design in equal amounts, such as 1, 2, 3, 4, 5, 6. **Alternating rhythm** does as its name implies—it alternates: 1, 2, 1, 2, 1, 2. Rhythm can also create a visual flow through a design, which can help move the viewer's eye to the most important parts of the design.

Placing and organizing various elements into a set format (or space) using different combinations of design principles is the foundation for all visual communication. What's important to understand is that no matter how powerful your computer system is, no matter how proficient you become in software applications, the computer does not design for you. It is you, the designer, who creates the wide array of designs that are produced every day. The computer is simply a tool that helps in the development, production, and execution of these designs.

FIGURE 1-27
Use of rhythm

FIND THE WORDS THROUGH COPYWRITING

What You'll Learn

 In this lesson, you will learn about who typically writes the copy for a design project.

What Is Copywriting?

While the designer works to create imaginative solutions that meet the client's needs, another process is going at the same time: **copywriting**, the creation of the words (copy) used in any visual project, such as an ad, direct mail letter, brochure, poster, or Web site. Copy, like design, is carefully developed to meet the needs of each individual project. (It's important to understand that "copywriting" is different from "copyrighting," although both are important terms in graphics. Copyrighting is the process of legally protecting your work from illegal duplication or reproduction.)

Who Creates Copy

Sometimes the client provides copy, especially if they are familiar with the technical aspects of the product, service, or information being covered in the design project. But in many cases, the client will hire a professional copywriter. Copywriting

can occur before, during, or after the design phase. In advertising, the words are often created before the visuals, and then turned over to the designer. Often, teams of copywriters and art directors work together to come up with copy and concepts that become the exciting ads we see all around us.

Skills Required

A good copywriter can communicate a message effectively and persuade an audience to buy a product or use a service. This ability requires top-notch writing skills as well as sales and marketing knowledge. Just because you got an "A" in English doesn't necessarily mean that you have the specialized skills to create good copy. Copywriters come from a variety of disciplines — some specialize in a particular area but the majority are able to write about many different subjects. How to obtain these skills? There are many on-line copywriting courses and some schools offer direct marketing courses that include copywriting skills.

Copywriting: The Job

Some copywriters work as freelancers; others are hired by larger design studios and ad agencies in full-time positions. Some form their own companies, either with other copywriters or with art directors or graphic designers, to provide a full range of services. But whatever the capacity, copywriters are the ones that bring to life many of the memorable headlines and catch phrases seen in ads and brochures and on the Web.

FIGURE 1-28
Creating words with copywriting

CREATE IMAGES WITH ILLUSTRATIONS

What You'll Learn

▶ *In this lesson, you will learn about who supplies illustrations when they are required for a design project.*

About Illustrations

While the design layouts and copy are being produced, the project may require another professional to become part of the process. If the designer has decided that illustrations would work best to solve the client's problem, an illustrator will be brought in.

The Illustrator's Job

Illustrators are artists who create drawings, paintings, or other types of hand-drawn or electronically created art specifically for graphic design and advertising projects. Many are fine artists who decided that fine art, although highly creative, doesn't always pay the bills. There are also programs at community colleges and universities that train people to become illustrators.

All illustrators develop a style or "look" that's unique to their work. Designers and art directors look for a particular style when they decide which illustrator to use on a project. If the art director decides on a loose, watercolor look, he or she will identify illustrators with that style. Whereas some illustrators still work in traditional media such as pencils, pastels, or paint, others now produce work in graphics software such as Adobe Illustrator or Adobe Photoshop. Some are even moving into 3-D software to create highly dimensional and realistic illustrations.

Few illustrators work for design studios or ad agencies. Most work on their own or with groups of other illustrators, each with a different style or technique, so they can market themselves as a team.

FIGURE 1-29
Creating art with illustration

TAKE PICTURES IT'S PHOTOGRAPHY

What You'll Learn

In this lesson, you will learn about how photography and photographers are part of the graphic design field.

About Photography

Although illustrations can create wonderful moods and styles in a design, many of today's graphics use photography for visual imagery. **Photography** is another area of employment in the visual communications industry. Many colleges and universities offer programs in photography. And some people gain the necessary skills to take a good picture through experience.

Photography requires many of the same skills used by designers, including proficiency in composition and the use of shapes, value, and texture. Photography,

like design, has moved rapidly into the digital arena. Traditional film-based photography is still very common, but many photographers have switched to using digital cameras. These cameras have become more powerful over the last few years and, in areas like product photography, have become the standard.

Photographic Styles

Like illustrators, photographers generally work on their own, and most develop a style that differentiates their images from those of other photographers. Some work in black and white, some use stark realism, and some use special effects. Some photographers specialize in a particular subject area, such as food, landscapes, sporting events, or portraits.

Jobs in Photography

Photographers generally work on their own, establishing a client base of agencies and studios that use their work for advertising and graphics projects. Some larger design studios hire a staff photographer who works specifically for that studio's clients and projects.

FIGURE 1-30
Creating images with photography

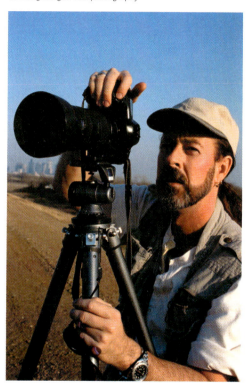

MOVE FROM DESIGN TO PRODUCTION

What You'll Learn

 In this lesson, you will learn how design projects move forward to the production phase.

The Production Process

The computer has dramatically changed how a project moves from the creative to the production phase of graphic design. Design and production used to be two completely separate areas of graphics; designers came up with the creative visuals and the **production** artists took those ideas and turned them into art for the printer to reproduce. But now the computer allows design and production to happen simultaneously. Designers now make production and creative decisions at the same time.

Designers use the software applications discussed in the following chapters to help create solutions to their client's design problems. But once the client approves the designs, the project then has to be prepared for output. This is where production takes over.

Production Artist Jobs

Good production artists are valued throughout the graphics industry. These jobs do require an eye for design, but they primarily focus on the technical aspects of creating electronic files that will output with minimal problems and a high degree of accuracy. Production artists must be highly proficient in vector-drawing, raster, page layout, and electronic publishing applications. They also must be proficient at creating work that adheres to the design principles you learned in this chapter.

FIGURE 1-31
Design and production in a studio

The concepts of creativity and design have a long history. But the introduction of desktop publishing in 1984 radically changed the tools and workflow of the graphics industry. Despite this change to an electronic environment, the basic skills necessary to produce quality design remain the same. The designer still needs to meet the needs of the client, using the design process to define and research the client's project, then work through thumbnails, roughs, and comprehensives to show the client as many alternative solutions as possible. Reviewing and refining the design then creates a solution that the client approves to move into the production phase.

During the design process the designer uses the basic elements and principles of design to create successful solutions. Line, shape, value, color, texture, and space are combined using the organizational concepts of balance, proximity, alignment, unity, emphasis, and rhythm. Working with the designer are copywriters, illustrators, and photographers, all of whom work together to produce dynamic designs that communicate the client's message.

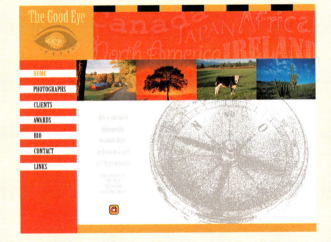

KEY TERMS & CONCEPTS

alignment

alternating rhythm

alternative solutions

asymmetrical balance

balance

camera-ready art

color

composition

comprehensive

contrast

copywriting

create thumbnails and roughs

creativity

define the problem

design elements

design principles

design process

emphasis

focal point

format

fundamentals of design

grayscale

grids

illustrators

line

mechanicals

negative space

pasteups

photography

positive images

prepare comprehensives

process cameras

production

progressive rhythm

proximity

research the project

review and refine the design

rhythm

rough

shapes

space

symmetrical balance

texture

thumbnails

unity

value

CHAPTER REVIEW

1. Why is creativity important for designers working on a computer graphics project?

   _____

   _____

   _____

2. Why is design different from fine art?

   _____

   _____

   _____

3. List the five steps of the design process, in order.

   _____

   _____

   _____

   _____

   _____

4. Give three examples of how you could research a design project.

   _____

   _____

   _____

5. Give an example of how line can be used in a design.

   _____

   _____

   _____

6. What are the three basic shapes used in design?

   _____

7. What is texture?

   _____

   _____

8. Arranging forms in space creates a(n):

   _____

9. Describe how format is used in design.

   _____

   _____

10. What is the difference between symmetrical balance and asymmetrical balance?

    _____

    _____

    _____

11. What is the difference between proximity and alignment?

    _____

    _____

    _____

12. How does unity help make a design easier to understand?

    _____

    _____

    _____

13. Explain how emphasis and contrast can improve the reading order of a design.

_____

_____

_____

14. What are the two main types of rhythm in design?

_____

15. What does a copywriter do in a design project?

_____

_____

_____

16. What does an illustrator do in a design project?

_____

_____

_____

17. What does a photographer do in a design project?

_____

_____

_____

You have been hired by an outdoor clothing company to help design the cover for their seasonal catalog. They would like you to design a logo-style image that represents one of the seasons.

1. Choose one season: winter, spring, summer, or fall.
2. Create at least 25 unique thumbnails that visually represent the season you selected. As you work, carefully consider the design elements and concepts that you will use to create this symbol. Produce your visualizations with a pencil or black felt-tip marker on a printout of the thumbnail sheets, **IG 1-01.pdf**, provided in the Chapter 1 folder in the location where you store your Data Files.
3. Print out several sheets and use them as a guide to help you focus on creating as many ideas as possible.

One Step Beyond

4. Take your two best ideas and attempt to make **comprehensive presentations**. Use colored pencils and/or colored felt-tip markers on marker paper. Make your presentation around 6" in size so the client can easily review your ideas.
5. Add the season name (winter, spring, summer, fall) to your symbol to make it look more like a logo.
6. Mount the marker comprehensive on presentation board as it would be shown to a client.

Two Steps Beyond

7. Take your finished marker comp and scan it. Then import (Place) the image in a vector-drawing software document and attempt to recreate it using the tools and commands available.

PROJECT BUILDER 2

You are speaking to a class of senior citizens who are learning page layout software. They need to understand basic design principles, and you want to show them examples of good and bad designs.

1. Look through magazines, newspapers, and the yellow pages, and find two ads. The first ad should demonstrate good design and creativity. The second ad should be poorly designed, the worse the better. Try to find two ads that are similar in size and format. Avoid color ads; black and white will work fine.
2. On two pieces of 8.5" × 11" paper, write a critique for each ad. Explain why you think the first ad is well designed and why you think the second is poorly designed. Use the terms you've learned in this chapter in your critique.

One Step Beyond

3. Take the poorly-designed ad you chose and redesign it. Look carefully at the well-designed ad and figure out what the designer did with design elements, composition, format, and design principles to make the ad look good. Then apply those same principles to the poorly designed ad.
4. Use a pencil or black felt-tip marker on marker paper to work on the redesign. Try at least three rough layouts. You must use the same format, all of the copy, and any imagery that was used in the original ad, but you can change the elements and layout and add any graphics you choose.
5. Mount the marker comprehensive on presentation board as you would show it to a client.

Your local community college is starting a computer graphics program. The department head wants you to create a logo for the program. The project requirements are:

- The logo must use the three basic shapes of design: a circle, a square, and a triangle.
- The logo must use the words "Computer Graphics" in a typeface that has a style that reflects a contemporary feel, yet is also easy to read.
- The logo must also include the name of the school. (Use the school you are attending, or the name of a local college or university if you are not a student.)
- The logo should be contemporary and modern in look and feel; avoid an old-fashioned or dated look.

1. Think up at least 20 different concepts for the logo, and sketch them on a printout of the thumbnail sheets, IG 1-01.pdf, provided in the Chapter A folder in the location where you store your Data Files. Print out several sheets and use them as guides to help you focus on creating as many ideas as possible, integrating the design methodologies, elements, and principles discussed in this chapter.
2. Choose the two best concepts and produce 6" finished comprehensives using pencils and felt-tip markers on marker paper.
3. Mount each comprehensive on its own piece of presentation board.

FIGURE 1-32
Logo samples

Figure 1-33 shows several examples of real-world design projects created by designers across the United States. Look carefully at each project, and write a summary of how each project reflects the design principles described in this chapter.

FIGURE 1-33
Designer-created projects

Steff Geissbuhler
NBC logo
National Broadcasting Company
www.cgnyc.com

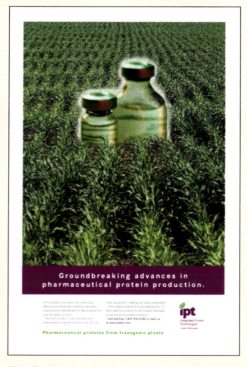

Diane Brody
IPT Ad for Monsanto Company
Genetic Engineering News *and other biotech publications*
www.brodymarketing.com

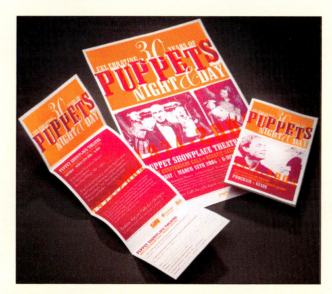

Collaborated, Inc.
Show Place Theatre
30th anniversary collateral
Boston area publicity

CHAPTER

VECTOR-DRAW SOFTWARE

VECTOR-DRAW SOFTWARE

A Brief Historical Perspective

Drawing started about 35,000 years ago, with the first cave paintings in Europe. Over time many new tools and techniques have been developed to create a vast array of visual imagery, all produced manually. Artists have used everything from pencils to pastels, charcoal to graphite, and crayons to air brushes.

Back in 1984, no software could match the artist's pencil. Applications like Apple's MacPaint created **bitmapped images**, which are composed of a series of dots called **pixels** (picture elements). Bitmapped images were **resolution dependent**, meaning that the quality of the image depended on the number of pixels per square inch: the more dots per square inch, the better the image quality, the fewer dots, the lower the image quality. This made bitmapped images difficult to work with and to output at the required resolutions.

Introducing Vector-Draw

In 1987, Adobe released Adobe Illustrator for the Macintosh. Rather than working with bitmap images, Illustrator worked with **vector paths**, which are mathematical points connected by paths that plot out the edge of an image, making them **resolution independent**. The advantage of these mathematically-calculated vector paths is that you can enlarge any art you create to

Manual versus electronic skills

Vector-draw software can create many different types of graphics, from the simplest icon to the most complex illustration. You can draw, or illustrate, almost any image you want. But if you don't know how to draw, the software isn't going to make it any easier. Knowing how to draw and paint is a major plus for working with vector-draw applications. So take an art class or drawing workshop and get out the old pencil and learn how to draw. It will help you get the results you want when working in Illustrator or FreeHand.

many times its original size and still retain high-quality output, as shown in Figure 2-2.

The following year, two more vector-draw applications were released: Aldus FreeHand and CorelDRAW. This book focuses on Illustrator and FreeHand because these are the two programs that are most commonly used by graphic designers today. Both applications have advanced over the years to include many types of tools and commands. But it is the strength of their basic drawing tools and their handling of vector paths to create electronic illustrations that has made them the leading drawing applications in the industry.

FIGURE 2-2
Comparison of bitmapped art vs. vector art

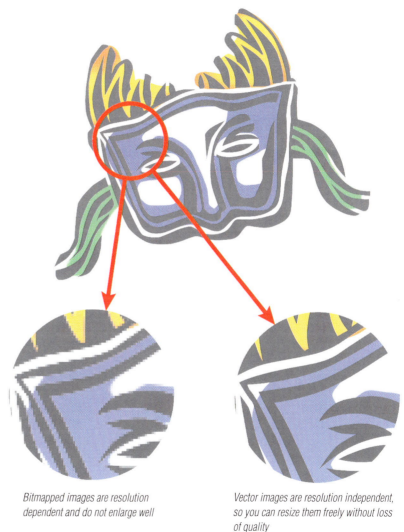

Bitmapped images are resolution dependent and do not enlarge well

Vector images are resolution independent, so you can resize them freely without loss of quality

FIGURE 2-1
Cave painting from Europe

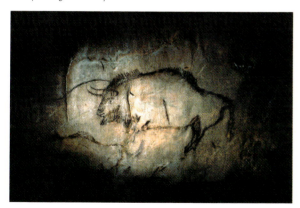

ILLUSTRATOR AND FREEHAND: AN OVERVIEW

What You'll Learn

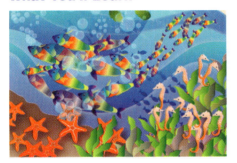

 This section provides a brief comparison of Illustrator and FreeHand.

Adobe Illustrator

Adobe Illustrator is a comprehensive vector-draw software application that has been the industry standard for many years. Illustrator (shown in Figure 2-3) is used to create almost any type of graphic illustrations, from logos and icons to the most complex renderings.

Artists use Illustrator's powerful drawing tools to produce fine art drawings with beautiful detail and style. Technical artists use Illustrator to create complex drawings of products and machinery with a high degree of realism. Graphic artists use the program to produce almost any type of graphic imagery, including maps, signage, posters, menus, special type treatments—the list is almost endless. Web and multimedia artists use Illustrator to create the graphic content for many Web sites and motion graphics productions.

Adobe continues to add new features to Illustrator. New tools can simulate airbrush and watercolor effects by controlling the transitions between multiple colors. Warp, liquify, and distort commands can now manipulate art in ways never before produced on the computer. Advanced typography and 3D effects combine to provide additional style and complexity to vector-based artwork. And integration between Illustrator and other Adobe products lets designers increase workflow speed and complete projects quickly.

Macromedia FreeHand

Macromedia FreeHand is similar to Illustrator in many ways. FreeHand is a vector-based drawing application that you can use to create a wide variety of print-based illustrations and Web-based graphics. FreeHand provides an easy-to-learn digital environment that features advanced drawing and editing tools to produce designs with maximum visual impact. The various attributes and special effects in a complex illustration can be organized for easy reference and fast accessibility. This helps designers work quickly and efficiently on any project, from the simplest symbol to the most complex rendering.

Although FreeHand (see Figure 2-4) can handle any print-based graphic with ease, its ability to work with Web- and monitor-based content makes the application useful in any media. FreeHand integrates easily with Macromedia's Studio MX 2004 products, which are the industry standard for Web-based projects. You can create graphics in FreeHand and drop them right into Flash animations or Fireworks Web layouts. And advanced effects such as bevels, drop shadows, and 3D extrudes make FreeHand the software of choice for many designers.

This chapter discusses menus, commands, and dialog boxes for both Illustrator and FreeHand. If you see only one instruction or command for a task, then it is the same for both applications. If the commands are different for the two applications, the Illustrator information will be listed first, followed by FreeHand information in parentheses.

FIGURE 2-3
Adobe Illustrator

FIGURE 2-4
Macromedia FreeHand

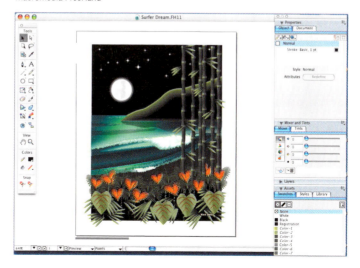

OPEN AND SAVE FILES

What You'll Learn

▶ This lesson shows you how to open a vector-draw application and save your files.

Opening Files

To begin a new vector-draw project, you have to launch (start up) the application. On a Macintosh computer you can locate and double-click the software icon in the Applications folder, or create an alias (shortcut) of the application icon in the Dock and click the alias. On a Windows computer, you click Start on the taskbar, point to Programs (or All Programs), and then select the software. See Figures 2-5 and 2-6.

Once the application is up and running, you can open an existing document or create a new one: Click **File** on the menu bar, and click either **New** or **Open**.

Selecting New opens the New Document dialog box in Illustrator (see Figure 2-7), or in FreeHand a blank 8.5" × 11" page will appear; you then go to the Document Properties panel (see Figure 2-8). The dialog box in Illustrator and the panel in FreeHand ask you specific questions about setting up a new document. Here you choose the Size

and the Orientation of the document. Although selecting initial document size and orientation is important when using other graphics software, it is less important in vector-draw applications because the software lets you resize drawings freely without loss of quality. You will most likely import the artwork you create into a page layout or other design application. So unless you are using vector-draw software for creating a page layout, work in a size and an orientation that is most comfortable for you. The standard letter size (8.5" × 11") will work great!

Saving Files

Once you create a new document, the next step is to **save** it. Saving your document makes it a permanent file on your hard drive or other storage device that you can open and close as often as you want. In most graphics applications, the **File menu** lets you **Save**, **Save As**, or **Save a Copy** of the open document.

FIGURE 2-5

Macintosh desktop

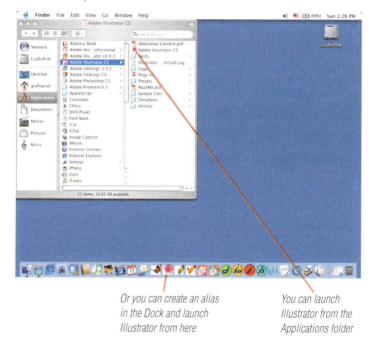

Or you can create an alias
in the Dock and launch
Illustrator from here

You can launch
Illustrator from the
Applications folder

FIGURE 2-6

Windows desktop

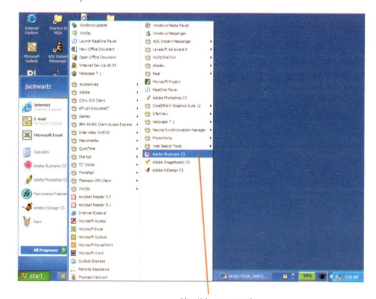

Use this command
to launch Illustrator

Save—Use this the first time you save a document, or when you want to save your work in progress. When you save a document for the first time, the Save as (Save) dialog box (shown in Figure 2-9) appears, asking you to name the document, indicate where you want to store it, and select the format in which you want to save it. Be sure to name your files to reflect the file's content and make it easy to search for later on.

Learning where to save your documents is also very important. Whether you're on a Macintosh or a Windows computer, be sure you understand where you are saving your files. Learn to create folders and navigate among them to organize your files for easy search and retrieval.

QUICKTIP

Many design studios and ad agencies assign a job number to every project. Using the job number as part of the file name makes it easier to track jobs as they move from computer to computer.

FIGURE 2-7
New Document dialog box—Illustrator

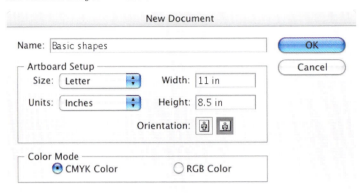

FIGURE 2-8
Document Properties dialog box—FreeHand

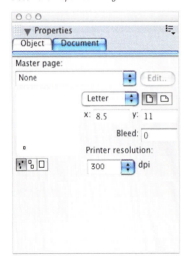

Save As—This option creates a duplicate of your document. If you are saving the duplicate in the same folder as your original, the name of the document must be different; if you're saving it to a different folder, drive, or network location, you can use the same name. When you save a document for the first time, the Save and Save As commands do the same thing—they open the Save as (Save) dialog box.

Save a Copy—Like Save As, this option creates a duplicate of your document but adds the word "copy" at the end of the filename. The big difference between Save As and Save a Copy is that after you use Save As, the new copy of the document remains open for your to work on, while the original closes. When you use Save a Copy, the original version of your document remains open, and the new copy is stored on your save location, but does not open. Any changes you make to your open original will not be reflected in the copy you saved. You might use Save a Copy if you want to create a backup in case something happens to your original.

FIGURE 2-9
Save as dialog box

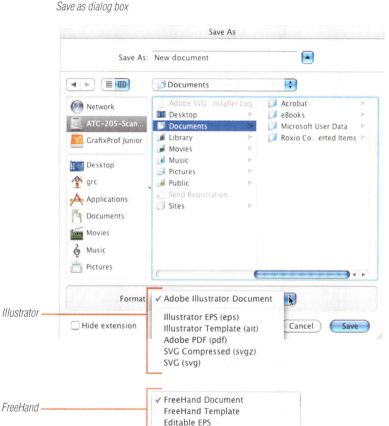

CHECK OUT BASIC TOOLS AND COMMANDS

What You'll Learn

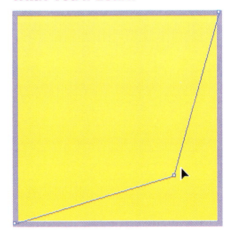

In this lesson, you will learn about some of the menu options and tools in vector-draw applications.

Learning the Application Interface

Every software application comes with its own menus, commands, and dialog boxes. The design or "look" of these items is called the software **interface**. In the past, several companies sold competing graphics software, and the interfaces were very different.

Two companies are now the main suppliers of graphics software: Adobe and Macromedia. Each company has attempted to give its family of software products a common interface so they look and act the same, in both the Macintosh and Windows operating systems. This is a big advantage for you—once you learn one application by a manufacturer, learning a second one is easier because you already know most of the commands. And many commands are the same in both Adobe and Macromedia software; they just might be in a different menu or group of commands.

Rulers and Guides

All graphics software lets you measure elements precisely on the page using **rulers** and **guides**. Click **View** on the menu bar and then click **Show Rulers (Page Rulers/Show)**. Horizontal and vertical rulers appear on the top and left edges of the project window (See Figure 2-10). By moving the pointer over either ruler, you can click and drag ruler guides onto your page. As you drag the guide, notice that a dashed line appears in the ruler, letting you position the guide exactly where you want it on the page.

QUICKTIP

In Illustrator, ruler guides are locked by default. To unlock them, click **View** on the menu bar, point to **Guides**, and then click **Lock Guides**. Release the mouse button and the guide unlocks. FreeHand guides are unlocked by default. To remove guides in Illustrator, click the guide to select it, then press [Delete]. In FreeHand, drag the guide back to the ruler.

FIGURE 2-10

Using rulers and rulers guides

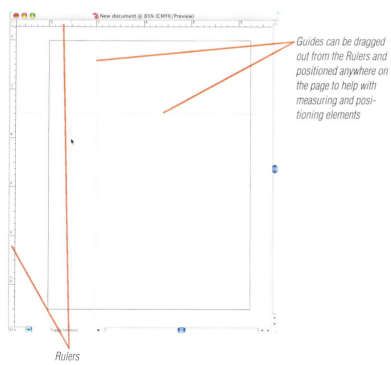

Guides can be dragged out from the Rulers and positioned anywhere on the page to help with measuring and positioning elements

Rulers

FIGURE 2-11

Illustrator toolbar

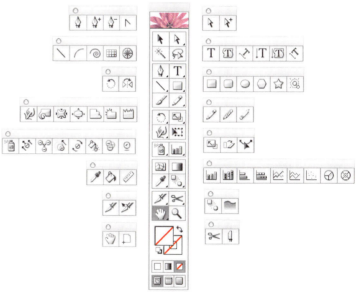

Toolbar

The **toolbar** contains the tools you use to create, modify, and move graphics and type in your project. As you can see in Figures 2-11 and 2-12, both Illustrator and FreeHand have many tools and features. For now you'll focus on the most commonly used ones.

Selection (Pointer) and Direct Selection (Subselect) tools—These tools let you select graphics and type that you have created. The Selection (Pointer) tool selects an entire shape, as shown in Figure 2-13. Once the shape is selected, you can move, resize, or modify it. The Direct Selection (Subselect) tool (see Figure 2-14) lets you select individual points within the selected shape. You can then drag these points to change the shape. This is one of the more powerful features of vector-draw software.

QUICKTIP

When resizing graphics using the Selection (Pointer) tool, you can resize either **non-proportionally** (which distorts the image) or **proportionally** (which does not distort the image). Clicking and dragging a handle resizes the graphic non-proportionally, but holding down [Shift] while dragging resizes the graphic proportionally. Either technique is fine; it just depends on the effect you're looking for!

FIGURE 2-12

FreeHand toolbar

FIGURE 2-13

Using the Selection (Pointer) tool

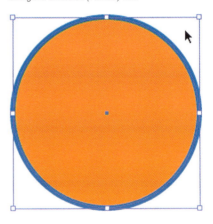

The Selection (Pointer) tool lets you select, move, scale, or delete the entire shape

Pencil and Line Segment (Line) tools—
At last, the tools that can actually draw something! Both of these tools do the same thing—create a line—but they go about it differently. The Pencil tool is a freehand tool that draws lines at any angle to match the movement of the mouse. To draw a line, you click the tool, move the pointer over the page, then click and drag, creating a line. See Figure 2-15. As long as you hold down the mouse button and drag, you create as long a line as you want. When you release the mouse button, the line ends.

The Line Segment (Line) tool is a precision-based tool, meaning that when you click and drag, you create a straight line, like the one shown in Figure 2-16. The line will then follow the angle that you drag in and, as with the Pencil tool, when you release the mouse button the line ends. Once you finish drawing a line, you can use the Selection (Pointer) tool to move the line or make it longer or shorter.

FIGURE 2-14
Using the Direct Selection (Subselect) tool

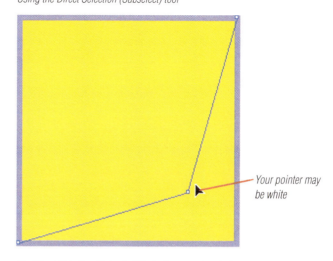

Your pointer may be white

The Direct Selection (Subselect) tool allows you to select individual anchor points so you can reshape any graphic

FIGURE 2-15
Drawing with the Pencil tool

Shape Creation Tools

All vector-draw software lets you create a wide range of shapes such as those shown in Figure 2-17. Both Illustrator and FreeHand have tools to make rectangles, ovals, polygons, stars, and more! The great thing about this software is that once you have drawn a shape, you can use the Selection (Pointer) tool to move or resize it, or use the Direct Selection (Subselect) tool to select and modify individual points within the shape. (In FreeHand you have to ungroup the shape before you can modify the individual points, with the shape selected click Modify, then click Ungroup). If you hold down [Shift] while dragging and drawing the shape, you can create geometrically perfect shapes, like squares and circles.

FIGURE 2-16
Drawing with the Line Segment (Line) tool

FIGURE 2-17
Several basic shapes

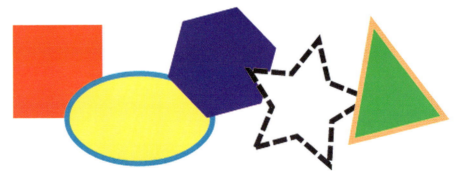

FIGURE 2-18
Creating a heart from a circle

DESIGNTIP Start with basic shapes

As you begin to learn vector-draw software, it's important to understand that you are working with **objects**, not pixels. These objects are the shapes you create with the application's various drawing tools. An advantage of working with objects is that you can easily create a complex shape by starting with a basic shape. By adding or modifying points, you can literally "reshape" the object into a more complex form. This technique can be much faster and more accurate than trying to draw a complex shape from scratch. Figure 2-18 shows how you can use the Direct Selection (Subselect) tool to create a heart-shaped object from a circle object, using a few simple tools and commands.

CREATE SHAPES USING STROKE AND FILL

What You'll Learn

 In this lesson, you'll learn how to create and work with basic shapes.

Stroke and Fill

Every line and shape has two attributes: stroke and fill. Each of these attributes also has a variety of possible "looks."

Stroke

Any line that you draw has a stroke applied to it. The **stroke** of a line is its thickness, color, and line style or texture. The thickness of a stroke is measured in points. A **point** measures 1/72 of an inch, so there are 72 points to an inch, and a 4-point stroke would be 1/18 of an inch thick. Illustrator can stroke to 1/1000 of a point, and FreeHand can stroke to 1/10,000 of a point! Both applications can color a stroke almost any color you like. They have various textures of strokes, as well as many styles, such as dotted lines, dashed lines, and multiple lines. You can also apply strokes to shapes; this makes a frame around the shape that can have all the attributes of a line stroke. Or you can turn off the stroke of a shape, so it has no stroke around it. See Figure 2-19 for examples of strokes you can use in your work.

> **DESIGNTIP An old printing measurement**
>
> A point is an old printers' measurement system that has been around since the 1700s. Printers used points to measure everything from lines of type to ad sizes. But the point as a measurement unit has slowly lost favor as the computer has become the major tool of the graphics industry; measurement in inches is now more common. Points are still used to measure the size of type, the vertical space between lines of type (called **leading**), and the thickness of strokes.

Fill

All shapes have an interior area called the **fill**. Fill can come in many variations, just like a stroke. A shape can have no fill, making it transparent, like a doughnut hole. Fill can also be black, white, a shade of gray, or almost any color imaginable. A shape can also have a **gradient** fill, where different colors or grades of one color flow through the shape. Fill can also be texture or almost any pattern you can imagine. Designers use fill to create flat or dimensional designs in vector-draw software. See Figure 2-20 for examples of fills.

FIGURE 2-19

Several types and styles of strokes

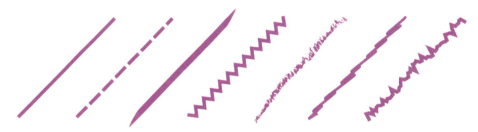

FIGURE 2-20

Several examples of fills

WORK WITH COLOR MODELS

What You'll Learn

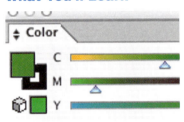

  In this lesson, you will learn about color and how it is used in vector-draw applications.

The concepts of stroke and fill lead directly to the use of color in vector-draw software. The topic of **color models**, or how color is described within a system of color reproduction, is very important in the design industry. Over the years, many technologies have used a variety of color models to reproduce color in graphics. This section focuses on two of the main color models used in the print graphics industry: grayscale and process color.

Grayscale

The most basic colors are black and white. In traditional color theory, black is the absence of color, and white is the combination of all colors. But the combination of black and white creates shades of gray, commonly called **grayscale**. In art, an almost infinite range of shades of gray can be produced. But computer graphics printers and other output devices can produce only 256 shades of gray.

Vector-draw software handles grayscale as a screen tint of black. **Screen tints** are a printer technique that takes a solid color and breaks it up into a series of dots that are uniform in size and in the spacing between the dots. These dot areas are measured in percentages. The larger the dots (a higher percentage), the darker the screen tint; the smaller the dots (a lower percentage), the lighter the screen tint. So a medium gray is a 50% screen tint, 10% a very light gray, and 90% a very dark gray. See Figure 2-21 for an example of grayscale values and Figure 2-22 for the grayscale setting in the palette.

Vector-draw software lets you choose black or white as colors, using either the **Color (Mixer and Tints) palette** shown in Figure 2-23 or the **Swatches palette**. You can make black any screen tint from 0% (white) to 100% (black), creating a value scale. And you can choose percentages up to 1/100 of a percent, such as 43.07% black!

FIGURE 2-21
A value scale

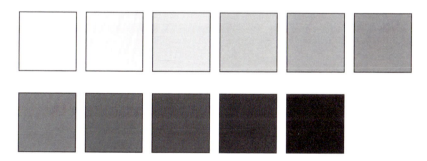

FIGURE 2-22
Color palette set for grayscale (Illustrator)

If necessary, click here to show options

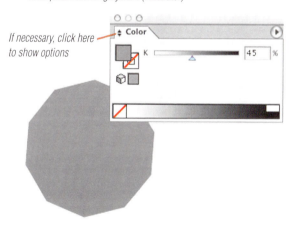

Grayscale is used frequently in newspaper and telephone book advertising, as well as in print projects where clients have limited budgets and can afford only one-color printing. Grayscale can be applied to either stroke or fill.

Process Color

While some artwork is produced in grayscale, more and more work is being produced in full color. To create full-color work, the designer has to develop the art in process colors. **Process color** combines four ink colors printed one on top of the other to re-create full color. Process color is commonly referred to as **CMYK**, which stands for the four colors: cyan, magenta, yellow, and black. Like grayscale, process color art is broken up into a series of dots. See Figure 2-24 for images created using CMYK.

FIGURE 2-23

Palettes that work with color

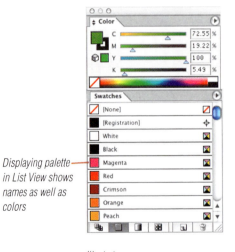

Displaying palette in List View shows names as well as colors

Illustrator

FreeHand

To use process color in vector-draw software, select any shape or type, then choose the **CMYK color model** in the **Color (Mixer and Tints) palette**. Instead of just one screen tint slider, which appears when you create grayscale tints, you will see four sliders, one for each process color (See Figure 2-25). By sliding each of the sliders to different percentages, you can create thousands of colors. For example, 100% Cyan/100% Yellow make a dark green, 50% Magenta/100% Yellow make orange, and so on. The Color palette previews the final process color as you move the sliders. Like grayscale, process color can be applied to stroke or fill.

FIGURE 2-24
Examples of CMYK art

FIGURE 2-25
Color palette set for CMYK (Illustrator)

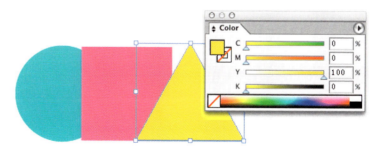

TRANSFORM PATHS AND SHAPES

What You'll Learn

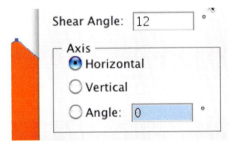

 In this lesson, you will learn about the tools used to transform paths and shapes into unique graphics.

Transform Tools

As you work in vector-draw software, you create basic shapes that you will usually have to modify in some way. There is a full collection of tools that let you modify, or **transform**, shapes in many different ways. Some of these transformation tools include:

Scale tool—to scale images larger or smaller, either proportionally or non-proportionally (see Figure 2-26)

Rotate tool—to rotate a shape either clockwise or counter-clockwise (see Figure 2-27)

Reflect tool—to show an image's reflection, as if it were being viewed in a mirror (see Figure 2-28)

Shear (Skew) tool—to shear or skew a shape in any direction (see Figure 2-29)

These four transformation tools are the most common. To access them, click **Object** on the menu bar, then point to **Transform** (click **Modify** on the menu bar, then point to **Transform**). Other tools such as warp, perspective, and free transform are also available, depending on the application. You can perform these transformations manually by clicking and dragging the mouse, or numerically through a dialog box (such as the one shown in Figure 2-30) for more precise control.

FIGURE 2-26

Scaling a shape (Illustrator)

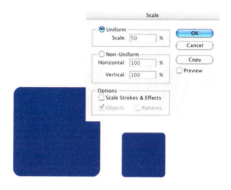

FIGURE 2-27

Rotating a shape (Illustrator)

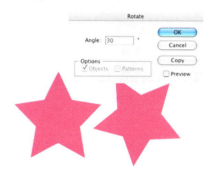

FIGURE 2-28

Reflecting a shape (Illustrator)

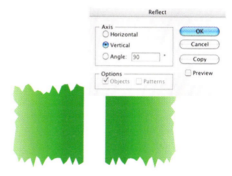

FIGURE 2-29

Shearing a shape (Illustrator)

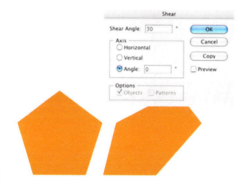

FIGURE 2-30

Transforming using a dialog box (Illustrator)

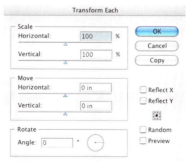

LEARN THE PEN TOOL AND BEZIER CURVES

What You'll Learn

 In this lesson, you will learn about the Pen tool and how to work with paths or Beziér Curves.

About Paths

The most important and unique feature of vector-draw software is the use of paths to create shapes. **Paths** (also called **Beziér Curves**) are made up of two components, **anchor points** (small square handles) and **direction lines** (lines that connect the anchor points). Paths are the foundation for everything you do in vector-draw software; they let you create just about any type of illustration.

The Pen Tool

The primary drawing tool is the **Pen tool**. This tool creates paths, and requires a particular technique to draw lines and shapes.

When you select the Pen tool and move it over the page, you can single-click to create an anchor point. If you move the Pen tool to a different location on the page and single-click again, another anchor point appears. A direction line also appears between the two anchor points. If you then click a third anchor point, yet another direction line appears, this time between the second and third anchor points. You can continue to click any number of new anchor points until you create the line or shape you want. If you are creating a shape, you should always close the shape by clicking the Pen tool on top of the first anchor point you created. Figure 2-31 shows the Pen tool as well as the tools used to add, delete, and convert anchor points from straight to **curved paths**.

FIGURE 2-31
The Pen tool and other path creation tools

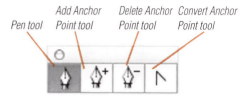

Add Anchor   Delete Anchor   Convert Anchor
Pen tool   Point tool   Point tool   Point tool

Illustrator

 Pen tool

 ✓ Bezigon tool (B, 8)

FreeHand

FIGURE 2-32
A straight path with anchor points and direction lines

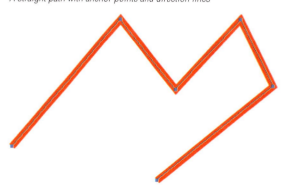

By simply clicking the mouse button, you produce **straight paths** with straight direction lines between the anchor points, as shown in Figure 2-32. But you can also create curved paths by clicking and dragging the mouse as you create a new anchor point. Dragging pulls out **handles** from the anchor point; these handles control the way the direction line curves into or out of the anchor point, as shown in Figure 2-33. This technique lets you create almost any line style or shape imaginable. It is a very controlled way of drawing, and it takes some time to get a feel for the technique. But creating paths is the way vector-draw software produces the impressive variety of electronic illustrations you see all around you.

Editing Lines and Shapes

Another advantage of vector-draw software is that once you've drawn a line or shape, you can go back and modify it until you get exactly what you want. This makes rendering much easier than with manual drawing tools, where once you've drawn something it's almost impossible to change unless you start over.

FIGURE 2-33

A curved path with anchor points, direction lines, and handles

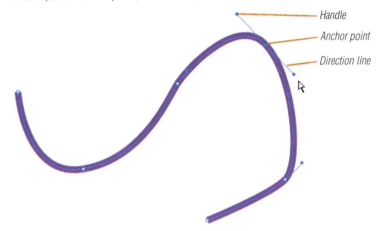

Handle

Anchor point

Direction line

FIGURE 2-34

A shape being modified with the Direct Selection (Subselect) tool

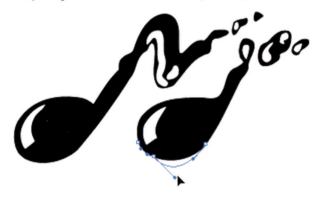

The **Direct Selection (Subselection) tool** lets you select individual anchor points, direction lines, and handles to modify a line or shape in almost any way you choose (see Figure 2-34). Vector-draw software also has tools to add and subtract anchor points, as well as tools that let you reshape paths. The trick to learning vector-draw software is to develop your ability to create and modify the paths that make up your "starter" shapes. So practice using the various path-related tools as much as you can.

FIGURE 2-35

A partially completed vector-draw illustration over a template photo

DESIGNTIP Don't start with a blank page

Very few illustrators create art in vector-draw software from scratch. Most find images that resemble what they want to create. They then scan the images, place them in their vector-draw document, and use them as tracing guides, as shown in Figure 2-35. This can help them create illustrations faster and with greater accuracy. But it hasn't totally replaced drawing with pencil and paper. In fact, people who already know how to draw tend to create better art more quickly. So practice your drawing skills!

TYPE IN VECTOR-DRAW SOFTWARE

What You'll Learn

In this lesson, you'll begin to learn about working with type in vector-draw applications.

About Type

The ability to work with **type**, including letters, numbers, and symbols, is an important skill in the graphics industry. But this skill is often overlooked when learning graphics, because so much emphasis is put on learning the software instead of learning graphics theory. This section focuses on the tools for creating and manipulating type in vector-draw software. You will learn more about type and typography in Chapter 4.

The Type (Text) tool

The simplest way to create type is to use the **Type (Text) tool**. Selecting the Type (Text) tool and clicking anywhere in a document places the flashing insertion point at the clicked location. As you type, characters appear on the page. When you are finished typing, the Type (Text) tool lets you go back and highlight (select) any part of the text to modify it. In Illustrator you use the **Character palette**, and in FreeHand, the **Properties palette** (see

Figure 2-36), to change the type style, size, leading, and other type properties. The following sections provide a brief summary of some of these type features.

Type Style

A **type style** refers to the design and shape of the letterforms. Some type designs are hundreds of years old, but new typefaces are designed every year. An example of an older typeface is Garamond, which was designed by the famous French type designer Claude Garamond in the 1530s. Helvetica was designed by the Swiss type designer Max Miedinger in the 1950s. The font you are reading now is Clearface, designed by Morris Fuller Benton in 1907.

Designers use type styles such as those shown in Figure 2-37 as design elements to create a certain look in their designs: some have a classic, more refined look, and some have a cleaner, more contemporary look. The number and variety of type styles you can use depends on what typefaces are installed on your computer. This and other aspects of type technology will be discussed in greater detail in Chapter 6.

Type Size

Like the thickness of strokes, **type size** (height) is measured in points (recall that one point equals 1/72 of an inch). Type that you read as the main body copy in magazines or books measures between 9 and 12 points. The type you are now reading measures 9.5 points. Headlines are usually much larger; the headline at the beginning of this section measures 22 and 29 points in height. The type sizes you select depend on how easy-to-read you want the text to be, how much emphasis you want it to have, and the amount of contrast you want between the text and other page elements. See Figure 2-38 for examples of type sizes.

Leading

This term describes the vertical space between lines of type. Leading (pronounced "ledding") is an old printers' term from when type was set in metal, and they used chunks of lead to separate the individual lines of type. Leading is also measured in points. The leading of the type you are now reading is 12 points. See Figure 2-39 for examples of leading.

FIGURE 2-36

Character palette in Illustrator and the Properties/Object palette in FreeHand

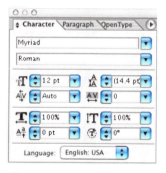

Illustrator

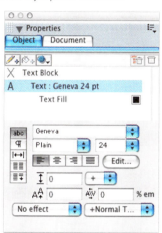

FreeHand

FIGURE 2-37

Several different type styles

Line Length

Line length describes the length of the lines of type you are creating. Line length is also a design decision: Combined with type size, style, and leading, line length can affect how easily text can be read. Line length is usually measured in inches. The line length of a column of type on this page is 2 3/8 inches. See Figure 2-40 for examples of line length.

Alignment

When type is set in columns or blocks, the lines of type align to each other in different ways. **Align left** means the type aligns on the left side of the column but varies in length on the right side. **Align right** is the opposite: the type aligns on the right side of the column but varies in length on the left side. **Align center** means the lines of type align to the center of the column but are different lengths, so neither side lines up. **Justified** alignment means the type lines up on the left

FIGURE 2-38

Examples of different type sizes

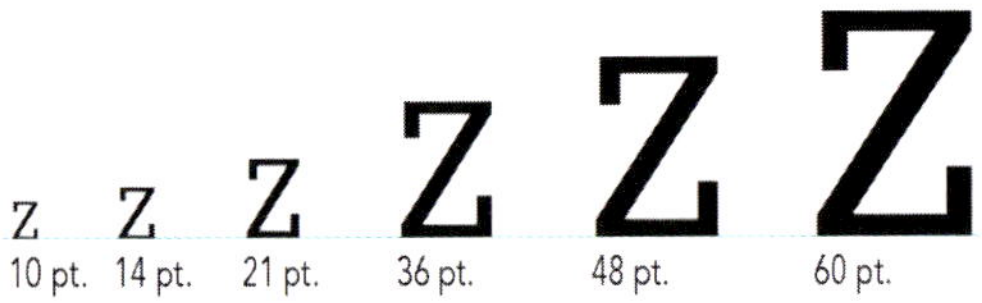

Z   Z   Z   Z   Z   Z
10 pt. 14 pt. 21 pt.   36 pt.   48 pt.   60 pt.

FIGURE 2-39

Examples of different leadings

Leading is the distance between lines of type and is measured in points. During the days of metal type, printers inserted extra strips of lead between long lines of text to make them easier to read. This procedure gave rise to the term "leading."

9 pt. type on 9 pt. leading

Leading is the distance between lines of type and is measured in points. During the days of metal type, printers inserted extra strips of lead between long lines of text to make them easier to read. This procedure gave rise to the term "leading."

9 pt. type on 12 pt. leading

Leading is the distance between lines of type and is measured in points. During the days of metal type, printers inserted extra strips of lead between long lines of text to make them easier to read. This procedure gave rise to the term "leading."

9 pt. type on 16 pt. leading

FIGURE 2-40

Examples of different line lengths

As lines of text get long, it can be difficult for the reader to move from the end of one line to the beginning of the next. On the other hand, short line lengths break up the text and interrupt the reader. The ideal line length depends on the design of the typeface, type size, line spacing, and length of the copy. Generally, a line should have 55 or 60 characters, or 9 to 10 words, for optimal readability.

1.25" line length

As lines of text get long, it can be difficult for the reader to move from the end of one line to the beginning of the next. On the other hand, short line lengths break up the text and interrupt the reader. The ideal line length depends on the design of the typeface, type size, line spacing, and length of the copy. Generally, a line should have 55 or 60 characters, or 9 to 10 words, for optimal readability.

2.25" line length

As lines of text get long, it can be difficult for the reader to move from the end of one line to the beginning of the next. On the other hand, short line lengths break up the text and interrupt the reader. The ideal line length depends on the design of the typeface, type size, line spacing, and length of the copy. Generally, a line should have 55 or 60 characters, or 9 to 10 words, for optimal readability.

3.875" line length

and right sides, as in many newspapers and magazines. Like all type features, alignment is a design decision. For example, left alignment is considered the most legible and easy-to-read alignment. Justified alignment creates a more organized layout because the lines of type are all the same width. See Figure 2-41 for examples of alignment.

More Ways to Modify Type

Once you've created type and modified it the way you want it to look, you can use the Selection (Pointer) tool to move the type anywhere you want in your design. You can apply color to type, and you can apply a stroke around type with any style or color you like. Finally, type set in vector-draw software can be attached to any shape path you want, which lets you create all sorts of interesting designs with type. See the examples in Figures 2-42 and 2-43 for unique type layouts and designs.

FIGURE 2-41

Examples of different alignments

The alignment of the text within text blocks contributes to the tone of your documents. When the text is aligned to one margin and ragged on the other, it can create an informal feeling. Left-aligned text is easier to read than right-aligned text. Avoid right alignment unless it is appropriate as a design treatment. Justified text aligns on both the left and right and is used in newspapers, newsletters, and in some books. Justified text is sometimes considered more formal than ragged text. It optimizes the amount of copy you can fit on a page.

Align left

The alignment of the text within text blocks contributes to the tone of your documents. When the text is aligned to one margin and ragged on the other, it can create an informal feeling. Left-aligned text is easier to read than right-aligned text. Avoid right alignment unless it is appropriate as a design treatment. Justified text aligns on both the left and right and is used in newspapers, newsletters, and in some books. Justified text is sometimes considered more formal than ragged text. It optimizes the amount of copy you can fit on a page.

Align center

The alignment of the text within text blocks contributes to the tone of your documents. When the text is aligned to one margin and ragged on the other, it can create an informal feeling. Left-aligned text is easier to read than right-aligned text. Avoid right alignment unless it is appropriate as a design treatment. Justified text aligns on both the left and right and is used in newspapers, newsletters, and in some books. Justified text is sometimes considered more formal than ragged text. It optimizes the amount of copy you can fit on a page.

Align right

The alignment of the text within text blocks contributes to the tone of your documents. When the text is aligned to one margin and ragged on the other, it can create an informal feeling. Left-aligned text is easier to read than right-aligned text. Avoid right alignment unless it is appropriate as a design treatment. Justified text aligns on both the left and right and is used in newspapers, newsletters, and in some books. Justified text is sometimes considered more formal than ragged text. It optimizes the amount of copy you can fit on a page.

Justified

FIGURE 2-42

Several different type layouts

FIGURE 2-43

Two unique type designs

WHEN IT'S TIME TO OUTPUT

What You'll Learn

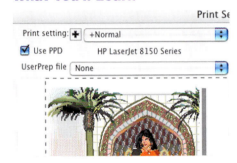

In this section, you will learn about printing options for your vector-drawing work.

Making Printing Decisions

As you work on a vector-draw project, you will want to check your progress by printing the file to a printer connected to your computer or network. The printed copy will more accurately reflect the image that you're viewing on your monitor. Printing in vector-draw software involves more than just clicking a Print button; you'll have a number of choices to make to get the results you want. You will learn different aspects of printing throughout this book; each type of software handles printing differently, as does each type of printer.

Both Illustrator and FreeHand have fairly complex Print dialog boxes (see Figures 2-44 and 2-45), but the following sections describe a few of the most important features:

Printer Selection

This is where you choose the printer to which you want to send your file. If you have one printer connected directly to your computer, you will have only one choice. But if you are part of a network, you may have several printers from which to choose. In this case, always make sure before you print that you have the correct printer selected.

Number of Copies

You can choose to print one copy or any number of copies. In FreeHand, this area of the Print dialog box also lets you choose which pages in a multipage document you want to print. Illustrator can produce only one-page documents.

FIGURE 2-44
Illustrator Print dialog box

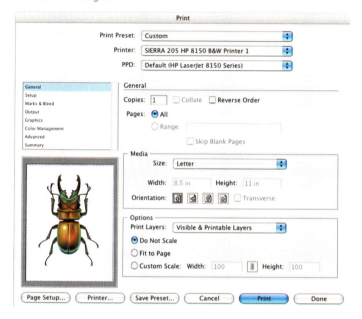

FIGURE 2-45
FreeHand Print Setup dialog box

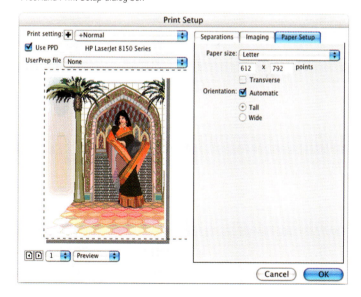

Media

Many printers can handle several sizes of **media** (paper as well as envelopes). This is where you would select the paper **size** and **orientation** (**portrait** or **landscape**), as shown in Figure 2-46.

Scaled outputs

Sometimes you will create designs that are larger or smaller than the paper sizes available with your printer. In this case, you will need to **scale** the output, enlarging or reducing it by a percentage you select. See Figure 2-47. For example, you can choose to shrink a large image so it will fit on an 8.5" × 11" piece of paper. Or you can create a very small design and scale it to 300% so it prints larger and is easier to see. Another way to print a large file is to **Tile** the output, which prints different parts of the file at actual size, but on separate pieces of paper. Then you just tape the pieces together to show a complete design.

FIGURE 2-46
Examples of portrait and landscape output

Portrait output

Landscape output

Vector-Draw Software   Chapter 2

Output Mode

Designers use two types of **output modes**: composites and separations. **Composite output** shows you all of the elements on the page in their correct positions and in their correct values and/or colors. **Separations** print each color used in the document as a separate output, simulating how the file will output to film or to printing plates to be used for printing the file on a printing press.

In print graphics, output goes far beyond just printing out a proof on a laser or inkjet printer. You'll learn more about separations and printing in Chapter 6.

FIGURE 2-47
Examples of scaled output

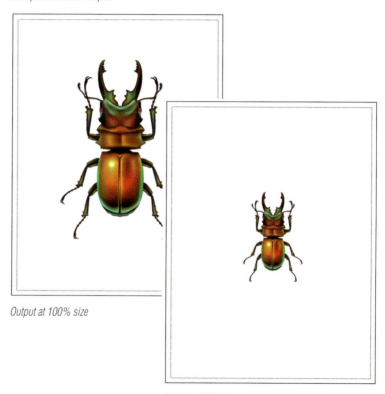

Output at 100% size

Output at 50% size

Vector-draw software is an important tool in computer graphics. With its wide assortment of tools, software helps designers draw and illustrate electronically with dozens of tools and commands, creating graphics for an array of design projects from simple to complex. The most important point to remember about vector-draw software is that it creates resolution-independent graphics, with their wide assortment of tools and effects, Illustrator and FreeHand let you create objects and type for almost any graphics application.

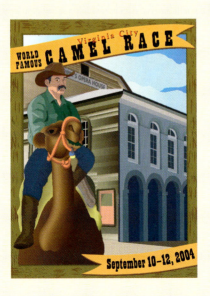

KEY TERMS AND CONCEPTS

alignment
anchor points
Beziér curves
bitmapped images
Character palette
CMYK
Color/Mixer and Tints palette
color models
composite output
curved paths
direction lines
fill
gradient
grayscale
guides
handles
interface
landscape
leading
line length
media
non-proportional
objects
orientation
Output mode
paths

pixels
point
portrait
Printer selection
process color
Properties/Object palette
proportional
resolution dependent
resolution independent
rulers
save
scale
screen tints
separations
size
straight paths
stroke
Swatches palette
tile
toolbar
transform
type
type size
type style
vector-draw software
vector paths

CHAPTER REVIEW

1. Compare how vector-draw and bitmapped images deal with resolution.

   _____

   _____

   _____

2. What two project features can you modify in the New Document dialog box?

   _____

   _____

   _____

3. What are the differences between the Save, Save as (Save), and Save a Copy commands?

   _____

   _____

   _____

4. What is the interface of a software application?

   _____

   _____

   _____

5. What are ruler guides used for?

   _____

   _____

   _____

6. What are the differences between the Selection (Pointer) tool and the Direct Selection (Subselect) tool?

   _____

   _____

   _____

7. Why is the Line Segment (Line) tool a better choice for creating straight lines than the Pencil tool?

   _____

   _____

   _____

8. What basic shapes can you create with the Shape Creation tools?

   _____

   _____

   _____

9. What is the difference between stroke and fill?

   _____

   _____

10. What variations can be applied to a stroke?

   _____

   _____

   _____

11. What were the two main color models discussed in this chapter?

   _____

   _____

   _____

12. Describe a screen tint.

   _____

   _____

   _____

13. What four colors make up process color?

_____

_____

_____

14. Name two Transform tools and describe what they do.

_____

_____

_____

15. What two components make up paths?

_____

_____

_____

16. Describe the difference in shapes you create when you click with the Pen tool and when you click and drag with the Pen tool.

_____

_____

_____

17. What are handles used for?

_____

_____

_____

18. Name four type features you can modify to change the appearance of type:

_____

_____

_____

19. What elements can you control in the Print dialog box?

_____

_____

_____

A local graphics industry group named Design Sessions has asked you to design a logo for them. The organization represents local designers and art directors, and has monthly meetings with speakers who discuss industry issues and new technologies. The group has given you some specific requirements for the logo. It must contain:

a. one rectangle or square shape
b. one oval or circle shape
c. one triangle shape
d. the words "Design Sessions"
e. the words "Your Local Graphics Community"

Include all five elements in the logo. Don't leave out any element, add any new elements, or repeat any elements. The three shapes can be any size, in any position, and have any stroke and/or fill applied. The words must have "Design Sessions" as the more dominant type (bigger, bolder) and "Your Local Graphics Community" as the subordinate type (smaller, less bold). Do some research on how four or five other graphics industry groups have designed their logos. Create thumbnails and roughs as described in Chapter 1, and then choose the best of your design ideas and create it in vector-draw software.

One Step Beyond

Use your finished logo in a design for a stationery package. Include letterhead (8.5" × 11"), a #10 business envelope (9.5" × 4.125"), and a business card (3.5" × 2" or 2" × 3.5"). Do some appropriate research into stationery packages, create some thumbnails and roughs, and choose your best design idea before you get on the computer. Make up an address and phone number to go in to the stationery

Two Steps Beyond

Take your logo and create an 8.5" x 11" flyer that promotes Design Sessions to high school and college design students. Create the flyer entirely in vector-draw software, and use the tools to create some graphics that work with the logo and call attention to the group. Again, research different types of graphics produced specifically for students (CD covers and fashion ads are a good place to start), and create thumbnails and roughs before you start working with the software.

Your friend is planning to open a seafood restaurant called Captain Nemo's and has asked you to help her design a flyer. You have decided to begin by tracing a fish shape from a template. In the drive and folder where your Data Files are stored, you will find three vector-draw files with the same image titled IG 2-1.ai (Illustrator), IG 2-1.fh (FreeHand), and IG 2-1.cdr (CorelDRAW). These files are templates of a fish.

1. Open the appropriate version of the IG 2-1 file with your vector-draw software application and immediately use the Save As command to save a copy of the file to your computer, using the filename Fish.
2. Using the fish image as a guide, draw the fish by creating shapes with your application's drawing tools. Use a 1-point stroke, with no fill.
3. Edit the paths you draw and make them match the template more accurately.
4. Fill the shapes with color to make your fish look more realistic. You can use gradients to create a 3D look. Work on mastering the Pen tool and on using stroke, fill, and color to make your fish look realistic.

One Step Beyond

Once you have completed the fish, select all of its elements with the **Select All** command, then group the elements together so they act like one graphic. Then use the **Copy and Paste** commands to create a school of fish, making them different sizes and colors. Create as many fish as you like.

Two Steps Beyond

Choose a picture of an image you would like to draw. Scan the image on a scanner as a .tif file with 150 dpi resolution. Then use the **Place** or the **Import** command to put the image in your document as a template. Use the Layers palette to create a layer on top of the image, then attempt to draw the image in paths.

You have been hired by Mountain PhotoMagic, a partnership of photographers who shoot traditional and digital photos. They develop traditional prints and slides and print high-quality, archival digital prints and burn them to CD-ROM. The company also does mounting and framing of photographic and digital prints. They want you to design full-color and grayscale versions of a Mountain PhotoMagic logo.

1. Begin by researching different logos for photographers. Notice that most logos have two parts, a symbol and type (usually the name of the company).
2. Design your logo to include a symbol and type. Do as many thumbnails as possible, then choose the two best designs and draw them as accurately as you can with pencils or markers at about 6" x 6" in size.

3. Show your roughs to several people, explaining what the company does. Get as much input as you can to help you choose one final design.
4. Create a comprehensive of the final design. Attempt to use color as a design element; what colors would present this company best?
5. Take the comprehensive and scan it at full size, 150 dpi, in TIFF format. Use the Import or Place command to put this scan into your vector-draw document. Use the image as a template and trace the symbol with the pen tool. Choose an appropriate typeface and create the type. Position the image and text elements so they create a unified design. Produce the grayscale version first, then use Save As to create a second document with the same artwork. Open this document and colorize all of the elements. Output both versions and mount them on a piece of presentation board for the client. See Figure 2-48 for examples.

FIGURE 2-48
Examples of comparable logo designs

Vector-draw software is very popular in the graphics industry. The vector-draw designs in Figure 2-49 use many of the principles discussed in this book. Write a critique of each design, focusing on the designer's use of shape, color, and layout

FIGURE 2-49

Examples of design work done in vector-draw software

Jussi Gamache
Freezepop logo
Freezepop collateral
www.archenemy.com/jussi

Laurence Dabek
Adler Planetarium logo

CHAPTER 3

RASTER/PAINT SOFTWARE

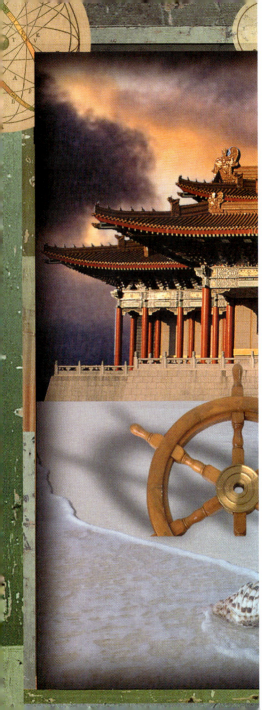

RASTER/PAINT SOFTWARE

Where It All Started

Humankind's fascination with recording the images around them dates back to primitive cave paintings. One ancient development, the **camera obscura** (Latin for "dark chamber"), used light to project life-like images on the wall of a darkened room (see Figure 3-1). By the 1800s, artists used compact versions of the camera to project and sketch images for finished drawings.

In 1826, in France, Joseph Niepce became the first person to produce a photographic image on a metal plate by using this technique (see Figure 3-2). After Niepce's death in 1833, his partner Louis Daguerre continued to perfect their photographic process.

The use of film-based photography exploded in the late 1800s, and continued to advance throughout the 20th century. George Eastman's development of the first **Kodak camera** (see Figure 3-3) in 1888 allowed everyone to take pictures of the world around them. Film-based photography became the foundation for graphic reproduction starting in the early 1900s and continuing up to only a few short years ago.

Digital Beginnings

As computers became more commonplace in the graphics industry, getting photographic images into the electronic environment became a necessity. The hardware was already developed—electronic scanners were able to capture traditional photographs digitally. But there was a need for software that could work with these scanned images. A breakthrough came in 1990, when Adobe Corporation shipped Adobe Photoshop 1.0. Originally developed by two brothers, Thomas and John Knoll, and called ImagePro, this software has grown to become the dominant image editing and electronic painting software in the world. Although there are several less expensive and less powerful applications, Photoshop has been able to maintain its top position throughout the years since its introduction.

FIGURE 3-1
Camera obscura

FIGURE 3-3
First Kodak camera

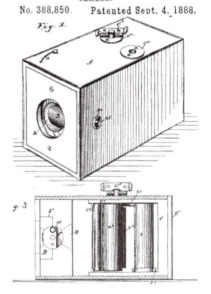

FIGURE 3-2
First picture taken by Joseph Niepce

PHOTOSHOP: AN OVERVIEW

What You'll Learn

▶ *In this lesson, you will be introduced to some of the powerful features of Photoshop.*

Photoshop is a bitmap-based application. This means that every image in Photoshop is made up of a series of dots, also called **pixels**. The first program created to work with pixels was MacPaint, an application that "painted" with electronic dots. But Photoshop was initially introduced as an image manipulation (rather than image creation) software, able to modify and manipulate photographic images in a digital environment (see Figure 3-4).

Since its introduction, Photoshop has grown into a powerful graphics application that lets artists work with existing bitmapped images and create original art. But Photoshop's ability to work with photographic images has always been its strength. Photoshop has a wide range of tools and filters that can adjust and correct the color, contrast, and dynamic range of any image. New tools such as the Healing Brush, Patch, and Color

Replacement can fix almost any damaged image. And with layers and layer effects, designers can create rich and complex visuals out of the simplest of images.

Recent versions of Photoshop also contain more powerful type handling capabilities.

Text can now be set along any shape path and specialized text effects can create exciting typographic designs with one mouse-click. Photoshop can work with numerous file formats, including the raw file format used by most digital cameras.

Finally, Photoshop has increased capabilities for creating graphics for the Web, including the ability to "slice" complex images and apply the correct compression and format settings for use in the HTML environment.

FIGURE 3-4

Photoshop program window

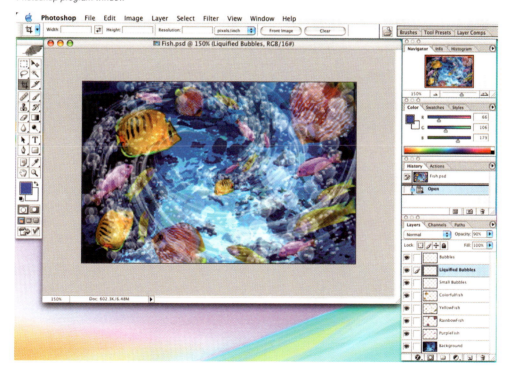

HOW ARE PHOTOGRAPHIC IMAGES CREATED?

What You'll Learn

▶ *In this lesson, you will learn where images come from and what devices are used to capture images electronically.*

Film-Based Images

Photographic images have traditionally come from film-based technologies. Film has evolved since the 1800s, but the basic concept of film has remained fairly constant: An emulsion, or coating, is applied to a thin, clear base material. This emulsion contains silver **halides**, small particles that darken upon exposure to light. When the film is developed, images appear within the emulsion. (See Figure 3-5.) These images are "fixed" on the film with development chemicals so they remain (somewhat) permanent. These images can be either on negative film, which is then exposed onto paper and developed as a **print**, or on positive film, also known as **transparency film**, which produces images on slides. (See Figure 3-6.)

Scanners

In the 1970s, the **electronic scanner** was introduced to capture illustrations and photographs electronically. The early scanner looked nothing like today's scanners; it was a large device that sometimes took up an entire room. The computer that ran the scanner was a DOS-based machine, meaning you had to program the scanner with a long series of typed-in codes; there were no drop-down menus or dialog boxes. (See Figure 3-7.) The light from the scanner would scan the image, then be split through a series of photocells that would break down the light into its four component color parts. These would travel through color-correction computers; the corrected light would then expose graphic arts film. Four pieces of film would be produced: cyan, magenta, yellow, and black.

Today, two types of scanners are used in the graphics industry: flatbed and drum. **Flatbed scanners** (see Figure 3-8) are the most common and least expensive; you can buy one for under $100. These scanners use **CCDs** (charged coupled devices), which are like electronic eyes, to capture the light that is reflected or shown through the image. This information is then converted to value and color, and the image is re-created electronically. In a flatbed scanner, the image remains stationary on the glass while the CCDs move across the image. Some high-end flatbed scanners sell for over $30,000 and are extremely accurate in capturing image color and detail.

FIGURE 3-5
Traditional film uses chemicals and light to reproduce images

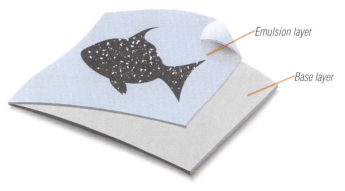

Emulsion layer

Base layer

FIGURE 3-6
Negative film, a print, and transparency film

Drum scanners use more expensive, and more accurate, **PMTs** (photo multiplier tubes) to capture images. This type of scanner mounts the image on a rotating drum. As the image moves, the stationary PMTs scan and collect the information electronically. Drum scanners can cost as much as $150,000. (See Figure 3-9.) Because flatbed scanners are becoming more accurate, drum scanners are not as common in the industry as they used to be; their hefty price tag makes them a major investment for any company.

Digital Image Capture

Although scanners are the primary technology used to capture graphic images electronically, another recent technology is slowly replacing scanners in some areas of the industry. The advance of **digital cameras** is revolutionizing the way images are captured. Several years ago a good, high-resolution digital camera cost over $5,000. But today excellent cameras are available for less than $800! (See Figure 3-10.)

FIGURE 3-7
Electronic scanner from the 1980s

FIGURE 3-8
Flatbed scanner

The advantages of digital photography are the ability to shoot any image, anywhere. And the files can be downloaded to almost any computer, anywhere in the world. The disadvantage is that digital photography still doesn't match the quality of a traditional scan. But it's getting better every day.

QUICKTIP

Like other areas of graphics, don't assume that you can buy a piece of equipment and become an instant expert. Learn to use your scanner by purchasing a good book, or by taking a class or workshop. The same goes for digital photography. If you want to be a good photographer (digital or otherwise), take a photography class, participate in a few good workshops, and practice.

FIGURE 3-9
Drum scanner

FIGURE 3-10
Digital photography is slowly replacing scanners

RESOLUTION AND COLOR

What You'll Learn

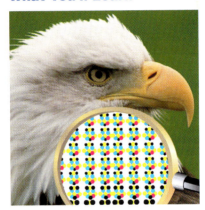

▶ *In this lesson, you will learn how resolution and color models are used in Photoshop.*

An Overview

Once you have created photographic images, what can you do with them? Unlike the vector-based art you learned about in the previous chapter, everything you work with in Photoshop is raster-based. **Raster artwork**, or **bitmapped art** as it is also commonly called, is made up of a series of dots arranged in a grid (see Figure 3-11). These dots vary in value and color, and work the same as the dots that make up the pictures on your television. To better understand what makes up a high-quality raster image, you need to look at three concepts: resolution, color models, and file formats. Resolution and color will be discussed in this concept; you will learn about file formats in the next concept.

Resolution

Resolution is the number of dots that make up an image. Unfortunately, the graphics industry has four ways to measure resolution, and they don't all work together. As shown in Figure 3-12, there are **lpi** (lines per inch) and **spi** (spots per inch) for analog dots on traditional printing film and plates, and **dpi** (dots per inch) and **ppi** (pixels per inch) for electronic dots on computer screens and electronic devices such as a scanner or printer. (Chapter 6 provides more detail on resolution.)

Dots are measured by the number of dots in one inch, both vertically and horizontally. More dots per square inch means more information can be displayed, providing a higher-quality image. In print graphics there is a wide variety of resolution requirements. Newspaper graphics print using an 85 lpi resolution, whereas high-quality color printing can go as high as 175 or 200 lpi. On a computer you will usually work with images ranging from 72 dpi to 300 dpi, and possibly higher, depending on how the image will be reproduced.

Why is all of this important? Because once you start working in Photoshop, you have to make decisions about the resolution of the images you work with. With raster images, the image resolution directly reflects the electronic file size on your computer. A 6" x 9" color image at 72 dpi is about an 820 K file, at 150 dpi is about a 3.5 MB file, at 300 dpi is about a 14 MB file, and at 600 dpi is about a 56 MB file! (The file size will vary according to the complexity of the image.) So, understanding what image resolution you need is very important,

and it's a decision you have to make—there's no drop-down menu in Photoshop that tells you what resolution or size your file should be.

This use of dots also makes raster files **resolution dependent**. As a raster image is enlarged, the number of dots does not increase; the dots in the image get larger.

This reduces the resolution of the image. If a 4" x 5" image at 200 dpi is enlarged to 8" x 10", the image size is doubled; therefore, the resolution is cut in half, because all of the dots are now twice as big. So the image resolution would be reduced to 100 dpi!

FIGURE 3-11

How bitmapped art uses dots

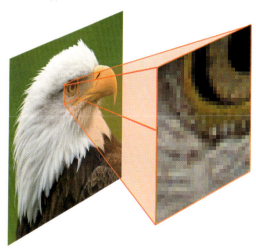

FIGURE 3-12

Different dot patterns in graphics

lpi   spi

Color Models

Photoshop supports several different color models. The three most important are **grayscale**, **CMYK**, and **RGB**. You learned about grayscale and CMYK in Chapter 2; the concepts are the same in raster software. In the **RGB color model**, red, green, and blue are known as the **additive primary colors**, meaning that these three colors added together make up white light. (See Figure 3-13.) Your computer's color monitor, like a television, uses RGB to re-create color. Raster software also uses RGB to re-create images electronically. RGB is Photoshop's "native color model," meaning that the software performs best when you use RGB as the working color model, whether you manipulate an image, adjust its color, or paint it electronically. The RGB color model also allows you to use all of Photoshop's tools and commands;

FIGURE 3-13

Combining RGB, the three additive primaries

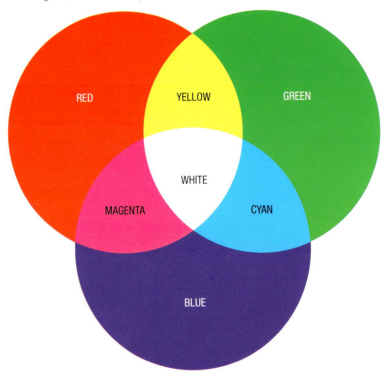

other color models limit your ability to use these tools. You can also use the CMYK model in Photoshop, because this color model is used in most printing processes. (See Figure 3-14.)

How do you determine which color model to use? If you are using Photoshop mainly as a design tool, use RGB. But if you are correcting color, using CMYK gives you a more accurate representation of how the final printed piece will look.

You'll learn more about the different ways to color-manage an image in Chapter 6.

FIGURE 3-14

Recreating full color art with CMYK using four colors

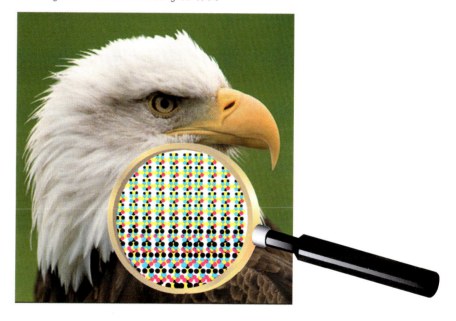

OPEN AND SAVE FILES

What You'll Learn

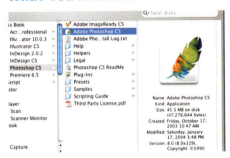

 In this lesson, you will learn how to open and save files and use the correct file formats.

Overview

The procedure for launching Photoshop is the same as launching vector-draw software. On the Macintosh, open the program from the Applications folder; on a Windows computer, use the Programs (or All Programs) submenu on the Start menu. (See Figures 3-15 and 3-16.)

Working with Documents

Once the application is up and running, you can click **File** on the menu bar, then click either **New** or **Open.** As in vector-draw software, the New command creates a new file with a blank canvas, and the Open command opens existing files.

Never manipulate an original!

When working in Photoshop always remember this rule: *Never manipulate an original.* Once you have modified a file in raster software, it's almost impossible to revert back to an earlier version of the file. Standard working procedure in the graphics industry is to open an original file, then immediately do a Save as and create a duplicate of the original using a different name. Put the original in a safe place where no one will accidentally open it. Then you can modify the duplicate file.

The New dialog box in Photoshop (shown in Figure 3-17) lets you set your document's size and orientation. The document size is an important consideration, because it affects the overall file size on your computer. You can also use this dialog box to set the document resolution, **Color Mode** (another name for the Color Model), and Background contents, which defines the background color of your new document.

Once you have created a new document, the next step is to save it. The commands for saving in raster software are similar to those in vector-draw software: Save, Save as, and Save a Version. The Save As dialog box is shown in Figure 3-18. Photoshop also has a Save for Web command, which displays an optimize window that lets you format images specifically for use on the Web. You will need to name your file and save it in the correct folder for future retrieval.

File Formats

Another important part of saving a Photoshop file is choosing the correct **file format**. As you can see in Figure 3-18, Photoshop can save in 18 different file formats! (Not all file formats are available every time you save a file, nor can all files be saved in all formats.) Which file format should you choose? It depends on what you plan to use the file for, and how you want to display or output the file.

FIGURE 3-15

Launching Photoshop (Macintosh)

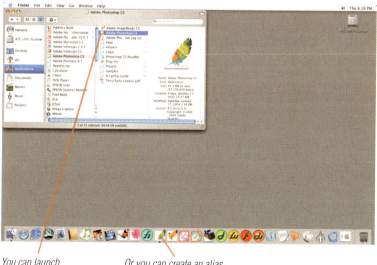

You can launch Photoshop from the Applications folder

Or you can create an alias in the Dock and launch Photoshop from here

FIGURE 3-16

Launching Photoshop (Windows)

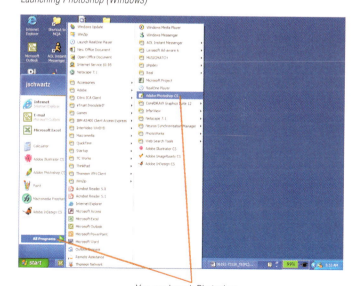

You can launch Photoshop from the All Programs menu

Fortunately, at an introductory level you can get by with knowing the following five formats:

- **.psd (Photoshop)**—This is Photoshop's native file format. This is the best format for your working files because it lets you preserve layers and, in the RGB color mode, lets you access all the tools and commands available in Photoshop. (You'll learn more about layers later in this chapter.)
- **.tif (Tag Image File Format)**—The original bitmapped file format developed by Aldus and Microsoft Corporations, this format can be any resolution, in grayscale or color, and is widely supported on both Macintosh and Windows computers. Designers use this format for graphics files that will be printed, instead of displayed on a computer.
- **.eps (Encapsulated Postscript)**—This is a specialized Postscript file used to store both bitmapped and vector graphics. Files in .eps format can be at any resolution and can be grayscale or color. Like .tif files, this format is also used for print graphics files.
- **.jpg (Joint Photographic Experts Group)**—This is a compressed bitmapped image format used in both grayscale and color, and works best with complex photographic images.

FIGURE 3-17
New dialog box

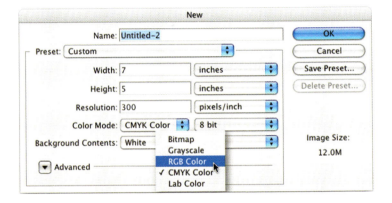

The .jpg format uses a compression system described as **lossy** (that is, the image loses quality when you open and resave the image). The .jpg format can be used for print graphics but is mainly used for computer-based presentations such as the Web and multimedia.

- **.gif (Graphics Interchange Format)**— This is a bitmapped graphics file format used specifically for the Web. Like the .jpg format, this is also a compressed file format, but it uses only 256 colors, as opposed to the millions of colors used by the other formats. The .gif format is effective for simple graphics and illustrations but not for color photos, which require many more colors.

In a nutshell, .psd is used for working with Photoshop files; .tif and .eps are used for print-based graphics; and .jpg and .gif are used for monitor-based graphics. So before you start a Photoshop project, be sure to decide what you'll need for resolution, color mode, and file format.

FIGURE 3-18
Save As dialog box

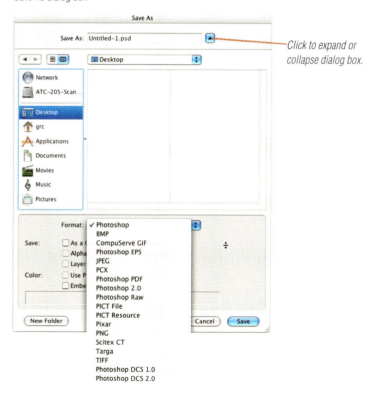

Click to expand or collapse dialog box.

EVERYDAY TOOLS AND COMMANDS

What You'll Learn

▶ *In this lesson, you will learn about the basic tools available in Photoshop.*

Overview

The first thing you'll notice when you open Photoshop is that the interface is similar to other Adobe applications. This will help you in learning about other Adobe applications as you progress through this book.

Rulers and Guides

Like vector-draw software, Photoshop also has rulers and guides to help you measure and position elements on the page. Click **View** on the menu bar and then select **Rulers**. The horizontal and vertical rulers will appear on the top and left edges of your project window. You can use any tool to drag guides from a ruler onto your page; they remain unlocked unless you click the View menu and click **Lock Guides** to lock them. To get rid of a guide, click the **Move tool** and then drag the guide back to the ruler and it will disappear.

Toolbox

The **Toolbox** in Photoshop, shown in Figure 3-19, is divided into four main areas: selection tools, modification tools, vector/type tools, and miscellaneous tools. As in vector-draw software, many tools have submenus with even more tools from which to choose.

The next sections provide a summary of the tools you will need at an introductory level. Some tools will be discussed in more detail later in the chapter.

Selection Tools

These tools let you select and move bitmapped images in a variety of ways. The main selection tools are the Marquee selection tools, Move tool, Lasso tools, Magic Wand tool, Crop tool, and Slice tools. The Crop tool lets you click-and-drag the mouse to make a cropping selection; when you double-click within this area, all other imagery outside the cropping selection disappears. **Cropping** is an old graphics term for selecting the parts of an image you want to show and deleting the parts you don't. Cropping is a design decision, but it also helps keep down your document's file size; retaining excess imagery can make your files larger than necessary. See Figure 3-20 for an example of cropping. The Slice tool allows you to select parts of an image and optimize that part for display on the Web.

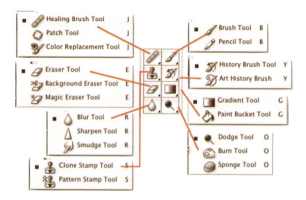

Modification tools

FIGURE 3-19
Photoshop Toolbox

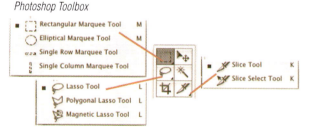

Selection tools

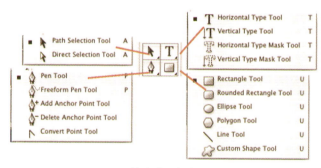

Vector/type tools

Miscellaneous tools

Modification Tools

You use modification tools to manipulate images in various ways. These tools include the Healing Brush and Patch tools, which can fix damaged photographs; the Brush and Pencils tools, which you use to paint or draw on images or create new images (see Figure 3-21 for an example of the Brush tool); and the **Clone Stamp tool**, which copies parts of images and allows you to "reproduce" them anywhere else on the image you like. The History Brush tools can restore pixels that have been deleted or erased; the Eraser tool (see Figure 3-22) erases pixels. The Gradient tool creates gradient blends of any number of colors you choose; the Blur and Sharpen tools let you "smudge" or sharpen parts of images; and the Dodge and Burn tools can make parts of images lighter or darker.

Vector/Type Tools

Although Photoshop was designed primarily to work with bitmapped images, it also contains a comprehensive array of type- and vector-based tools. These tools match almost exactly the basic tools available in Illustrator. When you use Photoshop to create type or vector images, the images exist on their own layer, independent of the bitmapped images with which you may be working. Be aware, however, that even

FIGURE 3-20

Example of cropping an image

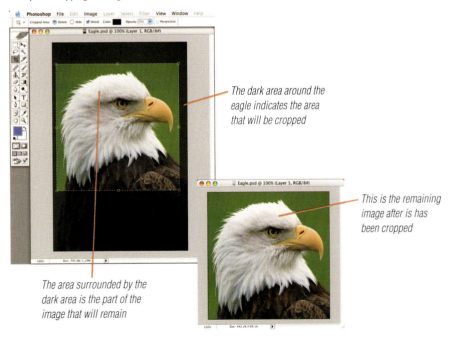

The dark area around the eagle indicates the area that will be cropped

This is the remaining image after is has been cropped

The area surrounded by the dark area is the part of the image that will remain

FIGURE 3-21

Drawing with the Brush tool

though you may be using vector shapes, they will eventually be converted to dots once you save your file to a format other than .psd and will print like any other raster-based image.

Miscellaneous Tools

Other tools include the Zoom and Hand tools you are familiar with from many other programs. The **Eyedropper tools** (see Figure 3-23) let you select color in your files so you can find out what makes up the color, or use that color in other areas of your image. The Notes tools let you create electronic "sticky notes" that you can use to attach nonprinting comments to any Photoshop file.

FIGURE 3-22

Using the Eraser tool

The Eraser tool has erased (deleted) this portion of the photograph

FIGURE 3-23

Sampling color with the eyedropper tool

The Eyedropper tool allows you to select, or sample, any color used in an image

THE POWER OF SELECTION!

What You'll Learn

▶ *In this lesson, you will learn how to select different parts of an image.*

One of the most important techniques to learn when working in raster software is selection. For some projects, the work you do will involve manipulating or modifying the entire image. But there will be times when you want to modify only a portion of an image. Or you may want to create a photomontage or other styles of original art that require you to choose only parts of an image. For this type of work you need to become proficient with the various selection tools in Photoshop, shown in Figure 3-24.

Marquee Selection Tool

The Marquee selection tool lets you make a rectangle or square selection or an oval or circle selection (see Figure 3-25), and lets you select a single row of pixels, either horizontally or vertically. The tool lets you quickly select simple rectangles and ovals.

Lasso Tools

There are three lasso tools: Lasso, Polygonal Lasso, and Magnetic Lasso. These tools are manually based, meaning that you either drag or repeatedly click the mouse button around an object to select it. With the Lasso tool you move the pointer over an image, then click-and-drag until you surround the image with a line, trying to get back to where you started dragging, and then release the mouse button. A selection (which looks like a series of moving dashed

---

DESIGNTIP **Using the Pen Tool**

Another way to make selections is to use the Pen tool. Draw an enclosed vector path, using the Direct Selection tool to reshape the path to match your proposed selection. Display the Paths palette (click **Window** on the menu bar, then click **Paths**), save the path, and then use the **Make Selection** command in the Paths palette menu to convert the path to a selection. If you are good with the Pen tool, this can be a very accurate way to make selections.

---

lines, commonly called "marching ants")
then appears. (See Figure 3-26.) The Lasso
tool is fast and easy to learn; however, the
accuracy of the selection depends on the
accuracy of your mouse movements.

FIGURE 3-25

Examples of rectangular and oval marquee selection

An Elliptical marquee selection

A Rectangular marquee selection

FIGURE 3-24

Photoshop selection tools

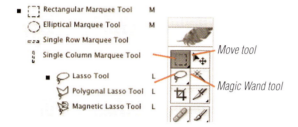

Move tool

Magic Wand tool

FIGURE 3-26

Lasso tool

A selection being made with the Lasso tool

FIGURE 3-27

Polygonal Lasso tool

A selection being made with the Polygonal Lasso tool

The other two Lasso tools let you select shapes more accurately. The Polygonal Lasso tool uses the same selection method as the Pen tool in Illustrator. Every time you click on an image, the Polygonal Lasso tool creates a direction change; the lines between the clicks form a straight line. (See Figure 3-27.) But you can't click-and-drag to create curved lines, and like the Lasso tool, you need to go back to where you made your first click to enclose the selection. The Magnetic Lasso tool attempts to judge the edges of your selection, then magnetically locks your selection lines to it. (See Figure 3-28.) This works best if your selection has a highly defined edge. If the edge lacks contrast, the Magnetic Lasso will have a hard time determining the edges, and the selection becomes less accurate.

Magic Wand Tool

The Magic Wand is an interesting tool that automatically attempts to select a range of values. Every image has different values within it, whether the image is grayscale or color. The Magic Wand tool can be set to recognize different ranges of value and select only that range within the image, as shown in Figure 3-29.

FIGURE 3-28
Magnetic Lasso tool

A selection being made with the Magnetic Lasso tool

FIGURE 3-29
Magic Wand selection

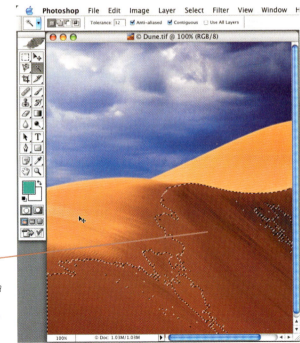

The Magic Wand tool selects an area of values within a range

When you choose the Magic Wand tool, the Options Bar at the top of the screen shows a text box labeled Tolerance. The smaller the number you type into this box, the narrower the value range (color and shades) of the selection. The higher the number, the wider the value range of the selection. See Figure 3-30 for an example of how different tolerance settings affect the range selected.

This tool works best if your image has well defined areas of value. If the values tend to blend together, the Magic Wand tool has a harder time making an accurate selection.

Both the Lasso tools and the Magic Wand tool have keyboard commands that let you add or subtract from the original selection, so you can refine the selection and make it more accurate.

Once you select an object or area using any selection tool, you can use the Move tool to move the selection around within the document. (See Figure 3-31.) When you select a specific part of an image, any changes you make affect the selected area only. This is the power of selection, and it's a skill that you should master to become proficient in any raster software.

FIGURE 3-30

How changing Tolerance affects the Magic Wand's selection

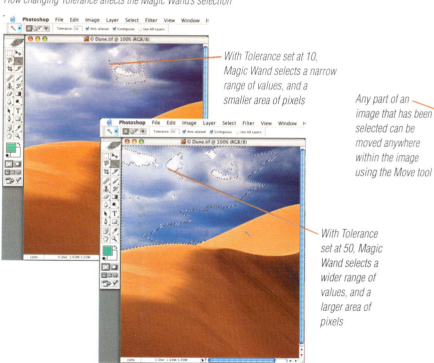

With Tolerance set at 10, Magic Wand selects a narrow range of values, and a smaller area of pixels

With Tolerance set at 50, Magic Wand selects a wider range of values, and a larger area of pixels

FIGURE 3-31

Using the Move tool

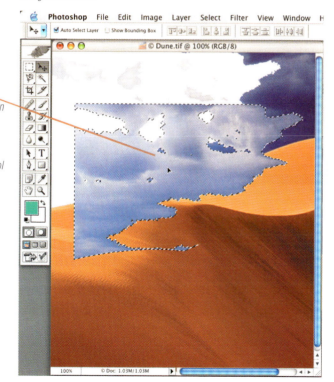

Any part of an image that has been selected can be moved anywhere within the image using the Move tool

IT ALL WORKS WITH LAYERS

What You'll Learn

In this lesson, you will learn how to work with layers in Photoshop.

Overview

When you're working with Photoshop and other graphics software, it's important to understand the concept of layers and the distribution of different images and effects onto layers within a document.

Using **layers**, Photoshop separates multiple images on different "levels," letting you manipulate each image without affecting the other images in your project. Without layers, working with complex files could be difficult. Photoshop also has many **Layer Effects** that can add excitement and dynamics to your designs.

Working with Layers

When you open a new file, one layer, called the **background layer**, is always present and locked. The **Layers palette** (see Figure 3-32) is the control center for layers in your file, so be sure it's showing at all times. (If it's not showing, click **Window** on the menu bar, then click **Layers**.) You can use the Layers palette menu to add, delete, or duplicate layers. When you copy and paste an image from one Photoshop document to another, Photoshop automatically creates a layer for that new image. If you use the Type tool to create type, Photoshop creates a separate type layer.

DESIGNTIP **Using layers for different versions**

In addition to using layers to build a project, designers also use layers to create multiple versions of the same design. By turning a layer's visibility property on and off, you can show many variations of a design while creating just one file. And the latest version, Photoshop CS, has a new palette called Layer Comps, which creates design variations more efficiently by saving different combinations of layers within the same file.

You can also change the **layering order** within the palette. Normally, the image on the top layer is the one you see on top of all of the other images. But by clicking-and-dragging any layer in the Layers palette, you can move it up or down in the layering order, changing how you see each image in your file. (See Figure 3-33.)

Finally, you can also adjust each layer's opacity, as shown in Figure 3-34. You can use this feature to make an image layer **transparent**, a very popular effect.

Layer Effects

Photoshop also has a collection of **Layer Effects** that you can add to any image on any layer. These are special effects that you

can use to add visual impact to your project. Layer Effects include Blending, Drop Shadow, Inner Shadow, Outer Glow, Inner Glow, Bevel, Emboss, Satin, Color Overlay, Gradient Overlay, and Stroke. As you can see in Figure 3-35, you can create incredible visual effects with these tools. To add a layer effect, click **Layer** on the menu bar, point to **Layer Style**, then click any effect.

FIGURE 3-32
The Layers palette

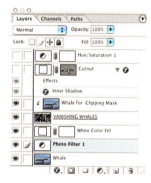

FIGURE 3-33
Adjusting the layering order

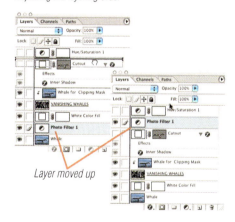

Layer moved up

FIGURE 3-34
Adjusting an image's transparency

FIGURE 3-35
Examples of different Layer Effects

TRANSFORMING IMAGES

What You'll Learn

▶ *In this lesson, you will learn how images can be transformed in Photoshop.*

Overview

Now that you've learned about creating, selecting, and adding effects to a raster project, you can explore various ways to transform your images. Photoshop has many of the same Transformation tools you use in vector-draw software. These include Scale, Rotate, and Shear. Photoshop also has shape transformation tools such as the Free Transform, Distort, and Perspective tools. See Figure 3-36 for examples of the Distort and Perspective tools.

But Photoshop's image transformation tools are what really give you power and control over your images. Summaries of the most popular image transformation tools follow.

Healing Brush and Patch Tools

The Healing Brush and Patch tools were new in Photoshop 7 and have quickly become two of the more popular tools. Both work in the same way to repair damaged areas of a photograph. In the past,

---

DESIGNTIP Learning Photography and Photoshop

Although it is possible to become proficient with Photoshop tools through learning the software, the designers who use Photoshop most effectively have a strong photography background. Take a couple of photography classes or workshops. It will greatly increase your skill in using Photoshop.

this type of repair was obvious, because you could see the changes in value between the repaired area and the adjoining areas. But these new tools work like magic; the areas they repair actually blend in with the adjoining image areas! (See Figure 3-37.) With both tools you use the Brush size to regulate the size of the area you can select

and modify. This is a valuable tool for fixing old and/or damaged photos.

Clone Stamp Tool

The Clone Stamp tool is a workhorse that's been around since the original version of Photoshop. Using this tool, you can select a particular section of

your image and re-create it over and over again. You can take a garden with just a few flowers and create a full flower bed by cloning the original flowers over and over again. (See Figure 3-38.) You can also use the Clone Stamp tool to cover up areas of a photo with different imagery.

FIGURE 3-36
Using the Distort and Perspective tools

FIGURE 3-37
Healing Brush seamlessly fixes a damaged image

Notice how all of the blemishes, spots and creases have been eliminated using the Healing Brush tool.

Eraser Tool

You use the Eraser tool to remove unwanted images or to clean up images that may have bits and pieces that you don't want to show. You can change the eraser size to erase large areas quickly or to be very precise in erasing small or tight areas of your file.

Blur, Sharpen, and Smudge Tools

The Blur, Sharpen, and Smudge tools let you alter specific parts of your image. As with the Eraser tool, you can change the tool's size to affect a small or large area, depending on your needs. Each of these tools works by clicking-and-dragging, and you can adjust the amount each tool alters your image in the Options bar at the top of the screen. The tool names are self-explanatory; you use them to blur, sharpen, and smudge any part of your image. (Smudge works almost like finger painting; it's a lot of fun!) See Figure 3-39 to see an image altered by the Blur and Sharpen tools.

FIGURE 3-38
Duplicating image areas with the Clone Stamp tool

The Clone Stamp tool was used to duplicate the canoe over and over again.

Dodge, Burn, and Sponge Tools

These tools relate to techniques common in traditional film-based photography that were done manually in the darkroom; they do the same thing in Photoshop. These tools also work by clicking-and-dragging, and you can adjust the size of the tool to modify large or small image areas. The Dodge tool lightens an image; the Burn tool darkens an image. (See Figure 3-40.)

The Sponge tool can **saturate** (heighten the color of) or **desaturate** (mute the color of) an image.

FIGURE 3-39

The Blur and Sharpen tools at work

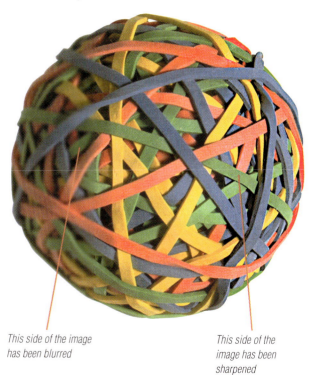

This side of the image has been blurred

This side of the image has been sharpened

FIGURE 3-40

Adjusting image lighting with Dodge and Burn tools

The Dodge and Burn tools have added highlights on the left side of the brush, shadows on the right side

PHOTOSHOP HAS TOO MUCH FUN WITH TYPE

What You'll Learn

▶ In this lesson, you will see how Photoshop can create impressive type effects.

Type in Photoshop Comes of Age

Because type is vector-based, early versions of raster software such as Photoshop had limited typographic tools and even more limited ways to work with type effectively. Back then, designers created their type designs in a vector-draw application, and then copied and pasted it into their Photoshop project. But once Adobe put type on a dedicated type layer, type in Photoshop has become increasingly powerful and easy to use.

Type Tools

Photoshop uses a **Type tool** similar to the one you use in vector-draw applications. Photoshop also has a **Character palette** that is almost identical to that in Illustrator; it lets you change the type style, size, leading, alignment, and other type attributes. However, there are a few things you can do with type that are unique to Photoshop.

Transformation Tools

All of Photoshop's transformation tools are available to manipulate type. That means you can scale, rotate, skew, distort, and

---

DESIGNTIP   Can you use Photoshop as a page layout tool?

Photoshop is a wonderful tool to create stylized type designs. Although you can set blocks of type and literally lay out pages in Photoshop, the raster makeup of Photoshop files makes type reproduction too dependent on file resolution and the power of the output device. So, use Photoshop to create unique headlines and other type effects, but use page layout software to create pages of text.

"perspective" type like crazy. See the examples shown in Figure 3-41.

Layer Effects for Type

You can apply any layer effect to type, including Blending, Drop Shadow, Inner Shadow, Outer Glow, Inner Glow, Bevel, Emboss, Satin, Color Overlay, Gradient Overlay, and Pattern Overlay. This creates all sorts of unique typographic designs. To add a text layer effect, click **Layer** on the menu bar, point to **Layer Style**, then click any effect.

Warp Text

Warp Text are a fairly new set of effects that you can apply specifically to type. These create some fantastic effects that used to take a lot of time and many steps to create. These effects include Arc, Arc Upper, Arc Lower, Arch, Bulge, Shell Lower, Shell Upper, Flag, Wave, Fish, Rise, Fisheye, Inflate, Squeeze, and Twist. The great thing about these effects is that text remains editable even after you apply a text warp. See Figure 3-42 for examples of some Warp Text effects. These effects have proven to be so popular that Adobe installed them in the latest version of Illustrator. To warp text, create type using the Type tool, then click the **Create warped text button** on the Options bar.

FIGURE 3-41
Examples of type transformed in Photoshop

FIGURE 3-42
Examples of Warp Text applied to type

HOW PHOTOSHOP FILES ARE OUTPUT

What You'll Learn

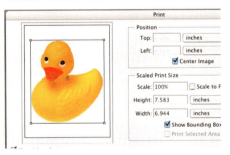

In this lesson, you will learn how Photoshop files are output.

Printing Directly from Photoshop

Designers don't normally output Photoshop files directly from the Photoshop application. Instead, they usually **import** most Photoshop graphics into another application, and then output from there. But lately, more artists and designers are creating original art and designs in Photoshop, then having the file output to a high-quality printing device. This reflects artists' growing proficiency in using digital tools and the dramatic increase in the quality of output devices. One type of output device that is becoming more affordable is large-format printers. These printers can produce images on large rolls of paper, sometimes several feet in length.

Printing Tools in Photoshop

Like vector-draw software, Photoshop allows you to select **printers, the number of copies, media, scaled outputs,** and **output modes**. The features in the Print

Width Preview dialog box (Figure 3-43) let you select these options. But Photoshop also lets you color-manage the output to create more consistent color output between different devices. This type of color management is being used more and more in the graphics industry, by both designers and printers. You'll learn more about color management in Chapter 6.

FIGURE 3-43
Photoshop Print dialog box

Select printer, number of copies, and media choices here

Color managment selected here

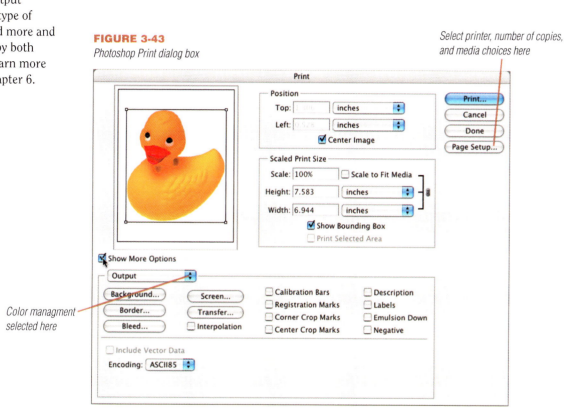

Designers use raster software every day in the graphics industry. By letting you optimize, modify, and manipulate images for print and digital media, Photoshop can create impressive designs for almost any project. Photoshop lets you adjust an image's color, save files in different digital formats, and use a variety of selection tools to help modify the smallest part of an image. Damaged images can be repaired and poorly shot photos can be adjusted to look like they were shot perfectly. Photoshop can also create a wide range of type effects. Many artists and photographers create original art in Photoshop, and Web designers use Photoshop to create the multitude of graphics required for the Web. The most important fact you should remember about raster software is that despite its power, it is resolution dependent, so understanding the resolution requirements of your job is a must.

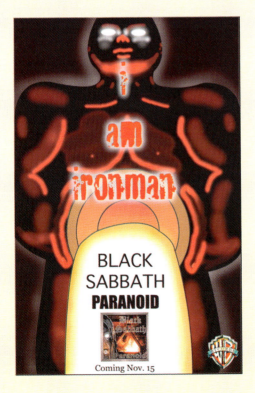

additive primary colors

background layer

bitmapped art

camera obscura

CCD

Character palette

CMYK

color mode

cropping

desaturate

digital cameras

dpi

drum scanner

electronic scanner

.eps

file format

flatbed scanner

.gif

grayscale

halides

import

.jpg

Kodak camera

layer effects

layering order

layers

Layers palette

lossy

lpi

pixels

PMT

ppi

Print dialog box

print film

.psd

raster artwork

resolution

resolution dependent

RGB

saturate

spi

.tif

toolbox

transparency (layers)

transparency film

transparent

Warp Text effect

1. What is a camera obscura?

   _____

   _____

   _____

2. What is the significance of the first Kodak camera?

   _____

   _____

   _____

3. What is the difference between print film and transparency film?

   _____

   _____

   _____

4. How does a flatbed scanner work?

   _____

   _____

   _____

5. What is the main difference between a flatbed scanner and a drum scanner?

   _____

   _____

   _____

   _____

6. How are digital cameras changing the way images are captured electronically?

   _____

   _____

   _____

7. Why are bitmapped images resolution dependent?

   _____

   _____

   _____

8. What are the four ways dots are measured in the graphics industry?

   _____

   _____

   _____

9. What are the additive primary colors?

   _____

   _____

   _____

10. What are the three main color models used in Photoshop?

   _____

   _____

   _____

11. Name the five main file formats for Photoshop that are discussed in this chapter.

_____

_____

_____

_____

12. What are three of the five primary selection tools in Photoshop?

_____

_____

_____

_____

13. How does the Magic Wand tool select images?

_____

_____

_____

_____

14. Why are layers important in Photoshop?

_____

_____

_____

_____

15. What are the Healing Brush and Patch tools used for?

_____

_____

_____

_____

16. Describe how the Eraser tool works.

_____

_____

_____

_____

17. What can you do with the Clone Stamp tool in a Photoshop file?

_____

_____

_____

_____

18. How do the Blur and Sharpen tools affect an image?

_____

_____

_____

_____

19. What can you use the Dodge and Burn tools for?

_____

_____

_____

_____

20. Name five of the Warp Text effects.

_____

_____

_____

_____

You have a new job handling photograph repair for the Valley Photo Shop. The owner has asked you to repair a badly damaged photo for a customer.

1. Open the file IG 3-1.jpg in the drive and folder where your Data Files are stored. Resave the file using the filename **young_woman.psd** and change the format to the Photoshop format. (Remember, never manipulate an original!)
2. Go to Photoshop's toolbox and select the **Healing Brush tool**. With this tool selected, note that the Options bar that runs along the top of your program window now shows options for this tool.
3. On the left side of the **Option bar**, note the Brush and its pixel size.
4. Begin fixing the photo. Bring the Healing Brush tool over an area of the file that looks good. Make sure this area is as close to the area you want to fix as possible and that your brush size closely matches the size of the damaged area.
5. [Option]-click (Mac) or [Alt]-click (Win) the **Healing Brush tool** over the good area; this loads this information into the brush.
6. Bring the brush over the damaged area and click once. This covers the damaged area with the good pixels you selected and blends those pixels to match the values in the damaged area.
7. Fix the photo to the best of your ability. Be sure to save your work as you go. Print the image to an output device to check your progress.

One Step Beyond

The young_woman.psd photo is very flat; it has little contrast. To fix this problem click **Image** on the menu bar, point to **Adjustments**, then click **Levels**. The Levels dialog box displays the **Histogram** of the image; it shows a visual representation of the values within the image and how these values are distributed throughout the image. Because this image is flat (low contrast), you'll notice that the values in the chart end well before they get to the left side or the right side of the chart.

Underneath the chart you will see three triangular sliders. Click the left slider and drag it slowly to the right until it lines up with the point where the values of gray start to rise. Then do the same with the right slider: move it to the left until it lines up with the point where the values in the chart end. The image now looks like it has more contrast and depth. Save your work and print it out.

Two Steps Beyond

The young_woman.psd file is very soft looking, meaning that it's out of focus. To adjust this, click **Filter** on the menu bar, point to **Sharpen**, then click **Unsharp Mask**. The dialog box that appears has a preview window so you can see how your work is progressing. You see three sliders at the bottom of the dialog box: Amount, Radius, and Threshhold. Slide each of these until you get a combination that makes the image look like it's more in focus. Save your work as you go, and print the image when it looks good.

You are a new designer at your local newspaper. Your first assignment is to create a vegetable head image (similar to Mr. Potato Head) that will be used as an advertising mascot for a local supermarket.

1. In the drive and folder where your Data Files are stored, open the file IG 3-2.jpg. Save the file as **selections.psd**.

2. Using the various selection tools in Photoshop, select, move, copy, scale, and rotate these shapes to make a head with a face. Be sure to make eyes, a nose, a mouth, ears, eyebrows, a tie, and a hat. Once you get a figure you like, save and print the file.

One Step Beyond

Create two new images from the image in IG 3-2.jpg. Make one head look like a man's face, and make a second head that looks like a woman's face. (To have more control over the various pieces, copy and paste the images onto their own layers.) Use the Layers palette to control your work and to determine which images are on top and which are on the bottom of the layering order. Save your work and print it out.

Two Steps Beyond

Find a series of images on your own and create a figure out of them. Be creative; try doing a little research and sketch out a few preliminary ideas with markers or pencils on marker paper.

Choose any Olympic sport you want; it can be an individual or a team sport, from the summer or winter games. Create a postcard that's 9" wide by 6" high. This postcard will put that sport in a completely different environment from where it is usually played. One example would be *Skiing in the Sahara*, where you would place skiers in the desert sand instead of the snow.

1. You must select at least five images from magazines or books of your chosen sport to put into a different environment; the environment would be a sixth scan. Work only in Photoshop, in RGB color (not CMYK), and keep your final resolution at about 250 ppi. This resolution provides a quality output while keeping the file somewhat reasonable in size. Grayscale is acceptable. As you work in Photoshop, remember that the final goal of this project is to make the sports images appear to be a seamless and natural part of this new environment.

2. The second part of this project is the type. In the previous example, you would set "Skiing in the Sahara" in Photoshop, then manipulate the type to further reflect your new sport and integrate it within the design. As with previous Design Projects, do research and work through thumbnails and

roughs to come up with the best possible solution to the project. Scan the images at the best possible quality; do not use images from the Web! If you have access to a digital camera, those images would work well for this project.

FIGURE 3-44
Examples of similar postcards

3. Try using as many Photoshop tools as you can. Use Figure 3-44 as a guide for your work. When you have completed the project, output your file and mount it to a piece of presentation board for final critique.

GALLERY

Designers and artists use Photoshop to create a wide range of graphic images. The examples in Figure 3-45 use many of the design principles discussed in this book. Write a critique of each of these designs; focus on the designer's use of color and images.

FIGURE 3-45

Examples of design work done in raster software

Amy Guip
ESPN The Magazine: "Freak Show Feast"
www.amyguip.com

Amy Guip
Time Magazine: Caleb Carr Fiction Series
www.amyguip.com

Amy Guip
ESPN The Magazine: "Freak Show Feast"
www.amyguip.com

PAGE LAYOUT SOFTWARE

CHAPTER

PAGE LAYOUT SOFTWARE

PageMaker Changed Everything

As you learned in Chapter 1, the "desktop publishing revolution" began in 1984 with the introduction of the Macintosh computer, followed by the LaserWriter printer. Aldus Corporation, named after the renowned Renaissance publisher Aldus Manutius, led the way in software with their PageMaker desktop publishing application. PageMaker was aptly named because it was the first software in which designers could "make," or build, pages of text, photos, and illustrations right on the computer screen. PageMaker represented an important advance in the concept of **WYSIWYG** (What You See Is What You Get) graphics software. What you saw on the screen looked reasonably close to what came out of the laser printer. With a computer, printer, and scanner, anyone could produce printed pieces such as newsletters, reports, and even entire books, all from his or her desktop.

QuarkXPress Battles Adobe

In the early 1990s, however, PageMaker was displaced by QuarkXPress, developed by Quark, Inc., as the industry standard for page layout. QuarkXPress was a more powerful and full-featured application, allowing designers to combine typography, graphics, and photographic images in highly accurate layouts. Even after Adobe Corporation acquired Aldus in 1994, PageMaker could never challenge QuarkXPress for industry dominance. So in 1999, Adobe released InDesign, a page layout application built from the ground up to challenge QuarkXPress. Since then, these software applications have battled each other to become the industry standard of the future.

Page Layout Software Today

Page layout software has evolved into powerful applications that designers use to create an almost endless variety of design and advertising projects. QuarkXPress and InDesign have become the workhorses of the graphics industry; their usefulness stems from strengths in four areas:

Typesetting: Page layout software has many powerful typographic controls, allowing designers to typeset text for almost any use.

Importing: These applications accept many different text and graphics file formats, letting designers integrate a variety of information in their publications.

Formatting: Page layout software lets designers lay out pages using color, special effects, and much more, to implement almost any creative idea.

Digital output: Page layout software suddenly made process cameras and **image assembly** (the process printers used to combine large amounts of film for the printing press) disappear; digital output became the norm.

Because QuarkXPress and Adobe InDesign are the most widely used page layout applications today, anyone working in the graphics industry needs to be as proficient as possible in at least one of them.

Aldus Manutius, famous Renaissance publisher

Items created in page layout software

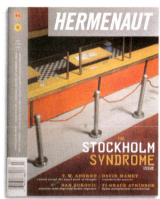

QuarkXPress and InDesign

INDESIGN AND QUARKXPRESS: AN OVERVIEW

What You'll Learn

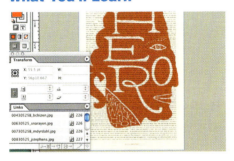

In this lesson, you will learn the major features of InDesign and QuarkXPress.

Adobe InDesign

Since its release, InDesign has been a strong contender in the field of professional-level page layout software. InDesign lets you produce designs with speed and accuracy, and has a user interface that resembles Adobe Illustrator and Photoshop.

InDesign, shown in Figure 4-4, integrates text and graphics easily and gives you an extremely high-quality preview of your work. You can specify page sizes from 1/6" to 18' in size, and view your pages from 5% to 4000% of original size. Using InDesign, you can measure or position any element on your page to within 1/1000 of an inch. Advanced type controls include precise kerning and tracking, optical (as opposed to measured) margin alignments, and Adobe's Paragraph Composer, an advanced system of optimizing the way letters and words in blocks of type lay out on the page. InDesign supports all of the popular image file formats and can import layered Photoshop and Illustrator files.

InDesign has many distinctive features, including the ability to create transparent type and images, drop shadows, and feathered edges. You can also create a full range of gradient blends in both graphics and type. InDesign can also export files directly to Adobe PDF documents, as well as many other popular formats. The application gives you a range of printing options; it also lets you preview separations and create special effects.

QuarkXPress

QuarkXPress is a very popular page layout application featuring powerful tools that let you write and edit text and combine your typography with images. QuarkXPress is used in all areas of the graphics and publishing industry, from advertising and corporate design to packaging and forms.

QuarkXPress, shown in Figure 4-5, lets you create different layouts (pages) within the same document; each layout can be a different size and orientation. You can import pictures and graphics in all of the major formats and modify them using scaling, rotating, cropping, and skewing. You can input or import text, editing and spell checking as you go. QuarkXPress lets you manipulate text to precise measurements and formats. Text can flow through multiple text boxes located on different pages of a long document, and this text can be easily controlled using character and paragraph styles.

You can output QuarkXPress files on almost any printing device, as well as export them to other popular formats, including PDFs. You can also move your designs to the Web: QuarkXPress has tools to export your files as HTML documents that you can upload and display as Web pages.

FIGURE 4-4
Adobe InDesign

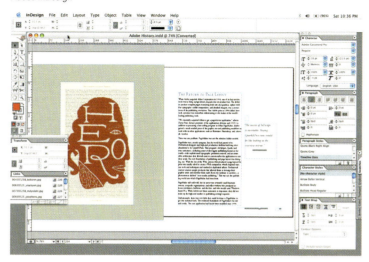

FIGURE 4-5
QuarkXPress

WORKING WITH DOCUMENT FORMATS

What You'll Learn

Number of Pages: 1	☑ Facing Pages
	☐ Master Text Frame
Page Size: Letter	
Width: 8.5 in	Orientation:
Height: 11 in	
Columns	
Number: 1	Gutter: 0.1667 in

▶ *In this lesson, you will learn how to create new files and choose formats.*

About Formats

The first decision you need to make when starting a design project in page layout software is the format. **Format** is the size of the project's working space; it is usually defined by client requirements or by the creativity of the designer.

There are many standard formats, such as 8.5" × 11" letterhead, a 9.5" × 4.125" (#10) commercial envelope, and so forth. Advertising must fit in predetermined formats based on the layout of the magazine or newspaper. Often a project needs to fit in a certain frame or on a particular billboard. The way a piece folds might also define the format of the job. But sometimes the designer gets to choose the project's format.

Setting Your Document Format

You launch InDesign or QuarkXPress the same way you launch the other programs in this book: by using the Dock or Applications folder (Macintosh) or the Programs menu (Windows). After the application starts up, you can either create a new document or open an existing document. And like vector-draw and raster software, page layout applications let you

---

DESIGNTIP Using Margins, Columns, and Gutters

Use margins for your project to create a "visual border" around your design to help viewers better understand your message. Larger margins can help frame your message; by making your text columns narrower, margins can help make certain typefaces more readable. Also consider the space between columns, called the **gutter**; working with this space can make type set in columns easier to read.

save your document using the Save, Save As, and Save a Copy (InDesign only) commands. The InDesign Save As dialog box is shown in Figure 4-6.

In this chapter, when InDesign and QuarkXPress have different commands for the same task, the InDesign command will be shown first, and the QuarkXPress command will follow, in parentheses.

To set up a new document (called a "project" in QuarkXPress), you click **File** on the menu bar and then point to **New**, and then click **Document (Project)**. The application will display a New Document (New Project) dialog box (see Figures 4-7 and 4-8) that lets you define the project's format and specify the **orientation** (tall or wide), margin sizes, and number of columns. **Margins** are the white space between the images on the page and the edges of the page. **Columns** let you divide the space between margins into a series of vertical spaces. Columns, shown in Figure 4-9, can help to organize

FIGURE 4-6

InDesign Save As dialog box

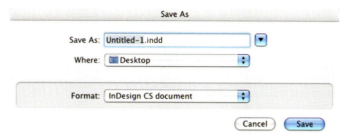

FIGURE 4-7

InDesign New Document dialog box

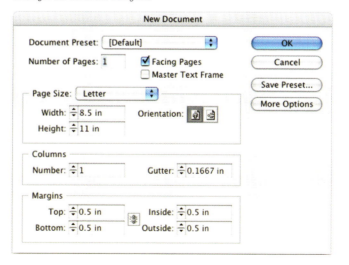

type and graphics in the professional manner you often see in newspapers and magazines.

Page layout software is unique in letting you specify **multiple pages** within the same document for large, multipage documents like books and catalogs. Both InDesign and QuarkXPress let you create a single document with 9,999 pages! The applications use a **Pages (Page Layout) palette** (shown in Figure 4-10) to help you manage and organize long documents.

QUICK TIP

Always make the format of your project file match the required finished size of the project. Don't use standard paper sizes (like 8.5" × 14") and design your project within that page size.

FIGURE 4-8

QuarkXPress New Project dialog box

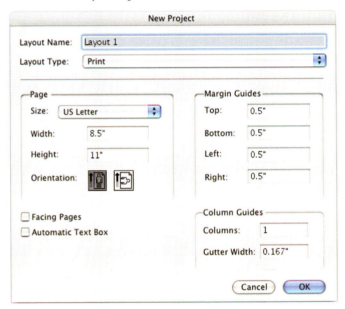

FIGURE 4-9

New document with margins and columns

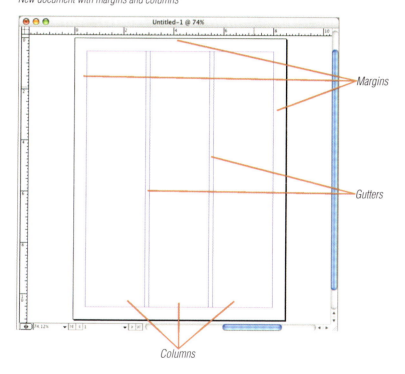

Margins

Gutters

Columns

FIGURE 4-10

Palettes help manage multiple pages

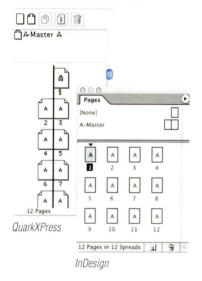

QuarkXPress

InDesign

BASIC PROCEDURES: SAVE MEASURE, AND ZOOM

What You'll Learn

▶ *In this lesson, you will learn about some basic page layout procedures.*

As with vector-draw and raster software, there are basic working procedures that are similar to all page layout applications. These include creating ruler guides and setting the zoom.

Ruler Guides

As you learned in Chapters 2 and 3, ruler guides are lines that you can drag onto your page to help you measure and place text and graphics precisely. Although other measurement units such as picas and centimeters are available, most people use inches for print-based work and pixels for digital media-based work. You can adjust the ruler's measurement unit in the Preferences dialog box, which you open by clicking **InDesign (Quark XPress)** on the menu bar, then clicking **Preferences**. Figure 4-11 shows the Preferences dialog box in each application.

The rulers at the top and left sides of your document window reflect the measurement unit you selected. To place ruler guides on the page, use the Selection tool to drag ruler guides out from the rulers. The ruler guides are a light color to set them off from the type and graphics on your page. You can position the ruler guides anywhere on your page (see Figure 4-12). Although you can see ruler guides on your document screen, the guides do not print when sent to a printer or other output device.

Zoom

As you work on your document, you may want to get a closer, more accurate look at how elements are positioned on the page. You'd be surprised how good many elements look in a normal view, only to be out of position when you zoom in. Or you may want to zoom out to get a better overall view of your page.

Both InDesign and QuarkXPress let you adjust the document view using the Zoom tool or by adjusting the view percentage in the main view window. The Zoom tools are shown in Figure 4-13. Figure 4-14 shows a document at three different zoom percentages. You can zoom in and out in InDesign from 5% to 4,000%. QuarkXPress zooms from 10% to 800% (100% is actual size). Now that's zooming!

FIGURE 4-11
Setting the measurement units

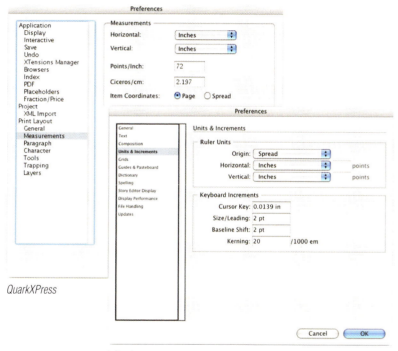

QuarkXPress

InDesign

FIGURE 4-12

Working with rulers and guides

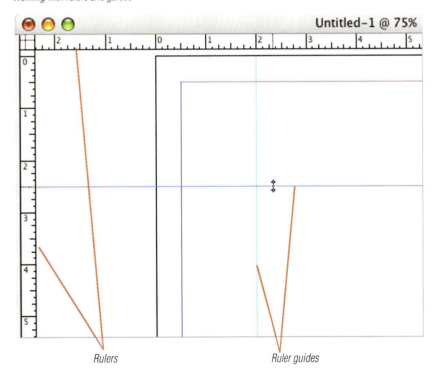

Rulers

Ruler guides

FIGURE 4-13

Zoom tool

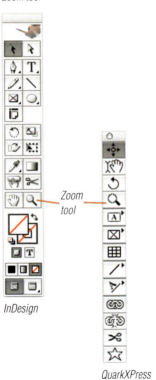

Zoom tool

InDesign

QuarkXPress

FIGURE 4-14

Zooming in to your document

100%

200%

400%

PAGE LAYOUT TOOLS AND COMMANDS

What You'll Learn

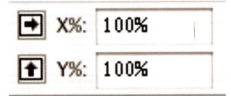

 In this lesson, you will learn about the basic tools and commands available in page layout software.

InDesign and QuarkXPress Tools

Because InDesign and QuarkXPress let you accomplish similar tasks, they have many tools and commands in common; sometimes they have identical names. In this section, when the tools have different names, the InDesign tool will be shown first, and the QuarkXPress tool will be shown in parentheses.

Selection tools—Both InDesign and QuarkXPress let you select text and graphic objects in your document. InDesign uses the **Selection tool** and the **Direct Selection tool**, which act like the same tools in Illustrator. QuarkXPress uses the **Item tool** as both a selection tool and a direct selection tool, as shown in Figure 4-15.

Shape creation tools—Both applications have a full range of shape creation tools that you can use to create lines, rectangles, ovals, polygons, and stars. InDesign tools

are somewhat different. The InDesign **toolbox**, shown in Figure 4-16, has two sets of tools; both sets create the same series of shapes. One set is called "Frame shapes," the other set just "shapes." What's the difference? Nothing, except the Frame shapes have two crosshairs that indicate the center of the shape. Sound familiar? These Frame shapes seem to exist to make QuarkXPress users feel more comfortable using InDesign. You can use either set to create the same shapes.

Figure 4-17 shows QuarkXPress shape creation tools. QuarkXPress uses the term Picture Box to describe its various graphic shapes; you can also create different types of borders (called **frames**). When you draw a shape in QuarkXPress, two crossed centering lines appear. These crosshairs don't print, but they do indicate the center of the shape and let you position the shape more accurately.

Pen tools—The Pen tools represent the biggest difference between the two software packages: InDesign has the same series of Pen tools (see Figure 4-18) that you find in Illustrator (Pen, Add Anchor Point, Delete Anchor point, and Convert Direction Point), and they work the same way. This allows an InDesign user to create fairly complex vector-based illustrations.

QuarkXPress also lets you create vector art. Its vector drawing tools are grouped with other drawing tools; there's a Bezier Text Box tool, a Bezier Picture Box tool, and a Bezier Line tool (see Figure 4-19). These tools are not designed for creating highly accurate drawings, so it's best to use them for just the simplest vector shapes.

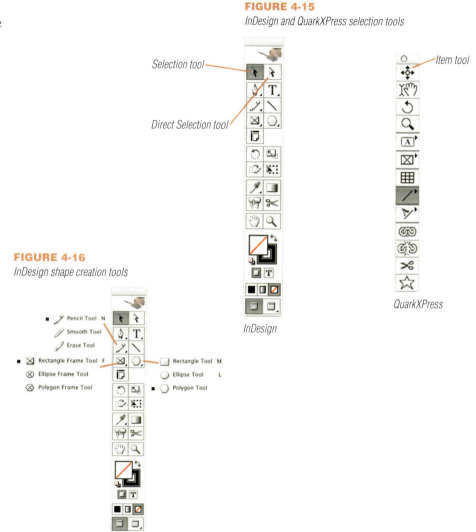

FIGURE 4-15
InDesign and QuarkXPress selection tools

Selection tool

Item tool

Direct Selection tool

InDesign

QuarkXPress

FIGURE 4-16
InDesign shape creation tools

Pencil Tool   N
Smooth Tool
Erase Tool
Rectangle Frame Tool   F
Ellipse Frame Tool
Polygon Frame Tool

Rectangle Tool   M
Ellipse Tool   L
Polygon Tool

Text creation tools—Both InDesign and QuarkXPress have a full range of typographic tools and commands. You'll learn more about these a little later in this chapter.

Transformation tools—Like vector-draw and raster software, page layout software has a wide range of object transformation tools, including Rotate, Scale, Skew, and Free Tranform. You will usually manipulate these tools with the mouse, but both InDesign and QuarkXPress also let you enter numeric settings for more precise transformations. InDesign uses the **Transform palette,** whereas QuarkXPress uses the **Measurements palette** (see Figures 4-20 and 4-21).

FIGURE 4-17
QuarkXPress shape creation tools

FIGURE 4-18
InDesign Pen tools

FIGURE 4-19
QuarkXPress vector tools

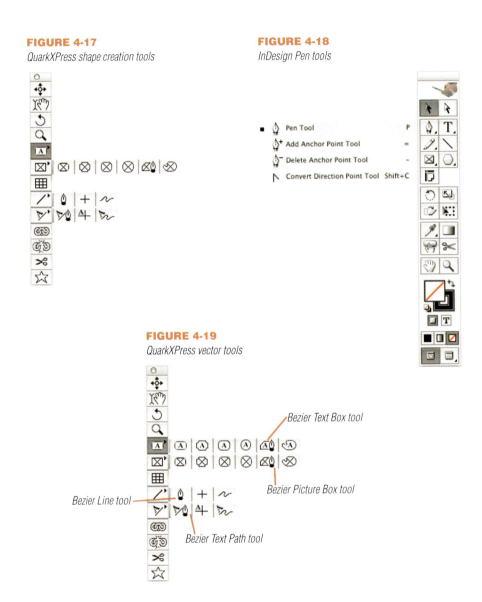

Bezier Text Box tool

Bezier Picture Box tool

Bezier Line tool

Bezier Text Path tool

Miscellaneous tools—Each application has some tools that are unique. InDesign has an **Eyedropper tool** to sample color, a **Gradient tool** to create and modify gradient blends, and a **Scissors tool** to cut shapes and lines. QuarkXPress also has a Scissors tool, as well as a **Tables tool** to create columnar tables. It also has **Linking/ Unlinking tools** to link text boxes so the type from one text box can flow into a different text box.

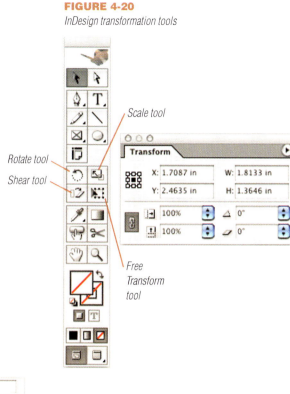

Scale tool

Rotate tool

Shear tool

Free Transform tool

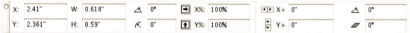

DESIGNTIP Create vector art in vector software

Although InDesign and QuarkXPress can create vector-based art, it's best to restrict their use to very simple art that is used only within the page layout document. For complex vector art, use Illustrator or FreeHand because they offer many more tools, commands, and effects specifically designed for this type of art. In addition, you can place Illustrator and FreeHand vector art into any graphics document created in any application, making the art much more useful.

GRAPHICS FROM SIMPLE TO COMPLEX

What You'll Learn

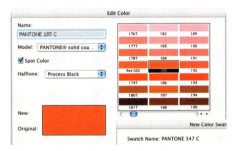

In this lesson, you will learn more about InDesign and QuarkXPress graphics tools.

Graphics Tools Get More Powerful

In the past, page layout software had limited graphics capabilities. But today many of the tools used in vector-draw software are now available directly in page layout software. Because designers can now use one software application to produce the majority of project artwork, they can work faster and more efficiently.

Rules and Lines

The most basic type of graphic is the **rule**, a simple **line** like one you can draw with a pencil or pen. In the days of pasteup, designers would use a technical pen to draw a specific-width line with permanent black ink. They would use tools such as T-squares and triangles to help draw the lines accurately. It was a tedious process, and one that most designers don't miss.

You can create rules most effectively using the **Line (Orthogonal Line) tool,** shown in Figure 4-22. You can also use the **Pencil tool (Freehand Line tool)** to draw lines by clicking-and-dragging the mouse. But the quality of Pencil tool lines depends on how steadily you can move the mouse. Because it is difficult to move the mouse in a perfectly straight line, most designers tend to avoid the Pencil tool and use the Line (Orthogonal Line) tool instead (see Figure 4-23).

To create a line with the Line tool, select the tool in the toolbox and then click-and-drag on the document; to create perfectly horizontal, vertical, or 45° lines, press and hold [Shift] as you drag.

FIGURE 4-22
InDesign and QuarkXPress Line tools

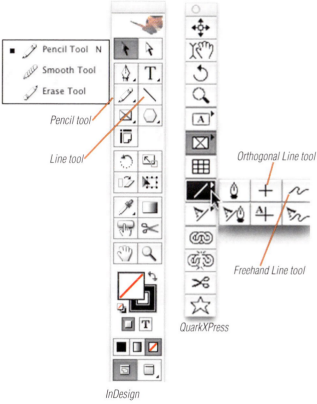

Pencil tool

Line tool

Orthogonal Line tool

Freehand Line tool

QuarkXPress

InDesign

FIGURE 4-23
The Pencil tool versus the Line tool

This was drawn with the Pencil tool

This was drawn with the Line tool

A selected line has an anchor point at each end (see Figure 4-24). To make a line longer or shorter, drag these points using the **Selection tool (Item tool)**. To move a line, click-and-drag any part of the line except an anchor point. To delete a line, click to select it, then press **[Delete]**.

You can also move or modify a line (or any selected shape) using the Transform palette (Measurements palette). The examples in Figures 4-25 and 4-26 show the settings for a 5" long line (L dimension) that has an x-coordinate of 3" and a y-coordinate of .5". The x- and y-coordinates show the position of the line on the document. In this example, the left point of the line is 3" from the left edge and .5" from the top edge of the document page.

To move a line using the Transform palette, type in the x- and y-coordinates for the desired top-left edge location, and then press **[Enter]([Return])** after each number you enter; the Transform palette will move your line accordingly. You can also type in any

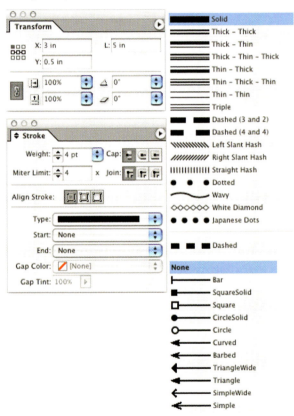

length in the L: text box, and the application will make your line match that length.

In addition to the length of the rule and its position on the page, a rule also has thickness and color. The thickness of a line is called its **stroke**, which is measured in points. The **Stroke palette (Measurements palette)** lets you apply a thickness (or weight) to a line using points. It also lets you choose different line styles, such as dashed, dotted, and multiple line rules, and different arrow heads and other start/end stroke graphics.

You can assign a color to a rule using the **Color (Colors) palette,** shown in Figure 4-27 (InDesign also uses the Swatches palette shown in this figure to store colors), using color systems such as grayscale, CMYK, RGB, and spot colors. **Spot colors** are ink colors that have been mixed to a specific

FIGURE 4-26
QuarkXPress line options

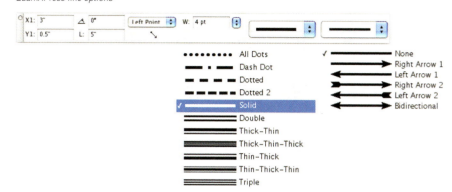

FIGURE 4-27
Displaying color

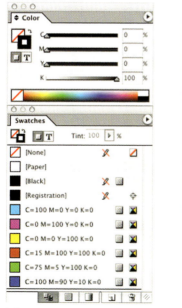

InDesign

QuarkXPress

hue. The most common type of spot color is the Pantone Matching System. Started in 1963, the **Pantone** system is a series of premixed colors that have a specific numbering system. These numbers let designers specify a particular color on the computer. The printer can then use that exact color to use on the printing press (see Figure 4-28). Spot colors can also use screen tints to create more colors while using just one ink color. A **screen tint** is a solid color of printing ink broken up into a series of dots. The larger the dots, the darker the value of the screen tint; the smaller the dots, the lighter the value of the screen tint. Screen tints are measured in percentages: 100% is solid color, 50% is a middle value, and 0% would be white. Screen tints let

The Pantone system of spot colors

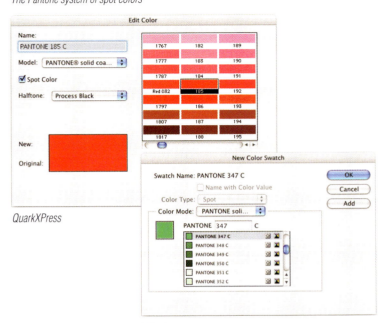

QuarkXPress

InDesign

FIGURE 4-29
Different shapes created in page layout software

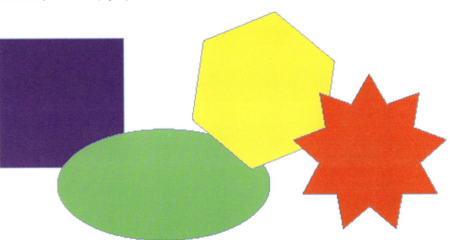

designers create graphics more economically, because printing with just one or two spot colors is less expensive than using CMYK, which requires four ink colors.

Today Pantone has competition; all graphics software lets you choose spot colors from Pantone, **Toyo**, **Focoltone**, and **Trumatch**. Once you've selected a spot color, you can store the color permanently in the **Swatches palette (Colors palette).** Then you can select the color and use it over and over again in your page layout project.

FIGURE 4-30
InDesign shape tools

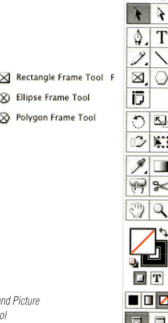

■ ⊠ Rectangle Frame Tool F

⊗ Ellipse Frame Tool

⊗ Polygon Frame Tool

☐ Rectangle Tool M

○ Ellipse Tool L

■ ○ Polygon Tool

FIGURE 4-31
QuarkXPress shape tools

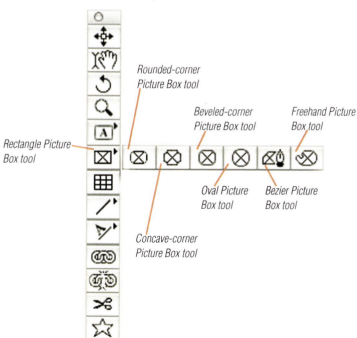

Rounded-corner Picture Box tool

Beveled-corner Picture Box tool

Freehand Picture Box tool

Rectangle Picture Box tool

Oval Picture Box tool

Bezier Picture Box tool

Concave-corner Picture Box tool

Shapes

Today page layout software can create a wide variety of shapes, like the ones shown in Figure 4-29. The tools available to make shapes are shown in Figures 4-30 and 4-31. Shapes are made up of two parts, stroke and **fill** (see Figure 4-32). You've already learned about stroke in creating lines; in shapes, a stroke creates a border that

FIGURE 4-32

Different types of stroke and fill

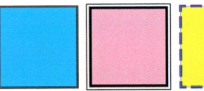

2 pt. black thick-thick stroke, blue fill

12 pt. black thin-thick stroke, pink fill

8 pt. purple dashed stroke, yellow fill

12 pt. black white diamond stroke, purple-to-orange fill

FIGURE 4-33

Controlling stroke and fill

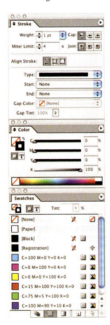

InDesign

QuarkXPress

totally encloses the shape. As with rules, shape strokes can be any available thickness (measured in points) and any available color, and can have several styles. Fill is the color that goes inside a shape, and it can be any color available in the application. Figure 4-33 shows the palettes (dialog box) in each application that control stroke and fill. InDesign and QuarkXPress can create rectangles and squares, ellipses and circles, and polygons. The Polygon tool even has an option to create star shapes.

FIGURE 4-34
InDesign special effects

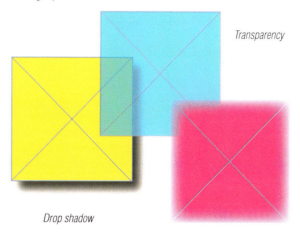

Transparency

Drop shadow

Feathered edges

The debate over special effects

InDesign has a series of special effects that are not available in QuarkXPress—Transparency, Drop shadow, and Feather—that you can apply to any line, shape, text, or image (see the examples in Figure 4-34). Before the debut of InDesign, these special effects were available only in other software such as Illustrator, FreeHand, and Photoshop. Designers had to create the effects in other software and import the objects into the page layout software. If any changes were necessary, they had to go back into the original application, make the changes, and then re-import the art, which was time-consuming. Letting designers use these effects directly in InDesign speeds up the design and production processes. But these special effects can cause output problems, especially with devices using older Postscript software. Quark Inc., the makers of QuarkXPress, decided to avoid these special effects, which generally makes QuarkXPress files easy to output.

POWERFUL TYPOGRAPHIC CONTROLS

What You'll Learn

 In this lesson, you'll learn about the full array of typographic tools and techniques available in page layout software.

Type is one of the major strengths of page layout software. But it is also an area that requires a lot of training and experience. Although the desktop revolution makes the magic of type readily available to almost everyone, it does not automatically help anyone to use type effectively. Working with type is both a science and an art, and possession of a computer is not a substitute for learning type basics. Anyone working with type should know how to use type styles, sizes, and spacing.

Type Styles

Type has thousands of styles or designs, many dating back hundreds of years. The two main style categories are serif and sans serif type.

Serif typefaces are based on the type designs the Romans cut in stone more than 2,000 years ago. This stonecutting technique created strokes of varying thickness as well as small brackets, called serifs, at the ends of strokes. We see these brackets in serif typefaces such as

Learning more about type

Learning how to use type creatively and effectively can greatly increase the quality of any graphics project. So how can you learn your serifs from your sans serifs? There are many excellent books on the subject. Adobe Corporation has an excellent type section on their Web site, and there are many more sites with insightful articles on type design and technology. Also dig into the history of type, which has directly influenced the way humankind communicates and stores information about our history and our future.

Garamond, Baskerville, Palatino, and many others. In **sans serif typefaces**, the strokes have a more consistent weight, and there are no serifs (*sans* is the French word for "without.") In sans serif type, the size of the lowercase letters are a little larger than in the serif types, making sans serif type appear visually larger than their serif counterparts set at the same size. San serif type styles are a more contemporary development; the first sans serif design appeared in 1816, and since then the design has become very popular.

There are several other type styles, including **Italic**, **Square (Slab) serif**, **Script**, **Blackletter**, and **Miscellaneous**. Examples of these styles are shown in Figure 4-35. The type styles available to you depends on the type files installed in your computer. (You'll learn more about type files in the Type Technology section of this chapter.)

Working with Type

Chapter 2 introduced you to the concept of type style. Here you will learn the five main type features you can use in different ways to design with type on a page.

Type families and styles—Type styles are based on families of type. A **type family**

FIGURE 4-35
Different type styles

Serif type

Garamond	Baskerville	Caslon	Times	Palatino

Sans serif type

News Gothic	Futura	Helvetica	Avant Garde	Myriad

Italic type

Jenson Italic	*Caxton Italic*	*Slimbach Italic*	*Optima Italic*	*Univers Oblique*

Square serif type

Century	Memphis	Rockwell	Glypha	Officiana Serif

Script and Blackletter type

Nuptial Script	*Palace Script*	*Caflisch Script*	*Banshee*	**Fette Fraktur**

Miscellaneous type

BEE/KNEE/	BERMUDA	Hobo	Viva	Shuriken Boy

consists of all the styles of type from the same design. For example, Helvetica is a type family. Helvetica comes in different weights (light, book, bold, and extra bold), different **postures** (**italic,** used more for serif type, or **oblique,** used more for sans serif type), and different widths (compressed or extended). Each of these variations is considered a different type style of the same type family.

Type size—Type is measured in points, the measurement system you learned earlier. A point is 1/72 of an inch, so 72-point type is approximately one inch tall. InDesign can set type from .1 point to 1296 points QuarkXPress can set type from 2 points to 720 points. Both applications can set type in 1/1000 of a point to 1-point increments (see Figure 4-36).

Leading—As you learned in Chapter 2, leading is the vertical space between lines of type. This distance is measured from the baseline of a line of type to the baseline of the next line of type. The **baseline** is where the bottom of most letters line up to each other. Some letters, such as g, p and y, have parts that drop below the baseline, called a **descender**. Remember that the term "leading" comes from the use of setting

FIGURE 4-36
Changes in size and leading

Aa 8 pt   Aa 13 pt   Aa 18 pt   Aa 24 pt   Aa 36 pt   Aa 36 pt

8 pt leading

Leading is the distance between lines of type and is measured in points. During the days of metal type, printers inserted extra strips of lead between long lines of text to make them easier to read. This procedure gave rise to the term "leading."

13 pt leading

Leading is the distance between lines of type and is measured in points. During the days of metal type, printers inserted extra strips of lead between long lines of text to make them easier to read. This procedure gave rise to the term "leading."

18 pt leading

Leading is the distance between lines of type and is measured in points. During the days of metal type, printers inserted extra strips of lead between long lines of text to make them easier to read. This procedure gave rise to the term "leading."

lead slugs between lines of metal type. Today's page layout software adds digital space for leading, at 1/1000 of a point increments. Figure 4-36 shows examples of leading.

Line length—Line length is the horizontal measurement of a line of type. It is the measure of the text box the type is set in. Text boxes are measured in inches and can be as wide or as narrow as the designer chooses (see Figure 4-37).

Alignment—You can set blocks of type to align in four major ways: **align left** aligns the type along the left edge of the text box, with the right edge set to varying lengths. **Align right** is the opposite of align left. **Align center** aligns the type along the center of the text box, with the left and right edges varying from short to long. **Justified** aligns the type on the left and right sides of the text box (see Figure 4-37).

FIGURE 4-37

Different line lengths and alignments

As lines of text get long, it can be difficult for the reader to move from the end of one line to the beginning of the next. On the other hand, short line lengths break up the text and interrupt the reader. The ideal line length depends on the design of the typeface, type size, line spacing, and length of the copy.

1" line length

As lines of text get long, it can be difficult for the reader to move from the end of one line to the beginning of the next. On the other hand, short line lengths break up the text and interrupt the reader. The ideal line length depends on the design of the typeface, type size, line spacing, and length of the copy.

1.75" line length

As lines of text get long, it can be difficult for the reader to move from the end of one line to the beginning of the next. On the other hand, short line lengths break up the text and interrupt the reader. The ideal line length depends on the design of the typeface, type size, line spacing, and length of the copy.

2.75" line length

As lines of text get long, it can be difficult for the reader to move from the end of one line to the beginning of the next. On the other hand, short line lengths break up the text and interrupt the reader. The ideal line length depends on the design of the typeface, type size, line spacing, and length of the copy.

Align left

As lines of text get long, it can be difficult for the reader to move from the end of one line to the beginning of the next. On the other hand, short line lengths break up the text and interrupt the reader. The ideal line length depends on the design of the typeface, type size, line spacing, and length of the copy.

Align center

As lines of text get long, it can be difficult for the reader to move from the end of one line to the beginning of the next. On the other hand, short line lengths break up the text and interrupt the reader. The ideal line length depends on the design of the typeface, type size, line spacing, and length of the copy.

Align right

As lines of text get long, it can be difficult for the reader to move from the end of one line to the beginning of the next. On the other hand, short line lengths break up the text and interrupt the reader. The ideal line length depends on the design of the typeface, type size, line spacing, and length of the copy.

Align justified

Type Tools and Commands

Both InDesign and QuarkXPress are built to work with type. You can input copy directly into the application, or you can type copy in word processing software such as Microsoft Word or Corel WordPerfect and place (import) it into a page layout document. Then you can modify the placed copy using InDesign or QuarkXPress tools and commands.

Type tool (Text Box tool)—Both InDesign and QuarkXPress let you create a **text box** to contain type. Basic text boxes are rectangular in shape, although in both programs you can also put type in any shape of text box. To create a text box in either program, select the **Type (Text Box) tool**, and then click-and-drag on the document. You can change the size and position of a text box using the **Selection (Item) tool**, or by using precise measurements in the **Transform (Measurements) palette**.

To edit text in an existing text box, use the Type (Content) tool to insert and modify type. As in a word processor, you can type

FIGURE 4-38
Selecting type with the Type tool pointer

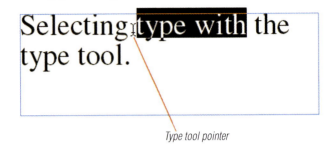

Type tool pointer

FIGURE 4-39
InDesign type options

DESIGNTIP **Guidelines for using type**

Here are a few design tips to help you use type more effectively:

- Don't use more than two type families in any design.
- If you use one type family, work with the different styles within that family to create variety while keeping the design unified.
- Avoid using all uppercase letters. If you want to emphasize a block of type, make it bigger, bolder, or both.
- Use contrast to add interest to your type designs. Work with big type, little type, different colors, and different styles of type within a type family.

---

in new text. Use the **Type tool cursor** (also called the **insertion point**) in a text box to add or delete text using [Backspace] or [Delete]. When you click-and-drag with the Type tool pointer you can **highlight** (or **select**) type (see Figure 4-38), then you can modify the highlighted type's style, size, leading, and alignment. Page layout software lets you select and modify a single letter within a text box or large blocks of type. To modify type in InDesign, use the Character and Paragraph palettes; in QuarkXPress, use the Character Attributes dialog box (click **Character** on the Style menu) and the Paragraph Attributes dialog box (click **Formats** on the Style menu; see Figures 4-39 and 4-40). You can use these tools to change the type style, type size, leading, tracking (adjusting the spacing between words), kerning (adjusting the spacing between letters), vertical and horizontal scaling (distorting the width and height of letters), baseline shift, and skewing.

Paragraph formatting—As you start to work with multipage documents, you'll find that formatting large amounts of text can be a daunting task; paragraph formatting can help. Paragraph formatting lets you modify paragraph settings such as left indent, right indent, first line indent, space before, and space after for entire paragraphs. Figures 4-41 and 4-42 show the Paragraph

FIGURE 4-40
QuarkXPress type options

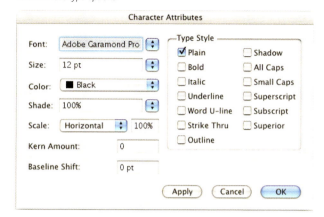

FIGURE 4-41
InDesign paragraph formatting

palette (Paragraph Attributes dialog box) where you can set this formatting. You can also add drop caps and rules between paragraphs.

Style sheets—As you start to work with longer documents, being able to control the many duplications of type styles becomes very important, and this task can become complicated. This is where style sheets come into play. **Style sheets** let you define type styles for any document element, such as headlines, subheads, body copy, bulleted type, and photo taglines. Style sheets help you define, organize, and apply almost any combination of text-formatting attributes, including size, leading, color, formatting, and alignment. For example, you might define a style sheet called "Caption" that is 12-point Bodoni, boldface, with 6-point letterspacing. Any type to which you apply the Caption style will then have the same type characteristics.

FIGURE 4-42
QuarkXPress paragraph formatting

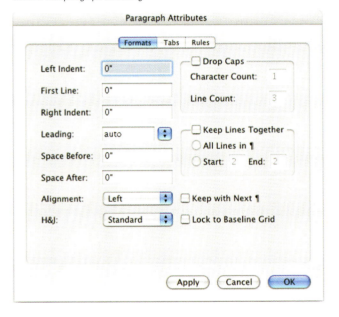

To apply a style to type, first highlight the text with the Type (Content) tool and then click any style in the Paragraph Styles (Style Sheets). The style is applied to the highlighted type, and you can apply the style to any other type throughout the document.

You create styles in the **Character Styles** and **Paragraph Styles palettes** (**Edit Paragraph Style Sheet** and **Edit Character Style Sheet**) dialog boxes, shown in Figure 4-43. Once you define (create) a style, it will appear in one of these palettes.

Styles not only let you control type formatting more effectively and make formatting consistent, they also let you modify formatting much more easily. For example, if you have created a long document with numerous type styles and then decide that your chapter headings need to be larger, you simply select the style in the palette, change its definition in the dialog box, and then click OK. All of the type throughout the document with that style applied to it then changes to match the new

FIGURE 4-43

An example of type style sheets (Quark XPress)

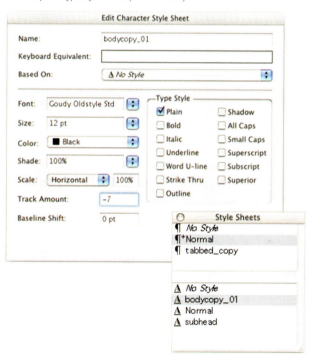

settings. Talk about simplifying a time-consuming task!

Special effects—InDesign and QuarkXPress special effects have both similarities and differences. Both applications let you set type on any path or shape, an effect that used to be available only in vector-draw software. But QuarkXPress does not have other, more complex special effects; its type modification capabilities are limited to traditional methods. Although designers must use other applications to create unique type effects, QuarkXPress files can be output with few issues or problems.

InDesign has two levels of special effects for type. You can make any headline, type block, or individual letter transparent, have a drop shadow, or have feathered edges (see Figure 4-44). InDesign also lets you create unique effects with type on a path, as shown in Figure 4-45. These options appear in the Type on a Path Options dialog box. You can

FIGURE 4-44
InDesign special effects applied to type

modify the relationship of the type to the path using Rainbow, Skew, 3D Ribbon, Stair Step, and Gravity positioning. While these effects are fun to use, they are difficult to output on older devices.

As you can see, when it comes to working with type, whether it's input directly into the software or imported from a word processing file, from short headlines to huge blocks of type, page layout software can handle just about any situation.

FIGURE 4-45
InDesign special effects for type

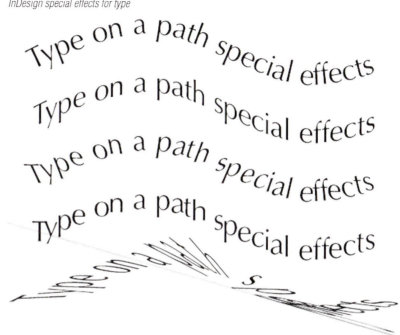

Paragraph Composer: A unique InDesign feature

When Adobe released InDesign, they included a concept unique to page layout software. In the past, designers have lamented that the computer is not the best typesetting tool. Old photocomposition machines controlled by experienced typesetters could create type blocks of beautiful, consistent letter and word spacing. Computer type never fully reproduced this typographic texture. But Adobe created the **Paragraph Composer**, which used a technology that attempted to re-create the visually pleasing texture in large blocks of type. Those who don't want to use the Paragraph Composer can switch to Single-line Composer in the Paragraph palette menu.

IMPORT AND MODIFY IMAGES

What You'll Learn

In this lesson, you will learn how page layout software lets you import and work with many image styles and digital file formats.

Using Image File Formats

Although InDesign and QuarkXPress support many image file formats, there are two common formats you should typically use in your page layout documents. For illustrations created in vector-draw software, the .eps (encapsulated PostScript) format works best for both InDesign and QuarkXPress. For photographs, the .tif (tagged image file) and .eps formats work perfectly in both applications. InDesign is pushing the technology envelope in the file format area by offering support for native Illustrator and Photoshop formats (.ai and .psd). But for most normal projects, and to assure that your file will output with minimal problems on most output devices, the .tif and .eps file formats are the best choices.

Use the Right Color Model

When you bring images into either an InDesign or QuarkXPress document, be sure that the images use the color model that matches the document's color requirements. For example, if you are

InDesign and native file formats

InDesign is the first software to accept native file formats, specifically Photoshop (.psd) and Illustrator (.ai) files. The advantage to using native files is that you don't need to create additional files (such as .eps or .tif) in the correct formats just to import them into your page layout documents. This speeds up the production process. The disadvantage is that because Photoshop keeps layers intact, the files are much more complex than those in a .tif format, which flattens all of the layers. Older output devices often can't handle this complex information.

working in grayscale or spot colors, then the images you import should be grayscale. If you are working in full color, then use CMYK as the color model for any imported graphics. In the past, RGB was never used for traditional print reproduction on printing presses. However, some digital printing devices prefer images in RGB, so in this case it's best to check with your vendor and verify what formats will work best with their specific output device (see Figure 4-46).

Understanding Links

When you import graphics into page layout software, you need to be aware of how the software handles the relationship between the page layout document and the original graphic. The most common way that page layout applications (and some other graphics applications) handle graphics is through the use of links. A **link** is a connection that exists between the page layout document and the original graphic (sometimes called the **source** graphic), as shown in Figure 4-47. In the early days of desktop publishing, PageMaker would

FIGURE 4-46
Different color models

Grayscale   Spot color   CMYK   RGB

FIGURE 4-47
How page layout software links to external files

Photoshop Files

Page Layout Document

Illustrator File

embed any imported graphics, meaning that the entire graphic was pasted in the document. This way, designers could send a PageMaker file for output without sending any other files along with it; all of the necessary file information was embedded in the PageMaker document. But embedding also made the PageMaker file extremely large, because it had to carry all of the information for all of the imported graphics. As graphics files became more complex, page layout files with embedded graphics became too large to manage and work with. To address this problem, QuarkXPress adopted the linking concept. Instead of embedding all of the file information for every imported image, QuarkXPress created an electronic link to the file. A small **proxy** (placeholder) image would appear in the QuarkXPress document. Designers could modify and manipulate this proxy just like an embedded image. But when the file was ready to print, QuarkXPress would link back to the original graphics file to get the necessary information for printing. This made QuarkXPress files much smaller, but it also

QuarkXPress

InDesign

FIGURE 4-49
Cropping an image

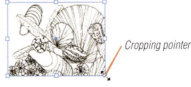

The lower-right corner of this image has been cropped

Cropping pointer

required the designer to send the QuarkXPress document and all of the original image files to the vendor for output. PageMaker adopted this link technique, which is also used by InDesign.

Importing Illustrations and Photos

To import images into page layout software, click **File** on the menu bar and then click **Place (Get Picture)**. In the Place (Get Picture) dialog box, navigate to the file you want to import, select it, and then click **Open** (see Figure 4-48), which brings the graphic into your layout. In QuarkXPress you have to create a Picture Box first, then import the picture into the box. With InDesign, you select the image, click **Open**, and when your pointer changes to an image icon, click on the document; InDesign creates a frame and puts this image inside it.

FIGURE 4-50

Scaling an image

Scaled 50%

Original (100%)

Scaled 200%

FIGURE 4-51

The scale tools in InDesign and QuarkXPress

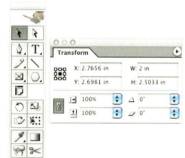

QuarkXPress

InDesign

Cropping and Scaling

After you import an image into your document, you can move it anywhere you want. You can also **crop**, or hide portions of the image, by adjusting the size of the Frame (Picture Frame). When you crop an image (see Figure 4-49), you are actually adjusting the frame through which viewers see the image. Because you're not cropping the original image, you can go back to the full image view at any time. You can also **scale** an image to make it larger or smaller (see Figure 4-50). You can scale an image manually with the **Scale tool** or numerically using the **Transform (Measurements) palette** (see Figure 4-51). You scale an image in percentages, with 100% being the original size. Any percentage smaller than 100% **reduces** the size of the image, and any percentage over 100% **enlarges** the image.

As you work with imported images in page layout software, be aware of each image's file format and the consequences of scaling. You can scale vector images larger than their original size (because they are resolution independent), but scaling a bitmap image larger than 100% decreases the resolution because bitmap images are resolution dependent.

FIGURE 4-52

The InDesign Links palette

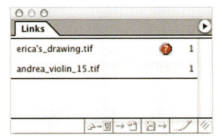

Managing Graphics

Once you start to place graphics into your document, you'll want to keep track of the images and make sure that you stay linked to the files so your document will print properly. InDesign keeps track of links using the **Links palette** (see Figure 4-52). This palette shows every graphic you've imported, what page of the document it's on, and if it is linked properly. In QuarkXPress, linking information is found in the **Usage dialog box.** Click **Utilities** on the menu bar, then click **Usage** and the **Pictures** tab (see Figure 4-53). This dialog box also lists the image links, what page they're on, and whether they are linked correctly. Broken links will affect output, so make sure your links are all up-to-date.

QUICKTIP

A smart way to help manage your links is to create a project folder, and inside that folder create a folder titled Links. Move or copy every file you plan to import into this folder. Then you will always know where your linked graphics are located, and you will be less likely to encounter broken links.

FIGURE 4-53

The QuarkXPress Usage dialog box

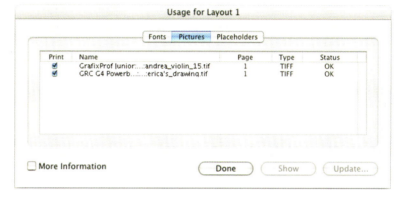

THE POWER OF OUTPUT

What You'll Learn

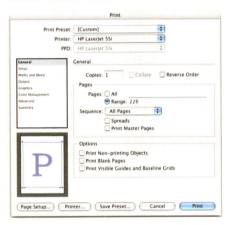

 In this section, you will learn how you can output your files using page layout software's powerful print features.

A strength of page layout software is its ability to print almost any file to almost any output device. It's certainly one of the reasons QuarkXPress has stayed popular for so many years—its files are made to output with as few problems as possible.

Both InDesign and QuarkXPress have complex Print dialog boxes, shown in Figures 4-54 and 4-55. Both have multiple tabs revealing a wealth of information. Both applications let you print between 1 and 999 outputs. You can print all of the pages in a multipage document, or any range of pages. You can also collate multipage documents.

The Print dialog box also lets you specify any paper size available on your printer and lets you scale the output to fit on whatever size paper is available. In addition, you can **tile** the output, meaning that instead of scaling a large file down to fit on one page, you can print it at 100% (actual) size. The software then prints different parts of the file on different pages, which you can then piece together to create output at actual size.

Both InDesign and QuarkXPress let you print composite and separation outputs. **Composite outputs** are what most people are familiar with; they show all of the elements in the correct colors and position. **Separation output** mimics how the file will output at the printer, with each ink color printing on an individual piece of paper, showing what information will appear on each printing plate (see Figure 4-56). This is a great way to check that you have used the correct colors in your document and that any imported images are also in the correct color model. It would be a very costly mistake to create a two-color file, only to have the file output in CMYK.

FIGURE 4-54

The InDesign Print dialog box

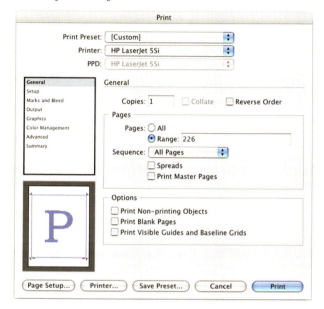

FIGURE 4-55

The QuarkXPress Print Layout dialog box

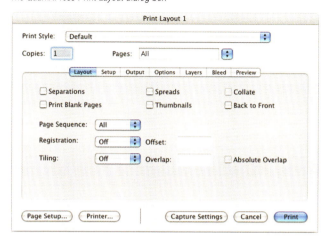

FIGURE 4-56

Example of separations

Composite

Separations

Designers use page layout software to produce everything from basic ads to the most complex catalogs to huge posters, banners, and billboards. Both InDesign and QuarkXPress can create and control single-page and multipage documents. The programs let you create a wide variety of graphic lines and shapes, including vector-based graphics. Typography is one of the major strengths of page layout applications, which include several different ways to apply special effects to type. The applications also support many different graphic formats that you can import and modify. Because it lets you accurately lay out and manipulate graphics, images, and type in almost any design possible, page layout software is a required skill for any designer.

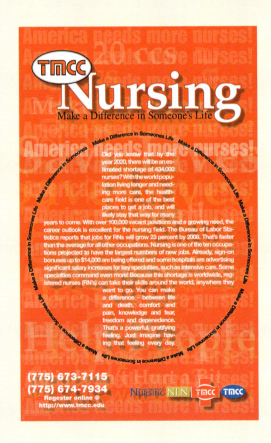

alignment

blackletter

baseline

Color (Colors) palette

columns

composite output

crop

descender

embed

enlarge

fill

Focoltone

format

frame

gutter

highlight

image assembly

importing

insertion point

italic

justified alignment

leading

line

line length

link

margins

Measurements palette

multiple pages

oblique

orientation

page layout software

Pages (Page Layout) palette

Pantone system

Paragraph Composer

paragraph formatting

postures

proxy

reduce

ruler

sans serif typefaces

screen tint

script

select/selection

separation output

serif typefaces

square serif

source graphic

special effects

spot colors

stroke

Stroke palette

style sheets

Swatches palette

text box

tile

toolbox

Toyo

Transform palette

Trumatch system

type family

Type tool cursor

type size

type style

WYSIWYG

zoom

1. What was the first true page layout software?

   _____

2. When you set up a new document, what is the format of a page?

   _____

   _____

3. Name three items you can specify in the Document Setup dialog box.

   _____

   _____

   _____

4. How do ruler guides help while working on a project?

   _____

   _____

5. Why is zoom helpful?

   _____

   _____

   _____

6. Even though page layout software can create vector art, why should you use vector-draw software instead?

   _____

   _____

7. What do transformation tools let you do in page layout software?

   _____

   _____

   _____

8. What is the thickness of a line called and how is it measured?

   _____

   _____

9. What are x- and y-coordinates used for?

   _____

   _____

   _____

10. What are spot colors?

    _____

    _____

    _____

11. What are two differences between serif and sans serif type?

    _____

    _____

12. What are the five main features of type?

    _____

    _____

    _____

    _____

13. What are the differences between left and justified type alignments?

_____

_____

_____

14. What does the Type tool cursor do?

_____

_____

_____

15. What types of modifications can you make using paragraph formatting?

_____

_____

_____

16. What are style sheets used for?

_____

_____

_____

17. Why are special effects (such as transparency) problematic in page layout software?

_____

_____

_____

18. What two image file formats work best in page layout software?

_____

_____

_____

19. How do links work?

_____

_____

_____

20. What is the difference between cropping and scaling?

_____

_____

_____

21. What is the difference between composite output and separation output?

_____

_____

_____

You have decided to go into business as a freelance graphic designer, and you need to create your business card. In your Chapter 4 Data Files folder, you will find two files containing business cards: IG 4-1.indd (InDesign format) and IG 4-1.qrk (QuarkXPress format). Both files have the same information.

1. Open the appropriate file; you will see the document size is set for a standard business card. All of the type and a graphic of a vector-based logo (named IG 4-2.eps) are already in the file.
2. Save the file as **buscard**.
3. Work with the type and graphic to produce a well-designed business card for yourself. Use the design principles you learned in Chapter 1, and try different type styles and sizes. Position the type and adjust the size and position of the logo. Stay in black and white and grayscale for now.
4. When you are done, print your file.

One Step Beyond

Delete the logo that's in your file and import the color version of the logo (IG 4-3.eps). Now work with color to make your business card more interesting. Save the file as **buscard_color**. Print your final version.

Two Steps Beyond

Create two additional files, one for a letterhead (8.5" × 11") and one for an envelope (9.5" × 4.125"). Using the same elements as in your business card, design a letterhead and envelope for your business. Try to create a unified design by keeping your type, graphic, and colors consistent. Save the files as **letterhead** and **envelope**. Print the documents.

You have been hired by Future Digital Workshops to produce a flyer promoting a digital imaging workshop. The marketing director wants the flyer to look dynamic and to promote the workshop effectively. She has electronic files that you can use for the flyer, including copy produced in a word processing file, three files of the same photograph manipulated in Photoshop, and a logo file produced in Illustrator.

1. Design the flyer, using the following files in the Chapter 4 Data Files folder: IG 4-4.doc, IG 4-5.tif, IG 4-6.tif, IG 4-7.tif, and IG 4-8.eps.
2. Review the project files and sketch three or four roughs for the flyer, following the project requirements listed below.
   - The format for the flyer is 8.5" × 11", and it must be a portrait orientation.
   - The intended audience for this flyer is company employees 25 years and older with little or no graphics training. These employees are being asked to work with photographs for the company newsletter and other printed literature.
   - Keep the type color black and the flyer background white.
   - The first two lines in the word processing files are a headline and a subhead; position them at the top of the flyer.
   - The three photos should appear right below the subhead.
   - Position the paragraph of body copy below the three photos.
   - The logo, with the company's address and phone number, should be at the bottom of the flyer.
3. Once you have determined which rough is the best design solution, launch your page layout software and create an 8.5" × 11" document. Name your file **fdw_flyer**.
4. Print the Word document and type in the copy. Then insert the images.
5. Use your knowledge of design principles to make the type and images generate enthusiasm for the workshop. When you are done, print the flyer.

One Step Beyond

Produce a version of the flyer using color throughout. How can you use color to make the flyer more visually interesting and promote the workshop more effectively? Name this file **fdw_flyer_color**.

Two Steps Beyond

Change the flyer format from portrait to landscape, and redesign it for an intended audience of high school students who already have some knowledge of graphics. How does this change the look of the flyer? Name this file **fdw_flyer_hs** and print a copy.

Your local library has hired you to create a poster that will be part of their "Giants of History" book series. Choose an individual who has had historic significance. Avoid people in entertainment and sports; choose someone who has made a social, political, or scientific impact on our nation or the world.

The format of the poster is 11" × 17", either landscape or portrait format. The headline must be the person's name, with a secondary headline containing a famous quote or saying attributed to that person. The text should be an essay about the life and the significance of the historical figure, and should be about 150 words long. The prominent graphic in the poster should be a scanned photograph or illustration of the person. The photo should be at least a head shot, but no more than from the waist up to the top of the head. Also include two additional images that relate to the person.

Work on making the headline, secondary headline, text, and all the images work together as a cohesive design based on the principles you learned in Chapter 1. Use two spot colors plus black. See Figure 4-57 for examples of this project.

1. Do at least ten thumbnails, then do three roughs using marker and pencils on marker paper.
2. Choose the best rough and re-create the design in page layout software. Save the file as **history_poster**. When you are done, print the file. This is the comprehensive that you could show to the client for input and/or approval.

FIGURE 4-57
Examples of two historical posters

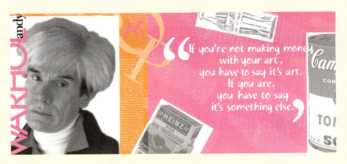

The projects shown in Figure 4-58 use many of the design principles discussed in this book. Write a critique of each of these designs, focusing on the designer's use of layout and type.

FIGURE 4-58
Examples of design work done in page layout software

Hirshorn Zuckerman Design
CHUCK NORRIS 6th Annual Kick Drugs Out of America
Tennis & Golf Invitational
Sent to invited guests
www.hzdg.com

James Evelock
Mills Corporation
Promotional campaign

Hirshorn Zuckerman Design
MEPT Quarterly Trust annual report design
Distributed to annual subscribers
www.hzdg.com

ELECTRONIC PUBLISHING AND PROOFING

CHAPTER 5

ELECTRONIC PUBLISHING AND PROOFING

The Paper Piles Up

By the 1990s, desktop computers were everywhere. Many major companies depended on computers in every facet of their business. Lawyers, accountants, bankers, educational institutions, and many other businesses had computers working day and night.

But all of these computers were connected to thousands of printers and were outputting more paperwork than ever before—mountains of it—making it increasingly difficult to store and retrieve information, and prompting environmental concerns.

An Adobe Solution

Adobe Corporation, the largest graphics software company in the world, dedicated itself to creating a paperless office, an office that could exchange and store all of its information electronically. One of

Adobe's founders, John Warnock, wrote, "Imagine being able to send full text and graphics documents (newspapers, magazine articles, technical manuals, etc.) over electronic mail distribution networks. These documents could be viewed on any machine and any document could be printed locally. This capability could truly change the way information is managed." ("The Camelot Paper," John Warnock, 1991)

The first version of this new technology was introduced in 1992 as Portable Document Format, or PDF. This new format didn't catch on at first, but today it is used worldwide not only to exchange electronic information but to produce files from graphics software that can be used as high-quality proofs or for output on any device, anywhere in the world, using the Adobe Acrobat software.

FIGURE 5-1

A mountain of paperwork...

FIGURE 5-3

The Camelot Paper

FIGURE 5-2

...that can be stored on any computer

The Camelot Project
J. Warnock

This document describes the base technology and ideas behind the project named "Camelot." This project's goal is to solve a fundamental problem that confronts today's companies. The problem is concerned with our ability to communicate visual material between different computer applications and systems. The specific problem is that most programs print to a wide range of printers, but there is no universal way to communicate and view this printed information electronically. The popularity of FAX machines has given us a way to send images around to produce remote paper, but the lack of quality, the high communication bandwidth and the device specific nature of FAX has made the solution less than desirable. What industries badly need is a universal way to communicate documents across a wide variety of machine configurations, operating systems and communication networks. These documents should be viewable on any display and should be printable on any modern printers. If this problem can be solved, then the fundamental way people work will change.

The invention of the PostScript language has gone a long way to solving this problem. PostScript is a device independent page description language. Adobe's PostScript Interpreter has been implemented on over 100 commercially available printer products. These printer products include color machines, high resolution machines, high speed machines and low-cost machines. Over 4000 applications output their printed material to PostScript machines. This support for PostScript as a standard make the PostScript solution a candidate for this electronic document interchange.

Within the PostScript and Display PostScript context the ¨view and print anywhere¨ problem has been implemented and solved. Since most applications have PostScript print drivers, documents from a wide variety of applications can be viewed from operating systems that use Display PostScript. PostScript files can be shipped around communication networks and printed remotely. "Encapsulated PostScript" is a type of PostScript file that can be used by many applications to include a PostScript image as part of a page the application builds.

ACROBAT: AN OVERVIEW

What You'll Learn

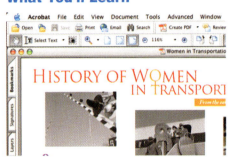

 In this lesson, you will get an overview of the PDF file format and Adobe Acrobat software.

PDFs and Acrobat

The **Portable Document Format (PDF)** is a file format that can be read and printed by any computer on any operating system. Documents in this format are used throughout the world to exchange and store electronic documents of all kinds. The PDF format has become the universal standard for electronic document exchange. You can create, view, and print PDF files using the **Adobe Acrobat** software application (see Figure 5-4). To date, over 500 million copies of Acrobat have been sold.

PDF files can be produced from documents created in any application. Once the original file has been converted to PDF, its layout, including graphics, images, and fonts, is preserved for viewing and printing. These PDF documents are also small in file size, because the format uses **compression**, an electronic process that "squeezes" all the file information into the smallest digital space possible. This makes it easy for PDF files to be exchanged over the Internet; many are small enough to be simple e-mail attachments.

A Multitude of Uses

Many companies and government agencies use PDF documents to simplify their document work flow and lower the amount of paper required to do jobs. Some use PDF to store millions of documents on one computer. Storing the same documents on paper would require warehouses of space. Many use this technology to let people access previously unavailable documents over the Internet. And many companies, such as book publishers, are using PDF files to distribute copies of long documents to employees and customers, to gain time in their schedules and cut shipping costs. (The page proofs for this book, for example, were distributed to the editorial and production teams in PDF format. The teams marked them using Adobe Acrobat and returned them for revision.)

FIGURE 5-4

Acrobat program window

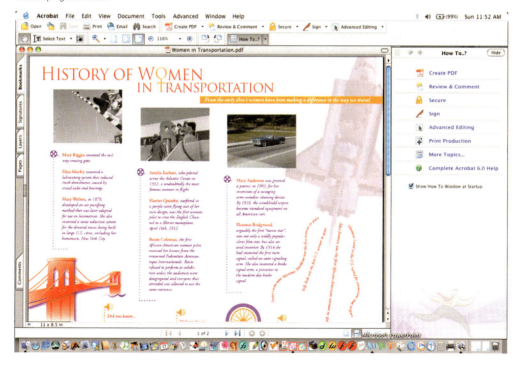

THE IMPORTANCE OF THE PORTABLE DOCUMENT FORMAT

What You'll Learn

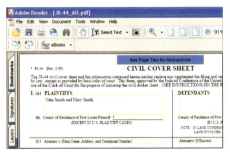

 In this lesson, you will learn about the Portable Document Format and why PDFs have become so important in computer graphics.

Adobe Creates the PDF Format

Adobe Corporation created the PDF format in an attempt to control their own growing mountain of internal company paperwork; they hoped to translate all of their paperwork into electronic documents that would be easy to store and distribute.

The problem was that there were many different models of computers running different software on different operating systems. Once you create a document on a computer, that document's file structure is based on the application it was created in and on the operating system on which that application was running. If you create a document in Adobe FreeHand, that file cannot be opened in QuarkXPress or Microsoft Word. Even if you are working in the same application, if the document was created on a Windows computer, it may not open on a Macintosh computer, or vice versa. If it does open, there is no guarantee that it will look the same as the original document.

So Adobe tried to create a file format that could not only preserve the look of the original document in the original application but would also look and print

---

DESIGNTIP PDFs give consistent results

Many applications provide filters to open files created in other applications. For example, InDesign will open most QuarkXPress documents. But when the document is opened, the fonts, layout, format, and color may not "translate" properly and the document will not look the same as the original. This is a big advantage of the PDF format: once a document has been converted to PDF it will look and print the same as the original, no matter what software or operating system it was created in.

the same way on any computer using any operating system. Adobe had already developed technology that was application- and operating system-independent: **PostScript**, the page description language that tells a computer or an output device how an electronic file is suppose to look and print out. Adobe also had developed an application that could view PostScript files:

Illustrator, which runs on both Macintosh and Windows computers.

So in 1992, using Postscript and Illustrator as a foundation, Adobe introduced the Portable Document Format as a **device-independent** electronic file format—one that could be viewed on any computer running almost any operating system. In 1993, they released Adobe Acrobat software

that could create, view, and print PDF files (see Figure 5-5).

What Are PDFs?

Because the PDF format is based on the PostScript page description language, it can "describe" to an output device how a page should look so it can print accurately. But because PostScript is a programming

FIGURE 5-5

PDFs work on any computer

language and not a file format, it cannot describe that page for viewing on your computer monitor. The PDF file format, however, contains all the necessary information for both viewing and printing documents accurately.

There is another advantage of using PDF over Postscript. When a Postscript file is sent to a printer, the printer needs a special software application to interpret the Postscript information. This software is called a **Raster Image Processor**, or **RIP**. (You'll learn more about this software in Chapter 6.) For now it's important to understand that this translation process is complex and problems can occur, making output of the same file appear different on different printers. When a PDF file is first created, it automatically goes through a similar translation process. So because a PDF file has already passed through a RIP, it prints much more consistently on different printers.

Business Uses of PDF

In business, PDFs are used for saving and storing **electronic documents**, cutting down on paperwork. Many companies are using PDF **electronic forms** instead of paper forms, allowing customers to fill out the forms on their computers and send them back to the company electronically. The company then processes and stores the information digitally, again saving paperwork. Many companies as well as the U.S. Internal Revenue Service and many state governments make their tax forms available in PDF format on the Web. Some forms, like the one shown in Figure 5-6, are interactive, meaning that you can fill them out and submit them electronically. Others are fill-in forms only; you can fill them out on your computer, then print and mail them.

FIGURE 5-6
An interactive PDF form

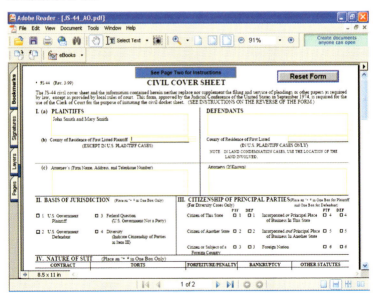

PDFs in Advertising

Computer graphics companies have made extensive use of PDF in all phases of their work flow. Has it saved them time and paperwork? The answer is an emphatic yes. The advertising industry quickly saw the advantages of using PDFs, and many advertising and graphics companies have joined with Adobe to advance the PDF concept into other areas of the industry. The PDF file format has now matured into several versions, each with its own distinct uses depending on a document's viewing or printing requirements. These include

Version 6, which supports layered graphics and special effects, and PDFX1a and PDFX3 for more robust and accurate file output.

Before the PDF format was introduced, ads produced for thousands of newspapers, magazines, and publications had to be output as pieces of graphic arts film, along with a **printed proof** of how the ad would look when produced from the film. (See the sidebar "Film goes the way of the dinosaur," below.) This was because the ads were produced using different graphics software applications, and each advertising agency (and each printing company) would use whichever application they preferred. This often created problems because, as you learned earlier in this chapter, a file produced in one application cannot always be accurately viewed and printed in a different application. In addition, the film and proof for each ad had to be shipped via an overnight delivery service, adding to the cost and creating the possibility that the package could be damaged or lost. Because film and proofs are very expensive to produce, replacing or duplicating them for other publications cost a lot of money.

Film goes the way of the dinosaur

Any new technology affects people and companies still using the old technology. For 15 years, the process of taking electronic files and producing graphic arts film was standard working procedure in the industry. These films would be used to produce printing plates, which would then be used to print the project on a printing press. But thousands of projects that once required film now use the PDF format instead. So the many graphics companies that used to output millions of pieces of film each year have either scrambled to adopt other technologies to replace that income, or have simply gone out of business. It's a sad reality, but for every company in the graphics industry that disappears, another one appears using a different, newer technology.

PDF files provide a solution to these problems; now files can be proofed and corrected electronically and imaged directly on a printing plate, bypassing film altogether. Advertising agencies now routinely convert ads to PDFs and send the files over the Internet as **e-mail attachments**. If the files are too large to be sent as attachments, they can be burned to a CD and sent using overnight delivery services. If the package is damaged or lost, replacing a CD costs only about 10¢, whereas replacing film and a proof can cost a couple of hundred dollars.

Many graphics companies are also setting up special Internet sites called FTP sites. **FTP** stands for the **File Transfer Protocol**, and it is used to transfer files over the Internet. Using FTP, users can transfer files to and from special computers used as central locations for file storage (see Figure 5-7). Many individuals and businesses use FTP sites to **upload** (send out to an FTP site) and **download** (get and save on a computer) files that are too large to attach to an e-mail message. By using

FIGURE 5-7

Downloading a file from an FTP site

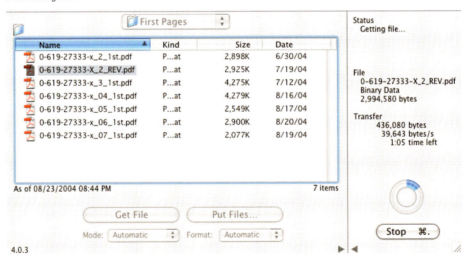

inexpensive or free software such as Transmit, Fetch, or other programs, anyone with permission and (in some cases) passwords can log onto an FTP site and transfer large files quickly and efficiently at any time.

Once an agency transmits a PDF file to a client, and the client approves it, the designer can send the file directly to the printer.

PDFs in the Rest of the Graphics Industry

Almost every area of the graphics industry has adopted PDFs in some area of its work flow. Many traditional print graphics projects, from posters and CD covers to annual reports, menus, and billboards, are either proofed or printed using PDF files.

Another area that uses PDFs is Web design. The traditional programming language for the Web, called **HTML**, cannot handle the complexities of graphics in a consistent manner. So companies are using PDFs to display graphic-intensive information accurately on the Internet.

Apple adopts PDF for OS X

Both Windows and Macintosh OS X operating systems need a file format to view documents on the monitor. For years Apple used a picture rendering file format called PICT (short for Picture) to view text and graphics using older versions of their operating system. But when Apple released the new OS X operating system, they adopted the PDF file format to render images. This makes every Macintosh computer a PDF viewer and allows any application developed for OS X to create PDF files through that application's Print function. Therefore, many applications on Macintosh computers running OS X don't even need the Acrobat software to produce PDFs.

IT ALL GOES THROUGH ADOBE ACROBAT

What You'll Learn

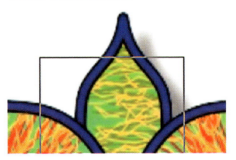

▶ *In this lesson, you will see how PDFs are produced using Adobe Acrobat software.*

But First, Adobe Reader

Many people are familiar with Acrobat and viewing PDF files on their computers. But the software most people use is the Adobe Reader application. **Adobe Reader** is a limited version of Acrobat, with only a small subset of its features that let you view and print PDF files. You cannot create or modify PDF files in Acrobat Reader. That's why Reader is free: anyone can download Reader from the Adobe Web site, and there are versions of Reader for both Macintosh and Windows computers (see Figure 5-8).

And Now, Adobe Acrobat

Adobe Acrobat is the version you have to pay for, and for good reason. Acrobat creates PDF files from many different applications. Acrobat also lets you modify existing PDF files. And Acrobat, like Reader, lets you print PDF files to almost any printer, whether the printer has Postscript or not.

QUICKTIP

Prior to the latest version of Acrobat, the Adobe Reader software was called Acrobat Reader. But Adobe, apparently wanting to distinguish Reader clearly from the full version of Acrobat, changed the name.

Opening PDFs in other applications

Two other Adobe applications, Illustrator and Photoshop, can also open and edit PDF files. Illustrator can open PDF files, and most of the content is still editable using Illustrator's vector-based tools. Photoshop opens PDF files just like any other bitmapped file, which can then be edited using Photoshop's raster tools.

Creating PDFs

Creating a PDF in Acrobat is as simple as opening the file. But Acrobat gives you several ways to do this. You click **File** on the menu bar, point to **Create PDF**, and then click **From File** (see Figure 5-9). You navigate to the file and select it, and the file will open in Acrobat as a PDF. Acrobat will convert the following file formats: HTML, PICT, BMP, Compuserve GIF, DOC, JPEG, JPEG2000, PCX, PNG, Postscript/EPS, Text, and TIFF.

You can also create **multiple files** at the same time, as shown in Figure 5-10; Acrobat will open them as one large, multipage PDF in which you can arrange the pages in any order. Acrobat also lets you connect to a scanner and **scan files** as PDFs (see Figure 5-11). Finally, you can open Web sites in Acrobat and download the **Web pages** as PDF files, as shown in Figure 5-12.

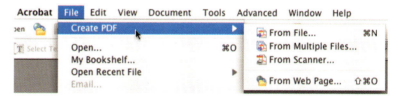

Producing PDFs in other Adobe applications

In previous chapters you learned about three different Adobe graphics applications: Illustrator, Photoshop, and InDesign. All can create PDF versions of the documents they create. In Illustrator and Photoshop, Adobe PDF is a Save As option. InDesign lets you use an Export command to create an Adobe PDF file. These applications let you create PDF files without having to purchase the Acrobat software, and it speeds up your work flow because you don't have to switch between applications.

Working with PDFs

Once you have a PDF document open in Acrobat, there are several ways you can work with it.

Zooming and Viewing—You can use the **Zoom tool** in Acrobat to get a closer look at a document. Zooming gives you a highly accurate view of the layout and any images within the document. Acrobat also has a **Loupe tool**, which lets you magnify a portion of a file while still viewing the file at actual size, as shown in Figure 5-13. The latest version of Acrobat also lets you preserve and view **multiple layers** created in Illustrator, FreeHand, or Photoshop documents.

Changing the Document Layout—Once a PDF document is open in Acrobat, you can modify its structure. In multipage documents you can change the page order, renumber the pages, and insert, replace, or delete pages. Acrobat also lets you rotate pages in 90° increments and crop pages to a new page format.

Comments and Review—Acrobat has a group of tools on the Commenting toolbar you can use to add **comments** and to **review** a document (see Figure 5-14.) These include the **Note tool**, which lets you add electronic sticky notes that float over the document. The **Text Edits tool** lets you add comments and make changes directly in the document text. The **Stamp tool** creates customizable graphics that you can place anywhere on the document, such as an approval stamp or a "reviewed by" stamp. The **Highlighter tool**

FIGURE 5-10

Create PDFs from multiple files

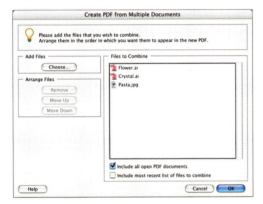

FIGURE 5-11

Create PDFs from scanner

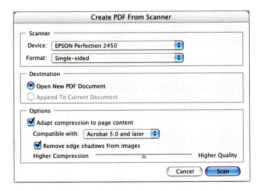

FIGURE 5-12

Create PDFs from Web page

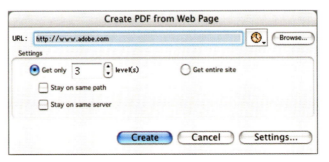

applies effects to text selected in the document, including underlining, strikethrough, and highlighting. The **Show tool** lets you see all of the comments in a document, sort them in any order, and select which comments can be viewed depending on the person viewing or the computer displaying the document.

The **Shape tools** on the Advanced Commenting toolbar let you use graphic shapes to highlight or to point to areas within the document. **Text Box tools** let you apply blocks of text directly on the document and make changes or insert comments. The **Pencil tool** is a free-form drawing tool you can use to draw markings

anywhere on the document. And finally the **Attach File tool** lets you attach other files within the PDF document. Attachments can include files with text changes too large to include in the document itself, or updated graphics or image files that need to be inserted into the document.

FIGURE 5-13
Loupe tool

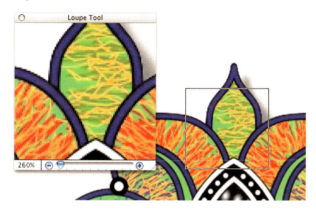

FIGURE 5-14
Acrobat Comments and Review tools

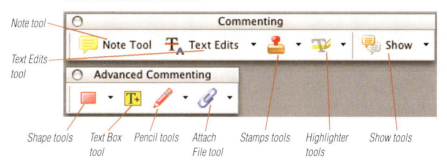

From printed to electronic books

Acrobat and PDFs have also created a new area of graphic communications called **electronic publishing**, and PDF now allows publishers to create magazines, books, and other publications in 100 percent digital form. PDF publications save paper and can be distributed anywhere to anyone who owns a computer. Many companies now produce their product and instruction manuals as PDF documents. In the '80s and '90s, when you bought computer software you used to get a thick manual on how to install and use the software. Now such a manual fits on a CD or DVD, and users can view the manual on their computers and print whatever part of it they want. Adobe and other software companies also put their PDF manuals on the Web, so people who buy the software can go online to download the manual.

PROOFING WITH PDFS

What You'll Learn

In this lesson, you will see how PDFs are used to proof projects.

The Proof's in the Pudding

After PDFs were introduced back in 1992, several graphics companies started to look into the possibility of using PDFs for proofing graphics projects. At the time, they had to produce film and proofs and deliver the proofs to the client for approval. Then they sent the proofs to the designer for revision and approval, and finally to the printer.

Dealing with Film

The first thing the industry wanted to get rid of was film, so work focused on producing printed proofs from the original application file, then electronic proofs using PDFs. The problem was that files created electronically use RGB as their color model, and output devices use CMYK to produce color. By the end of the 1990s the problem was solved, and many types of high-end printers, such as those shown in Figure 5-15, could produce accurate color proofs from electronic files.

Proofing without Paper

The final step in this process is still being worked on: the ability to proof an electronic file directly on the computer monitor. **Monitor proofing** eliminates the need for any printed materials or expensive output devices, and allows clients, designers, and printers to view proofs right in their own offices. The PDF format is part of this process, and some companies are already moving to this type of proofing system. But monitor proofing requires highly accurate (and expensive) monitors and the ability to keep the electronic color accurate and consistent no matter what computer or operating system is being used.

PRINTING WITH PDFS

What You'll Learn

▶ *In this lesson, you will see how PDF files are printed.*

More Printing Options

Many of the early problems associated with printing PDF files have been solved over the last several years. PDFs are being utilized to create the printing plates used in traditional printing processes, again removing film from the work flow. In addition, more printers are looking into digital printing processes. Electronic digital printing systems (such as the Xerox Docutech or Agfa Chromapress) use no printing plates, but instead use high-speed laser technology to print multiple copies of images on paper directly from electronic files. These systems are ideal for smaller printing jobs under 1,000 copies. The PDF format has increasingly become the standard in this area of the industry (see Figure 5-16).

The New Process

Today a graphic designer can create a design using any combination of software, then create a PDF and send it over the Internet to the client. The client can open it in Adobe Acrobat, make comments, indicate changes, and attach revisions, then send it back over the Internet to the designer. This goes back and forth until the client approves the job, usually using an electronic stamp in Acrobat. The designer then sends the PDF with comments and instructions to the printer. The printer mails a printed proof to the designer and the client (many clients still want to see one printed proof before approving a job); the client makes changes or approves the proof. The printer then prints the job and delivers it to the happy client, who e-mails the designer thanking them for a job well done, all thanks to Acrobat and PDFs.

FIGURE 5-16
Digital printing system

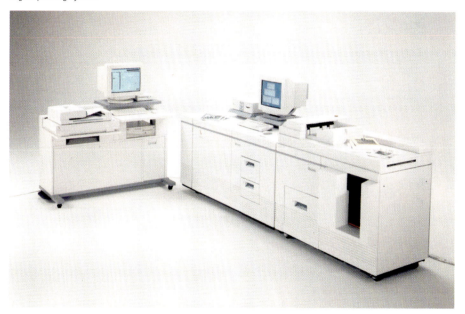

PDFs have become an important part of the graphics industry. The ability to create and modify PDFs makes Adobe Acrobat a valuable tool for anyone working in advertising, graphic design, production, printing, or the Web. Today PDFs are used to proof jobs throughout the design and production process, and to print jobs using a variety of traditional and digital processes.

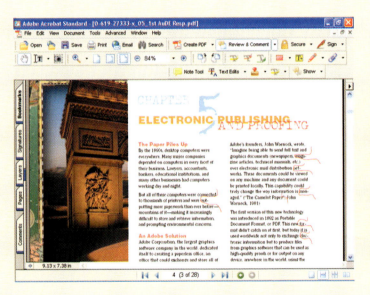

KEY TERMS AND CONCEPTS

Adobe Acrobat
Adobe Reader
Attach File tool
comments
compression
device-independent
document layout
download
electronic documents
electronic forms
electronic publishing
e-mail attachments
File Transfer Protocol (FTP)

HTML
multiple files
multiple layers
monitor proofing
Portable Document Format (PDF)
PostScript
printed proof
Raster Image Processor (RIP)
review
Review tools
scan files
upload
Web pages

CHAPTER REVIEW

1. What does PDF stand for?

_____

_____

_____

2. What types of computers and operating systems can read PDFs?

_____

_____

_____

3. Why are PDF files so small in size, compared to the original document file formats?

_____

_____

_____

4. How is a PDF file different from a Postscript file?

_____

_____

_____

5. Name two ways PDF files can be sent over the Internet.

_____

_____

_____

6. How is Adobe Reader different from Adobe Acrobat?

_____

_____

_____

7. Name three file formats that can be opened in Acrobat.

_____

_____

_____

8. Name the four ways Acrobat can open or create a PDF file.

_____

_____

_____

9. What does the Loupe tool do?

_____

_____

_____

10. List three ways you can modify the structure of a PDF document in Acrobat.

_____

_____

_____

11. What is the function of each of these comment/review tools?

Note: _____

_____

Stamps: _____

_____

Show: _____

_____

Attach File: _____

_____

12. What is electronic publishing?

_____

_____

_____

13. What are the advantages of monitor proofing?

_____

_____

_____

You have been working on several projects for Butterfly Foods. They have asked you to send over proofs of all the jobs in progress for an important meeting being held in three hours. Each project needed to be produced in a different application, and you work on a Macintosh computer. The computers in your client's office are Windows machines.

Fortunately, this client has a color printer hooked up to a computer with the latest version of Adobe Reader, so you've decided to convert the files to PDF format.

Open Adobe Acrobat, then open the following files from the disk or folder where your Data Files are stored: IG 5-1.ai, IG 5-2.tif, and IG 5-3.eps. Save each file as a PDF file, using the filenames

butterfly_logo_1.pdf, **package_cover.pdf**, and **butterfly_logo_2.pdf**, respectively. These three PDF files could now be sent to the client for printing in plenty of time to meet the required deadline.

One Step Beyond

Compare the size of the file created in the original application to the size of the PDF file you created. Write these down and compare how much smaller the PDF files are. Write a brief explanation as to why the PDF files are smaller. Note if there are any files that do not compress as much as the others.

You are working on a project for Butterfly Foods and have sent them a PDF proof to look over. The proof has come back and you have opened it up to review their comments and changes. In Acrobat, open the file IG 5-4.pdf in the location where you store your Data Files. Then open the original application files to implement the suggested corrections: If you are using Illustrator, open IG 5-5.eps; if you are using FreeHand, open IG 5-6.eps. (Note that the blue caret character indicates inserted text; hold the pointer over it to view the insert.) Save the revised file as **foods_logo**. Read the comments on the PDF and make those changes in the original application file. Make sure you go through and make every change. (*Hint*: Remember that you can use the Show tool to view all of the comments.) Save the revised file, print it out, and compare the printout to the PDF to make sure you have made all of the requested changes.

One Step Beyond

Produce a PDF of the revised file, name it **foods_logo.pdf**, and attach it to an e-mail. Send it to yourself or to a friend, then download the file from the e-mail and view it in Adobe Reader. Compare it to your printout, and write a brief paragraph on the differences you see between the monitor display and the printout. Look at color, layout, and fonts; be sure to write down any differences you notice.

DESIGN PROJECT

Create an 8.5" × 11" ad or flyer in any application that can save or export to a PDF. Be sure to make it as colorful as possible, and use several different type styles. Print out your file on the best color printer available to you. Then convert the file to a PDF, name it **ch5_design_project.pdf** and burn it on a CD. Make sure you use a CD format that both Windows and Macintosh can recognize.

Take the CD to a local printer service that prints to a digital device such as a color copier, and make sure they know how to print a PDF file. Ask to have one output of the file. (If it's a copier device, it should cost only one or two dollars for one output.) Take their output and compare it to your output. How close are they? Write two or three paragraphs on the differences between the two outputs.

FIGURE 5-17
Examining different digital proofs

PDFs are used in a wide range of industries, from graphics to law to education and more. Connect to the Internet, go to *www.course.com*, navigate to the page for this book, click the Student Online Companion link, then click the link for this chapter, which will take you to the Adobe Web site. Navigate to the "Customer stories" link. Here you will find dozens of articles of how different companies are using PDFs in their daily work. The page should look similar to Figure 5-18. Download three stories from three different industries and write a brief 1- to 2-page paper comparing how each company uses PDFs.

FIGURE 5-18
Adobe customer stories

PRODUCTION AND REPRODUCTION TECHNOLOGIES FOR PRINT MEDIA

CHAPTER 6

PRODUCTION AND REPRODUCTION TECHNOLOGIES FOR PRINT MEDIA

Moving a Project to Production

You have defined the client's visual problem and completed the necessary research. You've created and evaluated numerous thumbnails and roughs, presented several comps, and—with just a few modifications—a final design has been agreed upon. The project has been approved. So...where do you go from here?

The project now moves into the **production** phase. Before computers, moving to production was a clearly defined event when the creative team handed off the work to the production team. All the work produced during the creative process was in the form of hand-drawn comprehensives, usually done with felt-tip markers like those shown in Figure 6-1. These marker renderings looked quite realistic

and included as many details as possible. In production, these manual presentations would be re-created into artwork that could be reproduced on a printing press. Highly skilled pasteup artists would have the text typeset and the photos and illustrations shot on a process camera. All the elements would be pasted down to an **artboard**. The finished pasteup was called a **mechanical**, which was the art that the printer would use to reproduce the design on the printing press.

Today's Production Process

As you learned in Chapter 1, the current production process is completely electronic and, in many instances, overlaps the creative process. As designers create possible project variations on the computer, they can input the text and produce typographic layouts. Photographs can be shot on a traditional camera and scanned, or the designer can download digital photographs and place them in the layout. Illustrations can be scanned or produced electronically for inclusion in the final layout. Then it's up to production to bring all the files together and make sure they print properly, checking for color, fonts, file formats, and other issues that might affect output.

To ensure that the final product outputs correctly, designers must think about and plan for potential issues with images, fonts, and color *during the design phase*. If you do as much of this work up front as you can, the output and printing processes will go smoothly. If you do not address these issues early on, leaving them for the production staff to solve, the amount of time required to complete the project could push it over budget and create problems in meeting deadlines.

Felt-tip marker comps

IMAGE CAPTURE

What You'll Learn

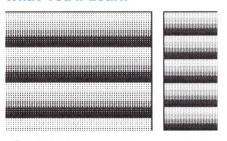

In this lesson, you will learn more about scanners and scanned images.

Scanned Images

In Chapter 3, you learned about scanner types and how they work. But once the scan is complete, what determines the quality of the image and what type of output it is best suited for?

A scanned image is a bitmapped or raster image in which the image's value and color are converted to a series of dots. The number of dots per inch describes the resolution (quality) of the image: the fewer dots per inch, the lower the resolution; the more dots per inch, the higher the resolution.

Before computers, these dots were measured in lines per inch (**lpi**), or how many rows (lines) of dots were measured left-to-right and top-to-bottom. If you magnified an image using lpi dots you would see the dots line up in perfect rows. In lighter value areas, the dots are small, with lots of white as the background. In darker value areas, the dots are larger, covering up more of the white background (see Figure 6-2).

DESIGNTIP All dots are not created equal

Because lpi describes dots on a printing press and dpi and ppi describe digital dots, the numbers used to describe the number of dots per inch don't match up. You need twice as many digital dots to convert to a specific number of printing dots. To solve this, it's best to use a 2-to-1 conversion, 2 being digital and 1 being printing. So a 120 lpi image would have to be scanned at 240 dpi or ppi to have an acceptable resolution for printed output.

As electronic production methods became more common, the industry looked at ways of recreating lpi dots digitally. First came **dpi** (dots per inch) and **ppi** (pixels per inch). Although both terms are used interchangeably, the graphics industry generally uses dpi to describe dots created by printing devices and ppi for dots on a computer monitor. Scanners may use dpi or ppi to measure resolution, depending on the manufacturer.

The graphics industry has now come up with a fourth way to measure dots: **spots per inch**, or **spi**. This technique spreads dots of equal size over the image. To make lighter values, the dots are fewer and spread apart; to make darker values, there are more dots placed very close together, or even overlapping each other, as shown in

FIGURE 6-2
LPI dots

Figure 6-3. Today lpi and spi are widely used in the industry, although many of the new platesetting devices use spi. So your scanner will scan an image in either dpi or ppi, but the imagesetter or platesetter will convert the image to either lpi or spi. Imagesetters and platesetters are discussed later in this chapter.

Resolution and Image Quality

Because a scanned image is a raster file, the resolution determines the quality of the image. **Resolution** is measured in both lpi and spi. The fewer lines or spots per inch, the lower the resolution, and the lower the quality of an image. More lines or spots per inch means higher resolution and higher image quality. In print graphics, a low resolution is between 45 and 95 lpi or spi. Newspaper images are usually printed at this resolution. If you look closely

FIGURE 6-3
SPI dots

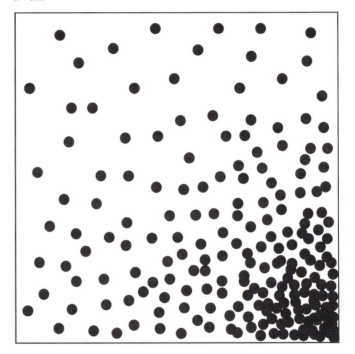

at a newspaper picture, you should be able to see the lines or spots in the photo. Average quality is between 100 and 133 lpi or spi; many flyers, catalogs, and business cards are printed at this resolution. The lines or spots are so small you would need a magnifying glass to see them. High quality is between 150 and 200 lpi or spi; most expensive printed pieces such as annual reports and posters are printed at this resolution. At this quality, the dots are so small that it takes expensive, highly accurate printing presses to reproduce the work. Figure 6-4 shows three different resolutions.

FIGURE 6-4
Different resolutions

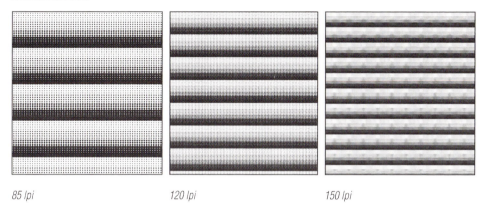

85 lpi   120 lpi   150 lpi

A cheap scanner won't cut it

Scanners are available in many prices, from inexpensive to very expensive. But it's important to understand that the cheap scanner you can buy at any computer chain store is *not* a graphic-arts quality scanner. Like anything else, you get what you pay for. An inexpensive scanner is great for scanning pictures for personal use that you will send as e-mail attachments. But most graphic-arts quality scanners start at over $500, and some can cost $30,000 or more. Most studios and agencies know that high-priced scanners are worth the cost; they scan at higher resolutions and reproduce color more accurately. Companies also know that scanner operators have to be very good at running the equipment and knowing how to make images look good. Scanner operators are some of the best-paid employees in the industry.

IMAGE AND FONT LINKS

What You'll Learn

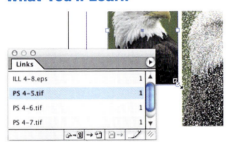

 In this lesson, you will learn how graphics applications link to images and fonts.

Preparing Files for Output

Once the client has approved a project, the designer or production artist now needs to prepare the electronic files for output. This includes checking to make sure that all components required for output are included with the original document.

Graphics Links

When designers and production artists create a graphics file, they import, or **place**, various raster and vector images into the file. They position, scale, and crop the images, like the images in Figure 6-5, based on the design requirements of the

The technology of type

Fonts are files that a computer accesses to create the font on the monitor or to print the font. There are three major font file formats: Postscript Type 1, TrueType, and OpenType. **PostScript Type 1** fonts, developed by Adobe in 1984, are used on both Windows and Macintosh computers. **TrueType** was developed in 1991 in a joint venture between Apple and Microsoft; these fonts are also available for both company's operating systems. But Postscript and TrueType font files on a Macintosh cannot be used on a Windows computer, and vice versa. However, a new font type called **OpenType**, released in 1999 by a partnership of Adobe and Microsoft, has solved this problem. OpenType font files can be used on either operating system, which makes moving and reading graphics files between the two much easier and more accurate.

project. But when you view these placed images on the monitor, you are seeing only a copy of what the original image looks like. This copy is accurate enough for layout purposes. But when the printer produces the proof or final output, the computer refers back to the original electronic file to obtain the complete image information so the printer can reproduce it accurately. This is known as **linking**, a concept made popular by QuarkXPress, and which you learned

FIGURE 6-5
Placed (imported) graphics

about briefly in Chapter 4. Figure 6-6 shows an InDesign document and its linked graphics. The use of links allowed the InDesign file to remain small.

Font Links

Graphics files also contain links to all the **fonts** used in the document. As designers and production artists build a file, they use fonts available on the computer they are using. Every computer has certain fonts available, depending on the font files that have been installed. This can create a problem when moving a graphics document from one computer to another: If the fonts used in designing the document are not installed in the output computer, the file cannot display the fonts correctly, and the layout doesn't look at all like what the designer intended. Nor can the output device print the file correctly, because it can't access the fonts used to create it.

FIGURE 6-6
Linking files

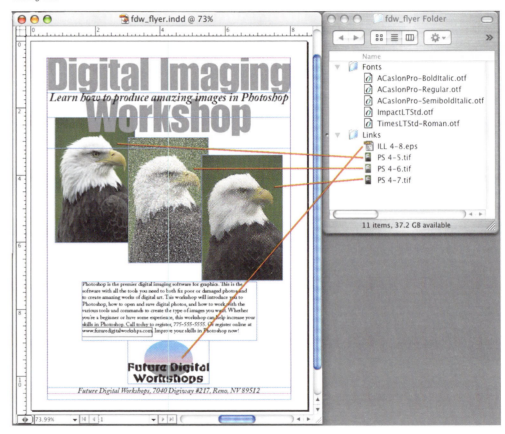

Packaging a File

When the production work on a document is complete, the designer or production artist must carefully manage images and fonts so the document file can be output properly. This used to be done manually, with the various image and font elements copied into common folders. But today both of the major page layout applications, InDesign and QuarkXPress, use an automated process. InDesign has a Package command that copies the graphics file into a new Project folder; it then creates a Links folder and copies all of the linked graphics there, and creates a Fonts folder for copies of the font files. QuarkXPress performs a similar process using the Collect for Output command. See Figure 6-7 to see how InDesign packages a file for output.

FIGURE 6-7

InDesign's Package command

PREFLIGHT AND PROOFING

What You'll Learn

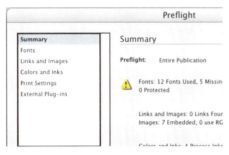

In this lesson, you will learn about the preflight and proofing processes.

Preflighting a File

When the designer or production artist has collected a file and all of its components, the file needs to be checked to make sure that it has been put together correctly. This process of checking a file is called **preflight**. Generally the company or vendor that will print or output the file does the preflight. But there are a few design studios and ad agencies that preflight files before they go to the printer. It depends on how much control they want over the output process, and if they have the time and the experienced personnel to do this additional work.

A preflight check is a software procedure you can run in either QuarkXPress or InDesign. The process checks to see if all of the linked graphics and fonts have been included with the file, and if all of the links are updated properly. It also checks the file's color models and linked graphics to make sure they match the project specifications. For example, a preflight check would reveal if a scanned image is RGB, but the project is printing CMYK. This

scanned image would have to be converted to CMYK in Photoshop and the link updated.

Preflight also checks the file formats of all linked graphics to make sure there are no formats that won't print properly. Formats like PICT, GIF, or PNG are not designed as high-quality print formats. Any special effects are also reviewed to make sure they will output correctly. Effects such as transparency cannot be output on older devices that use software that doesn't recognize or support these newer effects. See Figure 6-8 for an example of a preflight check in InDesign.

Proofing the File

As a file is prepared for output, it's important to print and check the work to make sure all changes have been made—a process known as **proofing**. The proofing process starts back during the design phase; the designer, and later the production artist, typically prints a **proof**, which is a laser or inkjet output copy, and check it, making design and layout changes as necessary. But these types of proofs are generally too low in quality to give an accurate rendering of color or other special effects within the file.

There are two major types of proofing processes: analog and digital. **Analog proofs** are made from the films that will be used eventually to print the job on a printing press. But **digital proofs** made from the electronic files used for output are becoming more commonplace in the industry. See Figure 6-9. Digital proofs include the following:

- **Black-and-white laser prints**—By far the most common way to proof a job, because almost every design studio and ad agency has at least one laser printer. This is the quick way to see how a file looks, but it only shows black and white.

- **Inkjet prints**—Another common device for proofing; the advantage over black-and-white laser prints is the ability to show color. However, the disadvantage is that the color is not accurate. The ink used by inexpensive inkjet printers is meant to make color photographs print in bright, vibrant colors, not to match colors in a graphics file.

- **Color laser prints**—Another device used for proofing color files but with similar color-matching limitations of inkjet printers. Color laser printers also tend to be more expensive than comparable inkjet printers, so they are not as common in the industry.

- **Large format inkjet prints**—Originally very expensive devices, these printers are becoming more prevalent in the industry because prices have dropped over the last few years. They use more accurate ink systems and can also print to large formats. Most are 24" to 48" wide and can print rolls many feet in length.

- **Digital color proofs**—These are high-quality color proofs that come in two types, halftone and continuous-tone (contone). Both types use different printing technologies and work with expensive equipment. **Halftone proofs** are intended to match the dots used on the printing press and therefore provide a highly accurate match to the final printed piece. **Contone proofs** are a little less expensive, but work well in simulating the spi dots used in many newer direct-to-platesetting systems.

FIGURE 6-8
A preflight summary

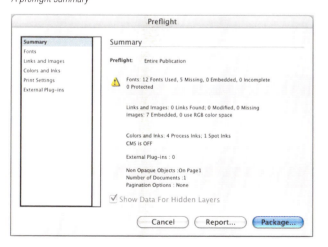

FIGURE 6-9
Various digital proofers

COLOR MANAGEMENT

What You'll Learn

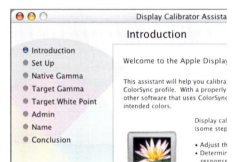

In this lesson you will learn about color management in the electronic environment.

Computers Manage Color Differently

Before computers, printing professionals managed color. Designers would create many colors within their designs, and it was up to the printer to match the designer's vision as accurately as possible. However, both the designer and the printer knew there were limitations in the machines and materials used to re-create color, and that not every color could be reproduced accurately. But at least the designer and the printer both used the same color models: So as long as the designer understood grayscale, spot colors, and CMYK, then he or she could work together with the printer to get the best color possible.

With the advent of the computer, color became a more difficult proposition. Printers had to deal with RGB color, and somehow convert what the designer saw on a computer monitor as accurately as possible on a printing press using CMYK.

This required a system of **color management**, a process that standardizes color from input (scanners and graphics software) to output (the thousands of output and printing devices used in the industry). Figure 6-10 shows a few of these color management settings.

Managing Color

Color management is a complex topic, but there are two basic concepts you should understand. First, when a scanner operator scans an image, a color profile is assigned. The scanner can be set up to assign the profile automatically, or the profile can be assigned by the operator. This **color profile** is a setting attached to a file that designates the type of device it will be printed to. The color profile will follow the file to every computer system that it may be viewed on, and ensures that each monitor will view the file color consistently, and that the designated output device will accurately re-create the color of the file.

But assigning a color profile electronically is only the first step: Someone has to set up each device with the ability to read color profiles. This person, a color management specialist (CMS), **calibrates** the scanners so they read the color of images consistently. This type of calibration is a hardware adjustment to achieve a specific effect or result. The CMS will adjust the graphics software in all computer systems to recognize color-managed files. All monitors have to be calibrated so they can accurately re-create color profiles, as shown in Figure 6-11. The CMS also has to calibrate all output devices and printers so they can recognize and print color-profiled files accurately. And all of these devices need to be recalibrated at least every month to make sure they stay within a consistent range of input and output.

As you can see by this brief overview, color management requires quite a bit of work. Many large studios, agencies, and print shops have a CMS as a full-time employee, or hire an outside service to keep their color management systems up-to-date.

FIGURE 6-10

Color management settings

FIGURE 6-11

Apple monitor settings

IMAGESETTERS AND PLATESETTERS

What You'll Learn

In this section, you will see how film and plates are output.

RIP It!

Once all production work has been completed on a job and all proofs have been approved, the finished files can be sent to an imagesetter or a platesetter. **Imagesetters** (like the one shown in Figure 6-12) output graphic arts film that is then used to expose printing plates. **Platesetters** output printing plates directly from electronic files without the need for film. The printing plates are then mounted on traditional printing presses.

Both imagesetters and platesetters require a computer loaded with special software that can translate graphics files for output. These computers are known as **Raster Image Processors**, commonly called **RIPs**. Raster Image Processors convert all of the type and images in any graphics file into dots. There are two types of RIPs: software and hardware. (In Chapter 5, you were introduced to software RIPS.)

Software RIPs can be installed into most desktop computer systems. There are RIP applications for Macintosh and Windows computers. Once a RIP is installed, the computer can process graphics files for imagesetter or platesetter output. Either output device can be connected directly to the computer with the RIP software, or the computer can be part of a network that includes either device. The advantage of software RIPs is that you don't have to purchase a separate computer; you can use one you already own. When the software becomes outdated, you can purchase an upgraded version. The disadvantage of software RIPs is speed and productivity: When a computer is processing a file through the RIP, it usually can't do any other work because it would be too much of a drain on the central processor. The RIP can usually process just one job at a time.

Hardware RIPs are computer systems that include the necessary RIP software. Figure 6-13 shows a hardware RIP system. Although it may look like a standard desktop model, this computer is dedicated to processing files and *only* processing files. The advantage of hardware RIPs is speed;

they can process files faster than a software-only RIP and in many instances can process multiple files at the same time. The disadvantages are cost and upgradability: Because you have to buy the software and a computer, it's a more expensive purchase up front; when it's time to upgrade, you have to upgrade or replace the computer as well as the software.

Output It!

Once a graphics file has been processed (commonly called a RIPed—pronounced "ripped"—file), the information is sent to a marking engine. A **marking engine** is the exposure and processing unit on an imagesetter or platesetter. Inside the marking engine a laser exposes either film or plate material under the control of the RIP computer. The film then goes through the traditional film development process. Plates can go through a couple of different processing methods, depending on the manufacturer and model of platesetter being used. See Figure 6-14 for one example of a platesetter system.

The graphics industry has been purchasing more platesetters and is moving away from imagesetters. The use of film has always raised environmental issues, especially with film disposal and the chemicals used to develop the film. Film also requires an additional step, because it is then used to expose the printing plate. By using platesetters to produce printing plates directly from the RIPed files, the industry is able to eliminate the film stage altogether.

FIGURE 6-12
An imagesetter

FIGURE 6-13
A hardware RIP system

FIGURE 6-14
A platesetter

PRINTING TECHNOLOGIES

What You'll Learn

▶ In this lesson, you will learn how film and plates are output.

Gutenberg Started It All

In 1440 in Germany, Johannes Gutenberg started the commercial printing revolution. Since then the technologies have gone through many variations, but the concept of using ink on a printing plate to transfer an image to a piece of paper has been the same. However, new digital technologies have advanced the concept of printing without the use of a printing plate or ink. There are now two main groups of imaging technologies: plate-based and nonplate-based.

Plate-Based (Impact) Technologies

The **plate-based (impact) printing technologies** use a printing plate to transfer an image to paper. This plate must impact, or press against, the paper to make the transfer. There are four types of plate-based printing: letterpress, offset lithography, gravure, and screen printing.

Letterpress printing: Gutenberg developed a system of printing using a raised image area on the plate. Commonly called **letterpress printing**, the raised part of the printing plate was the image area; the recessed part was the **nonimage area**. When a roller coated with ink was rolled over the plate, the raised area was covered with ink; the recessed area didn't receive any ink. The inked plate was then pressed against a piece of paper, and the inked image transferred onto the paper. And like magic... a printed page was created! Figures 6-15 and 6-16 show how the letterpress process works and a current letterpress press, respectively.

Letterpress was the main commercial printing process up until the early 1900s. Today most letterpress printing is reserved for cardboard and paper packaging materials using plastic or hard rubber plates; this specialized letterpress process is known as **flexography**.

Lithography: Letterpress was replaced by **lithographic printing**, a process that uses chemistry to ink an image on a printing plate. A thin, aluminum printing plate with a special, light-sensitive coating applied to it is exposed to light. When the light hits the plate, the coating hardens onto the aluminum surface. Any coating that is not exposed to light remains soft and can be washed off the plate with a special chemical wash.

Printers would photographically "shoot" artwork and mechanicals (pasteups) on graphics arts film. This would be negative film: When the film was exposed, any image areas on the art would become clear areas on the film and any nonimage areas would remain black areas on the film. The negative film would then be positioned on top of an unexposed piece of plate material on a device known as a **plate burner**. The plate burner would shoot high intensity light at the film and the plate. The clear image areas of the film would allow the light to expose the plate coating (hardening it), while the black nonimage areas would block the light, leaving the coating soft so it could be washed away, leaving the bare aluminum of the plate showing. The exposed, washed plate would then be mounted on a printing press.

FIGURE 6-15
Letterpress process

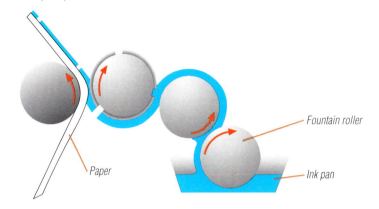

Fountain roller

Paper

Ink pan

FIGURE 6-16
Letterpress printing press

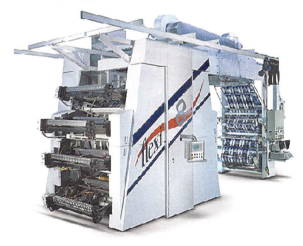

A lithographic press has three main cylinders, placed close together. The plate is mounted on one of these cylinders. As the cylinder turns, the plate runs under two sets of small rollers. The first set lays down a thin film of water on the plate. The aluminum (nonimage) area of the plate accepts water, but the coated (image) area rejects water, so the water doesn't stay on the coated area. The plate then runs under the second set of rollers, which lays down a thin film of ink. The coated area accepts ink, but the aluminum area that's covered by the thin film of water rejects the ink.

The plate with the inked areas and water areas pushes up against the second main cylinder of the press. This cylinder has a hard rubber plate mounted to it, and the inked image transfers, or **offsets,** to the second cylinder—thus the term **offset lithography**, which is the process normally used in commercial printing. This transfer allows most of the water that was applied to the metal plate to evaporate so it won't transfer on to the paper, because too much water can make paper buckle and warp.

This second cylinder then rotates against the third cylinder, which pushes the paper against the second cylinder, transferring the inked image onto the paper. The Sheet transfer cylinder (#4) guides the paper out of the press (see Figures 6-17 and 6-18).

FIGURE 6-17
Offset lithography process

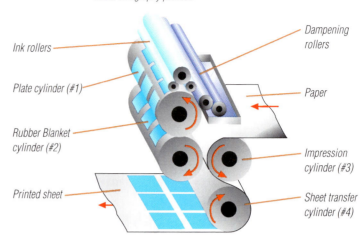

Ink rollers

Plate cylinder (#1)

Rubber Blanket cylinder (#2)

Printed sheet

Dampening rollers

Paper

Impression cylinder (#3)

Sheet transfer cylinder (#4)

FIGURE 6-18
Offset lithography printing press

Gravure printing: The third plate-based process, called **gravure**, works with a large metal plate cylinder; the image area is **etched,** or recessed, into the cylinder. These etched areas are called **cells**. The plate cylinder then turns under an inking cylinder, which lays a thin film of ink over the entire cylinder, including putting ink into all of the recessed cells (the image area). The plate cylinder then rotates under a squeegee, called the Doctor blade. The squeegee pulls the ink off of the surface of the cylinder, but leaves the ink in the recessed cells (the image area). The plate cylinder then presses up against an impression cylinder, which guides paper through the press. The impression cylinder presses against the paper and transfers the inked image onto the paper. Gravure's advantage has been with printing large quantities. Unlike letterpress or lithography, gravure cylinders handle the impact of printing well and can last for millions of impressions (see Figures 6-19 and 6-20).

Screen printing: The fourth plate-based process is **screen printing**, which uses a fine mesh plastic, metal, or silk screen to print images. The screen has a light sensitive **stencil** material applied to the mesh. When the stencil material is exposed to light, the nonimage area hardens onto the mesh, and the image area remains soft and can be washed away with water. This creates openings in the stencil where the porous mesh represents the image to be printed. Ink is then put onto the mesh, and a squeegee spreads the ink over the mesh

FIGURE 6-19
Gravure process

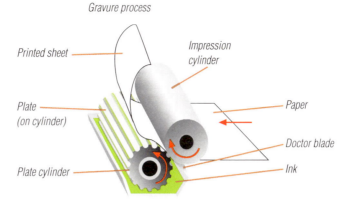

Printed sheet

Impression cylinder

Plate (on cylinder)

Paper

Doctor blade

Plate cylinder

Ink

FIGURE 6-20
Gravure printing press

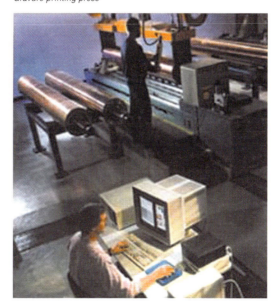

screen. When the ink hits an open area, the ink is pushed through the mesh and prints on the paper or material put underneath the screen. Because a metal plate isn't being used, almost any material, from glass to metal to T-shirts, can be printed using this process (see Figures 6-21 and 6-22).

Nonplate-Based (Nonimpact) Technologies

Nonplate-based technologies do not use a printing plate to transfer an image to paper, and they don't require impact. There are quite a few of these systems in use today; some of the most popular are xerography, electrostatic, and inkjet technologies.

FIGURE 6-21
Screen printing

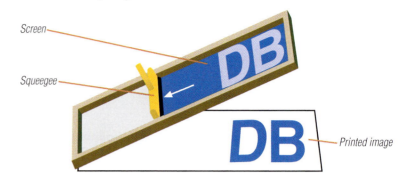

FIGURE 6-21
Screen printing

Screen

Squeegee

Printed image

FIGURE 6-22
Screen printing

Xerography: Xerography is an everyday photocopier system. The first working photocopier system was developed in 1937 and was later improved on in the 1950s by a company that would eventually become known as Xerox. The technology works by placing a positive electrical charge on a flat or cylindrical surface. When an image is exposed onto the charged surface using light, the nonimage area loses its charge and the exposed image area retains its charge. Negatively-charged toner particles are spread across the surface, and the particles stick only to the charged image area. A piece of paper is then placed over the surface, and a positive charge is applied behind the paper. This attracts the toner particles onto the paper, which is then heated, fusing the particles to the paper (see Figures 6-23 and 6-24).

(see Figures 6-23 and 6-24)

FIGURE 6-23
Xerography

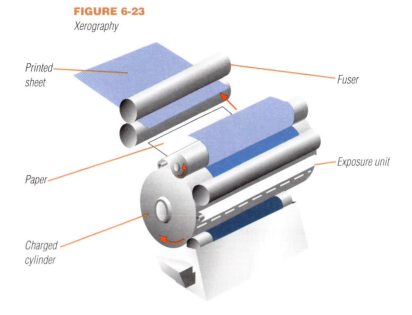

Printed sheet

Fuser

Paper

Exposure unit

Charged cylinder

FIGURE 6-24
Xerographic printer

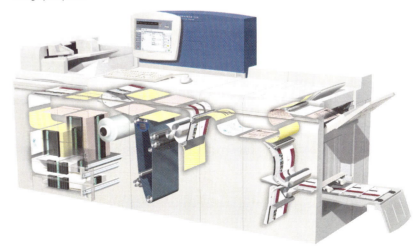

Electrostatic printing: Another process, similar to xerography, is called electrostatic printing. **Electrostatic printing** uses the same concept of attracting positive and negative charges, but uses a liquid-based toner made up of superfine particles that create a highly detailed and accurate image. Some of these electrostatic printing systems are beginning to challenge impact-based systems in quality and economy (see Figure 6-25).

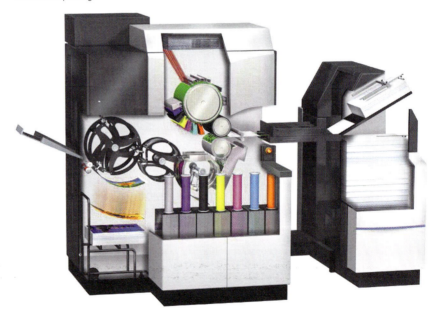

Inkjet printing: Earlier in this chapter, you learned about how inkjet printers are used in the proofing stage. This technology is growing throughout the industry. **Inkjet printing** uses small nozzles to spray ink onto a page. This fine spray allows inkjet printers to work in very high resolutions. These printers are used for high-quality photographic reproductions, including large-format printing all the way up to billboards and displays covering several stories of a building. Inkjet is taking over much of the work formerly done with screen printing, because, like screen printing, inkjets can spray onto almost any surface (see Figure 6-26 and 6-27).

FIGURE 6-26
Inkjet printing

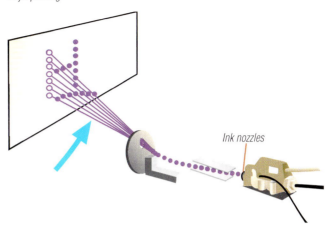

Ink nozzles

FIGURE 6-27
Inkjet printer

Print graphic production and reproduction encompasses important concepts and technologies that designers need to understand. These include scanning and scanning resolutions, graphics and font linkage, file preflight and proofing, color management, imagesetters, platesetters, and printing processes, including plate-based and non-plate-based processes. Designers should always know how their designs are going to be printed; this allows them to balance their creative ideas with the realities of the technologies they choose. Production people are vital to the process because they are the ones who make those creative ideas come to life. Their thorough understanding of production applications and technologies is an important component of the graphics workflow.

analog proofs
artboard
black-and-white laser prints
calibrate
cells
color laser prints
color management
color profile
contone proofs
digital direct color proofs
digital proofs
digital color proofs
dpi
electrostatic printing
etched
flexography
fonts
gravure
halftone proofs
hardware RIP
imagesetter
inkjet printing
inkjet prints
large-format inkjet prints
letterpress printing
linking
lithographic printing
lithography

lpi
marking engine
mechanical
nonimage area
nonplate-based (nonimpact) printing
offset
offset lithography
OpenType
Package command
place
plate-based (impact) printing technologies
plate burner
platesetter
PostScript Type 1
ppi
preflight
production
proof
proofing process
Raster Image Processor (RIP)
resolution
screen printing
stencil
software RIP
spots per inch (spi)
TrueType
xerography

CHAPTER REVIEW

1. What does lpi stand for?

2. How are dpi and ppi dots different from lpi dots?

3. How does resolution relate to the quality of an image?

4. Describe how linkage works in a graphics file.

5. Name the three major font file formats.

6. In a graphics file, what areas will a preflight check look at?

7. What is the difference between analog proofs and digital proofs?

8. Name three digital proofing systems.

9. Give a brief description of color management.

10. What is calibration?

11. What is the main difference between an imagesetter and a platesetter?

12. In production, what does RIP stand for?

_____

_____

_____

13. Name three plate-based (impact) printing technologies:

_____

_____

_____

14. What kinds of materials can screen printing print on?

_____

_____

_____

15. What is the difference between xerography and electrostatic printing?

_____

_____

_____

16. Describe how inkjet printing works.

_____

_____

_____

Your production supervisor at Horizon Advertising has an ad that needs to be checked to make sure it will output properly. Open the file IG 6-1.indd or IG 6-1.qrk from the folder where you store your Data Files. (Make sure you are working on a copy of the original folder, containing the file and all linked graphics, to preserve the original. Saving the file under a different name using the Save As command could break links.) Check the graphics links and the font links. You will find that several are broken and you will have to relink to the files and fonts that are located in your Chapter 6 Data Files folder. (In InDesign, in the Fix Links dialog box, click Fix Links automatically. If the images don't relink automatically, use the Browse button in the Relink dialog box to find the correct file.)

When relinking fonts, you may have to substitute different fonts, depending on the fonts installed on your system. If so, check the layout and adjust it as necessary. Once you have updated all of the links and made any necessary layout changes, print the file to verify that everything is printing properly.

It's another normal day at Amazing Graphic Designs, until the phone rings. It's the production department at Incredible Color Printers, letting you know they are sending over a file that needs to be checked for color. Open IG 6-2.indd or IG 6-2.qrk from the folder where you store your Data Files. (Make sure you are working on a copy of the original files, to preserve the original. Saving the file under a different name using the Save As command could break links.) This file is supposed to print CMYK (full color). The linked files are provided in a Links folder. Open all of the files in Photoshop and check to make sure each image has the correct color model, using the Mode command on the Image menu. If they are not the correct color model, change them as necessary.

Relink all graphics. (In InDesign, in the Fix Links dialog box, click Fix Links automatically. If the images don't relink automatically, use the Browse button in the Relink dialog box to find the correct file.)

When relinking fonts, you may have to substitute different fonts, depending on the fonts installed on your system. If so, check the layout and adjust it as necessary. Print out a set of separations. (Specify the separation settings on the Output tab of the Print dialog box.) Check the separations to make sure the file is printing CMYK. If you see any additional colors, change them to CMYK. Print out a final set of separations to verify that everything outputs properly.

DESIGN PROJECT

Schedule a visit to a printer in your area. Have them give you a tour of their facility, showing you the equipment they use in production, preflight, file output, and printing. Be sure to ask your tour guide the following questions:

1. What types of graphics files do they accept from designers?
2. Do they have a scanner in their facility, and what type of scanner is it?
3. How do they preflight and proof files?
4. Do they have an imagesetter and/or platesetter in their facility?
5. How do they handle color management?
6. What types of printing presses do they have in their facility?

Write a summary of what you learned from the printer and how it compares to what you learned in this chapter.

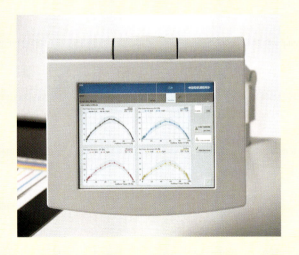

Open the files shown in Figure 6-28 from the welding_brochure_folder. Use a word processor or a spreadsheet to create a table like the one shown, and fill in each of the file characteristics listed. Then print black-and-white composite and separation proofs of the file. (Print color composite proofs if you have the appropriate equipment available.)

	Project
Number of bitmapped images	
Number of vector images	
Resolution of images	
Color model of project	
Type of fonts used	
What printing processes can this job be produced in today? (Choose the ones that make sense based on the type of job and knowing that the client needs 10,000 printed.)	

FIGURE 6-28
An artist-designed brochure

Dan Bouweraerts
Welding department brochure
Truckee Meadows Community College

ELECTRONIC DESIGN FOR DIGITAL MEDIA

ELECTRONIC DESIGN FOR DIGITAL MEDIA

New Technologies Appear

At the start of the 20th century, the field of graphic design and production was in the middle of a "machine makeover;" the industrial revolution of the 19th century had mechanized many areas of the industry, raising both the speed and the quality of the graphics being produced. This mechanization helped bring about the development of the daily newspaper. Publishers could collect news throughout the day and then write, edit, typeset, proof, print, and deliver newspapers overnight (see Figure 7-1). By the 1920s, many types of graphics and advertising that used to take months to produce could now be produced in a few days.

During this explosion of technology, artists and designers explored other areas of visual communications—areas that would move graphic images off the printed page and onto the movie screen, television, and computer monitor.

Giving Images Depth

Before 1900, most pictures in books and periodicals consisted of drawings or illustrations. But the first few decades of the 20th century saw an ever-increasing use of photography that brought images to life with a greater sense of realism and depth.

Fine artists have always had a fascination with three-dimensional space. Sculpture, crafts, and architecture all deal with solving a design problem using three-dimensional forms. Artists applied these concepts to a new medium—**motion pictures**, where the sensation of three-dimensional space reached new levels. The audience in a movie theater could now view images as they had never seen them before. Past events, today's stories, and visions of the future could be created as if they were actually happening. This re-creation of reality was then transported to another new medium: **television**. TV brought these images into everyone's homes.

As video technology progressed and computer use became common during the 1980s, so did the designer's ability to create three-dimensional designs. Simple computer programs let designers create more realistic three-dimensional models, like the illustration shown in Figure 7-2. Animators, too, began to use the computer to model their animated figures more realistically. Even simple two-dimensional pictures looked more realistic on a computer monitor able to display millions of colors.

FIGURE 7-1

Newspapers appear overnight

Giving Images Motion and Sound

Motion pictures provided two additional dimensions to the recording and re-creation of reality: motion and sound. **Motion** is an aspect of time, the fourth dimension of design, and has created many new job areas within the graphics and other related industries. Motion pictures, television, video games, and the Internet all use motion to give graphics a dynamic presentation (see Figure 7-3).

Sound, in the form of speech, music, and other audio effects, further enhances the visual experience. Motion pictures and radio were the first to introduce sound; now recorded sound technologies range from vinyl records to audio tape to the digital technologies of CD, DVD, and MP3.

The Arrival of the Internet

The ultimate integration of graphics, motion, and sound was the development of the Internet. During the 1950s, the U.S. military wanted a way to have all its nuclear-missile-targeting computers communicate with each other. The military worked with numerous university researchers to develop a computer **network**—a group of computers that can communicate with each other. The network quickly began to grow beyond just targeting missiles. The university researchers used it for sending communications to each other (using an early form of e-mail) and posting information on computers that could be shared by other computers connected to the network.

FIGURE 7-2
Three-dimensional image

During the 1970s, computer networks sprang up all over the world. But there were no common computer languages; a computer in Japan couldn't communicate with a computer in Germany, and a German computer couldn't communicate with a computer in Chicago. So in 1989, **Tim Berners-Lee**, a programmer working for **CERN** (European Laboratory for Particle Physics) in Geneva, Switzerland, became interested in solving this problem. Berners-Lee developed the foundation for **Hypertext Markup Language** (**HTML**), the programming language that is the foundation of the Internet. He developed a network protocol named **hypertext transfer protocol (http)** that connected collections of hyperlinked pages at different locations on the Internet. Berners-Lee also created the first **Web browser** software that allowed computers to display the content of an HTML-programmed Web page with text and pictures instead of lines of code. Amazingly, Berners-Lee gave all of this technology away for free!

Since 1990, the Internet has grown at a tremendous rate. Today **e-mail** (electronic mail) is as common as sending a letter through the postal service. Thousands of companies such as Amazon.com do business completely over the Internet. Businesses have discovered they can use advertising on the Internet to reach a new and potentially huge market. And the Internet is becoming a more visually dynamic environment, with motion, sound, and interactivity now commonplace.

FIGURE 7-3
Motion comes to design

CREATIVITY AND DESIGN FOR DIGITAL MEDIA

What You'll Learn

QUIET LAKE SCENE

▶ *In this lesson, you will learn how creativity and the steps of the design process are applied in digital media.*

Skills for Digital Media

How is designing for digital media different from designing for print media? The principal differences are:

- Print media is presented on paper or other two-dimensional material, whereas digital media is presented on a monitor, which is capable of two- and three-dimensional display. Therefore, digital media requires a much greater understanding of three-dimensional space than print media.

- Print media is much more predictable because it is normally produced on a stable, consistent product such as paper. But digital media is dependent on variable factors such as the viewer's computer platform, operating system, monitor resolution, browser type and version, and so forth. And because digital media can present events over a period of time, it requires a greater understanding of "time design" and storytelling than print media.

You don't have to be creative to get a job—Part 2

As you learned in Chapter 1 with print media, there are numerous jobs in digital media that don't require a lot of creativity. These types of jobs require a strong understanding of the technologies associated with digital media. They include computer programmers, database specialists, network experts, production engineers using motion and sound, and many other jobs. Designers have a high regard for good production people, who help them to realize their creative vision. Production people are invaluable contributors to the execution and completion of any successful print or digital media project. So don't become discouraged if you find you're not the most creative person. There are still many opportunities out there.

- Digital media requires print designers to learn a new set of technologies and applications, such as Web programming, video editing, and timeline design.

What's Included in Digital Media?

So what areas of the industry fall under the umbrella term "digital media?" Although the boundaries of each area overlap, digital media is any technology that is viewed on a monitor and, for the purposes of this book, includes:

- **Web design**: the creation, design, and production of pages that are intended for display on the World Wide Web.
- **Web animation**: the creation, design, and production of graphics that incorporate motion on a Web page. This generally refers to two-dimensional animation, although more three-dimensional animation is appearing.
- **Digital video**: the use of motion picture-based moving pictures on the computer and on the Web. This can include film-based video that has been converted to digital format, as well as images captured using a digital video camera and 2-D and 3-D animation.
- **Multimedia**: the use of motion graphics on the computer, including designs, images, video, and sound, for example, CDs for interactive instruction for education.

- **3-D modeling and animation**: the creation of three-dimensional images that move and include sound. For example, the original *Toy Story* movie was the first computer generated 3-D movie.

Creativity and Digital Media

Designers need the same creativity for digital media that they do for print media. Being able to work through the design process and use the basic principles and elements of design are important, regardless of media type. As with print media, many people working in digital media have come to the industry knowing how to use the software, but they have not necessarily learned creative design skills. But books, workshops, and classes can help develop anyone's creative skills for working in digital media.

Designers in digital media still need to pay attention to the designer/client relationship. They must understand and satisfy the client's needs, whether it's creating a Web site, a multimedia presentation, or an animated commercial.

The Design Process for Digital Media

Design for digital media follows the same process as for print media: Define the problem, research the project, create thumbnails and roughs, prepare comprehensives,

and review and refine the design. For example, the personal watercraft company whose brochure you considered in Chapter 1 could ask you to create a Web site for their company. As with the brochure, you need to define the problem. What information needs to appear on the Web site? Will it have only general information about the company, or will it include the products they sell? Who will be the audience viewing the site? Will the viewer be able to download a company brochure or catalog? Will the company want the viewer to type information about themselves in a form and send it to the company, requesting information? Who will collect and organize this information? Does the company want to sell products over the Internet?

As you can see, there are a lot of questions to ask to help you define the problem. But once the problem is defined, you can begin research on the design project. To start, research other Web sites for personal watercraft and other sports vehicles and see how these sites are designed.

Preliminary Work

After research, the designer creates thumbnails and roughs of the proposed site, sketching alternative designs for each Web page. But for a Web site, there is an additional and very important piece to develop: a site layout. Very few Web sites contain only one page; the **site layout** is a sketch of each page arranged in a tree diagram. It establishes the number of pages the site will need and how each page will be connected to all of the other pages in the site. An example of a site layout is shown in Figure 7-4. A well-designed site layout ensures that the site is logically organized. It also ensures that users can easily navigate among the site pages and won't become "lost" in its structure or reach a "dead end," with no way to navigate out of a page. You'll learn more about site navigation in Chapter 8.

As with print design, it's important to work through thumbnails and rough layouts using felt-tip markers on marker paper. The computer would slow down the process; remember that thumbnails and roughs are meant to be quick sketches that establish creative direction and basic layout parameters. Doing this process manually allows you to move quickly through a number of creative solutions. And the more solutions you create, the better chance you have of creating a design that the client will accept and approve. Remember that you, not the computer, are the designer. Use your creative skills to come up with dynamic designs that you can enhance even further using the computer.

FIGURE 7-4
Site layout

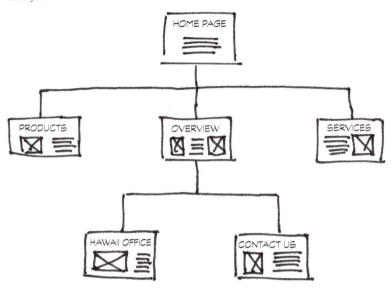

Motion graphics and storyboards

In animation, multimedia, and video, storyboards replace the site layout in Web design and thumbnails and roughs in print design. A **storyboard** is a scene-by-scene presentation of how a motion graphics project will progress (see Figure 7-5). Virtually all filmmakers use storyboarding extensively to establish the overall story concept and define every individual scene within the movie before one frame is shot. Anyone creating motion graphics should be proficient in creating storyboards.

Comprehensive Presentations

Comprehensives in digital media take on a different form than in print media. Because so much of what happens in digital media includes motion, sound, and **interactivity** (where the viewer interacts with the project), flat, two-dimensional comprehensives can't adequately represent the content. Instead, the designer must create a working version of the project, called a **prototype**. For a Web site, the designer would create a working model of the site, with all of the pages laid out and the navigational links installed so the client can move from page to page.

In multimedia, a prototype would be a working model of the multimedia project, with all of the components working as designed. It's also useful to develop prototypes of videos and animations, known as **rough cuts**, that show the project as it would appear in the final presentation.

Reviewing and Refining the Design

As with print media comprehensives, the client reviews the prototypes and submits any necessary changes and updates to the designer. This process repeats until the client gives the final approval. Once approved, the prototype then enters the final production phase.

FIGURE 7-5

Storyboards

Keeping your creative muscles in shape—Part 2

As you learned in Chapter 1 with print media designers, digital media designers need to be out in the real world, observing design all around them. There are thousands of well-designed Web sites: you need to find them and figure out what makes them successful. For anyone interested in motion graphics, it's important to go to movies and watch television, observing how stories are told and what computer techniques are used. Computer games are a fast-growing area of graphics and a great way to see the latest digital animation techniques in use. Keep on top of the latest developments—read books, subscribe to industry magazines, and join an industry organization to keep your knowledge and skills current.

DESIGNING IN 3-D

What You'll Learn

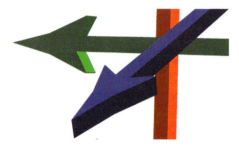

▶ *In this lesson, you will learn how design elements and principles are used to create three-dimensional projects.*

Design Elements in 3-D Design

It's important to understand that although digital media uses different technologies and applications, the concepts of design are no different than in print media. But the concepts of three-dimensional design do require a review of how these elements and principles apply in the 3-D space.

Lines and Shapes

The use of lines and shapes in three-dimensional design is as varied as in two-dimensional design. But as you move into the **three-dimensional space**, lines and shapes have their own unique properties.

The 3-D space is defined by **width**, **height**, and **depth**, or on the computer as the **x-, y-, and z-axes** (see Figure 7-6.)

When designers define shapes in three dimensions, they use two common drafting methods—orthographic projection and perspective drawing—to create 3-D representations of 2-D concepts. **Orthographic projection** is a technique that accurately represents a form's structure: the six sides of an object (top, bottom, front, back, left side, and right side) are projected around the object on an imaginary cube. This creates a three-dimensional representation of

---

DESIGNTIP   **These techniques help you to think in 3-D**

Orthographic projection and perspective drawing are great ways to understand how 3-D works. Learning to "think" in 3-D is important for anyone interested in working in the digital media industry. When using 3-D software applications (which you'll learn more about in Chapter 12), you move beyond these techniques and actually build objects in 3-D space, as opposed to projecting 2-D images into the 3-D space.

---

the form, as shown in Figure 7-7. This technique is often used in manufacturing and in set design for television and movies.

Perspective drawing is a more accurate representation of the form in space. Through the use of a horizon line and vanishing points, the form appears to be moving back into space toward the vanishing points (see Figure 7-8). Architects use perspective drawings to show how proposed structures will look in the environment for which they are being designed.

Once the designer puts shapes into the three-dimensional space, the shapes can now take on two additional design elements: volume and mass. **Volume** is an enclosed area of space. There are many geometric shapes with volume, including cubes, cylinders, cones, and spheres (see Figure 7-9). Designers create a multitude of three-dimensional shapes using these basic forms.

Mass is the amount of matter in a 3-D form, generally one made of a substance, such as stone, wood, or clay. Sculptors and architects use mass to make sure their three-dimensional designs have substance and are noticed by the viewing audience. The pyramids in Figure 7-10 show how the Egyptians used stone to create a mass of monumental proportions.

Value, Color, and Texture

In 3-D design, the use of value, color, and texture parallel two-dimensional design applications. Value and color can also help

FIGURE 7-6

Three-dimensional space

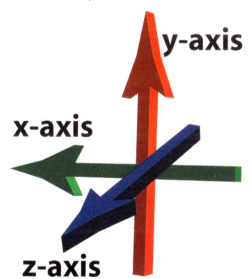

FIGURE 7-7

Orthographic projection

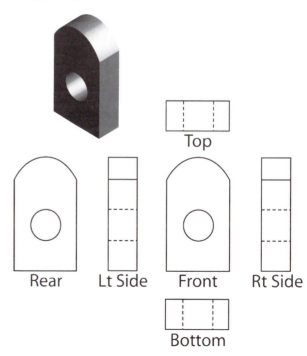

define a three-dimensional form and make the shape appear more dimensional. In Figure 7-11, value helps to define the phone as a three-dimensional shape, and the use of a shadow establishes that the form is sitting on a defined area in space. Because color has value, it can be used in the same way.

Texture takes on more importance in 3-D design than in 2-D design. People understand particular forms because of the material from which they are made. Wood, metal, and fabric are all easy to recognize because the texture of each material is familiar. Using familiar textures is an important aspect of 3-D design; many 3-D computer applications have features that attempt to re-create these textures accurately.

Space

Space in 3-D design is much more important than in two-dimensional design, because with the third dimension (the z-axis) there's so much more space to work with! There is the space that the three-dimensional shape occupies, the space around the shape, and the position of the viewer in relation to the shape. Space

FIGURE 7-8
Perspective drawing

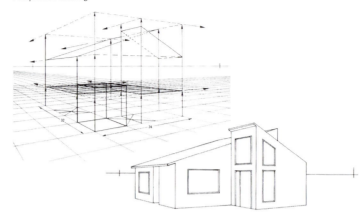

FIGURE 7-9
Volume

FIGURE 7-10
Mass

becomes even more important when the three-dimensional form starts moving within a space.

Light

Light can work in two ways when you create a 3-D design. It can illuminate the shape itself to either define, add to, or subtract from its volume or mass. Light can also add to a form's emotional quality, both positively and negatively. And the form itself can emit light, creating various visual effects and eliciting different responses from the viewer. The hallway rendered in Figure 7-12 shows how light can become a major element in design.

Design Principles

As you learned in Chapter 1, design principles are the rules designers use to organize elements in space. A designer's ability to apply these principles determines how well he or she can organize elements into an effective, coherent design. These design principles include balance, proximity, alignment, unity, emphasis, and rhythm. Each principle plays an important role in 3-D design; they are the foundation that all designers use to create and execute effective visual communication in digital media.

FIGURE 7-11
Value in 3-D design

FIGURE 7-12
Light in 3-D design

THE DESIGN OF TIME

What You'll Learn

▶ *In this lesson, you will learn how time is used as both an element and a design principle.*

Time Design in History

The use of time in design is as old as the cave paintings shown in Chapter 1. These paintings were society's attempt to keep track of the events that occurred over time. Many artists have painted the same scene at different times of the day, or over a period of weeks, months, or years, to show the effects of time.

Digital media has brought time into the design process, both as an element and a principle of design. Radio and television commercials, video productions, multimedia presentations, animation, and moviemaking all require a strong understanding of time and its effects on design.

The Elements of Time

Time design has the following six features:

Duration—The amount of time it takes to tell the events of the story and the amount of time the story covers is called **duration**. An example would be the movie *Forrest Gump*: the viewing time duration is 141 minutes, and the duration of the story is the first 40 years of the lead character's life.

Tempo—The speed at which time passes, called **tempo**, can be controlled by both the events being recorded and the individual recording the event. The control of the tempo can affect how we perceive a specific event or an entire sequence within a piece.

Intensity—The amount of perceived or actual energy in a particular scene or event is known as **intensity**. In the movie *Saving Private Ryan,* the re-creation of the D-Day landings in France was so intense that some people had to leave the theater. Many automobile commercials use intense, fast motion to give you the feeling that driving their car will be an exciting experience.

Scope—The overall breadth of ideas and events being presented is called **scope**. Many filmmakers attempt to show a large amount of information in a short amount of time; it takes a great deal of production skill to ensure that the audience is not overwhelmed by too much information all at once.

Setting—One complex aspect of time design is **setting**. This term refers not only to the project's physical location but to all of its other visual aspects, including the wardrobe, props, historical references, and so forth.

Chronology—The sequencing of events in time is known as **chronology**. Certain projects require the chronology to be highly accurate in presenting events in the correct order. Others may go back and forth in time between the past, present, and future. In these cases, the correct sequencing is not as important as telling the story in an interesting way. Time designers use **editing** to cut and paste events into any sequence they wish (see Figure 7-13).

The Art of Storytelling

Like print media, digital media communicates images and ideas. But the addition of time allows the digital media designer to expand the presentation to deliver more complex concepts. A 30-second television commercial, a 5-minute Web animation, and a 30-minute video production all have the potential to deliver a multitude of messages that can take the form of a story.

With the ability to use and manipulate time, the digital media designer now becomes a storyteller. One of the oldest forms of communication, **storytelling** can convey a client's message more effectively than thousands of printed pieces. A story can be a powerful vehicle to supply information, to increase awareness of an important issue or concern, to inspire, and to develop a deeper understanding of almost any topic.

FIGURE 7-13
Time design

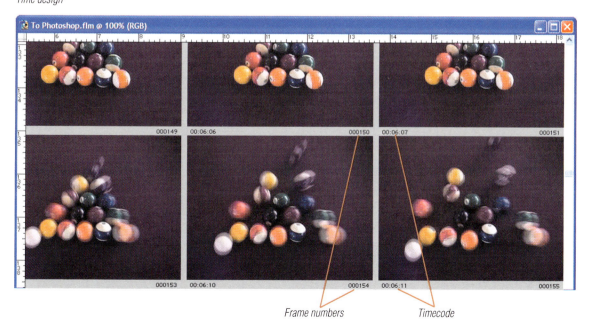

Frame numbers   Timecode

SOUND FINDS A VOICE

What You'll Learn

In this lesson, you will learn how sound has become an important design component in digital media.

The Design of Sound

Sound is the invisible element of a digital media project. Sound can enhance a project's mood and emotion and advance its pace. Sounds can include actors' voices, music, natural or environmental sounds, and specialized sound effects. Each of these sounds can be modified through six sound properties:

- The **volume**, or loudness, of the sound. This can be based on a volume setting on the device playing the sound, or on the environment in which the sound is being played.
- The **pitch**, or how high or low the sound is. High-pitched screams are very effective during horror movies.
- The **duration**, or the length of time the sound is audible. Some sounds last for a few seconds, others can go on for minutes or hours at a time.
- The **rhythm**, or a sound's cadence. Some musical forms, such as marching bands, disco, and rap, have rhythm as their most distinguishing characteristic.
- The **fidelity**, or the connection between the sound and its source. Many movie soundtracks attempt to use music to support and advance the story. Some feel, however, that in some recent movies, soundtrack music has little fidelity to the story on the screen.
- The **environment**, or the place where the music is being played. A popular rock band may sound extremely loud in a small, indoor auditorium, yet may seem almost quiet when heard in a large, outdoor stadium.

The Technology of Sound

The use of sound is becoming more common because the technologies to store and deliver sound are advancing dramatically. Sound used to be almost nonexistent on the Internet, due to the limitations of delivering sound through a slow dial-up connection. But with faster connections and more compact digital sound files, the Web is fast becoming a sound-based medium. And sound has always been a major component of multimedia presentations and video projects. Figure 7-14 shows a sound clip being edited digitally.

FIGURE 7-14

Sound

THE PROJECT MOVES TO PRODUCTION

What You'll Learn

 In this lesson, you will learn how digital media projects move forward to the production phase.

The Production Team

As with print media, the production phase of digital media is a highly technical area that includes many different processes and software. This phase is also team-driven; the **production team** includes an appropriate group of artists, programmers, and other specialists working together to produce a digital media project. The makeup of a production team depends on the complexity of the project and the technologies required.

The first step in production is defining the content required for the project. **Content** includes all of the graphics, images, text, video, sound, and animation required to complete the project. Like print media, many digital media projects require

traditional copywriting, illustrations, and photography. Graphic designers create logos, icons, and type treatments, and manipulate photographic images for effective presentation on a monitor. **Programmers** work to create digital media using the various programming languages used on the Web and in other digital media applications. Selling products and services on the Web requires highly specialized database, networking, and security programming knowledge. **Video** and **sound specialists** are used when these components are required for a Web site, multimedia presentation, or video production. And more digital 3-D imaging and animation is being used both on the Web and in motion pictures, television commercials, and video game design.

Jobs in Production

In addition to these production specialists, creative Web, multimedia, animation, and video designers are in great demand. Using the principles discussed in this chapter, designers can create projects that not only meet client demands but are visually dynamic and communicate the visual message effectively.

FIGURE 7-15

Production team

Digital media is a rapidly growing area of the graphics industry that requires many of the same creative and design skills as print media. Even though digital media's final product is a monitor-based presentation, designers still must follow the formal design development process, using design elements and principles to create successful solutions to a client's design problem. Digital media designers also need to understand the unique requirements of motion, sound, 3-D design, and time design; all are important components of digital media projects.

3-D animation
3-D modeling
CERN
chronology
content
depth
digital video
duration
editing
e-mail
environment
fidelity
height
HTML (Hypertext Markup Language)
http (hypertext-transfer protocol)
intensity
interactivity
light
mass
motion
motion pictures
multimedia
network
orthographic projection
perspective drawing
pitch

production team
programmers
prototype
rhythm
rough cuts
scope
setting
site layout
sound
sound specialist
storyboard
storytelling
television
tempo
three-dimensional space
Tim Berners-Lee
time design
video specialist
volume
Web animation
Web browser
Web design
width
x-, y-, and z-axes

CHAPTER REVIEW

1. How did motion pictures and television change the way audiences viewed visual images?

   _____

   _____

   _____

2. What European programmer was instrumental in developing the World Wide Web? List three concepts this programmer developed for the Web.

   _____

   _____

   _____

3. Name one of the differences between print media and digital media.

   _____

   _____

   _____

4. List four of the five major areas of digital media.

   _____

   _____

   _____

   _____

5. In Web design, what is a site layout?

   _____

6. What is a storyboard?

   _____

   _____

7. Preliminary work in digital media requires the creation of a working version of the project, called a(n):

   _____

8. What three terms define three-dimensional space on a computer?

   _____

   _____

9. Which drafting method accurately represents the structure of a form?

   _____

10. What is the difference between volume and mass?

   _____

   _____

   _____

11. How does light affect a three-dimensional shape?

_____

_____

_____

12. List four of the six elements of time design.

_____

_____

_____

_____

13. How can storytelling be used to convey a client's message?

_____

_____

_____

14. List four of the six elements of sound.

_____

_____

_____

_____

15. What individuals can make up a production team?

_____

_____

_____

You have been hired by the local zoo to design a Web site for its grand opening after remodeling. The zoo has received a complete face-lift, with new exhibits and new animals. It needs an opening page that will announce its grand opening, and several pages showing the new animals it will have on display.

Go online and research zoo Web sites. See how they are designed, and also notice how the sites use navigation to move from page to page. Find information on at least five different animals that would be in a zoo, including a couple of pictures and a few paragraphs of copy that describes the animal, its habitat, and the like.

Using markers and marker paper, draw 8" wide × 6" tall rectangles on your paper, reflecting a standard format for a Web page. Design three different visual concepts, each with its own layout, graphics, and navigational concepts. Use the design elements and principles discussed in this chapter and in Chapter 1 to come up with three exciting concepts.

One Step Beyond

On a separate piece of marker paper, create a site layout rough of your proposed Web site. Show each page of the Web site and how each page connects to the other pages. Keep the representation of each page simple; this is only intended to show how the site works. The layouts you drew earlier will show the design of the pages.

Two Steps Beyond

Re-create your best layout concept on the computer, using any software you feel comfortable with, to help the client better visualize the site. Name the file **zoo_site**. Also create the site layout on the computer, then print everything to present to the client.

The Overpowered Speedboat Company has called your studio and would like you to produce a 30-second commercial promoting their new line of powerboats, the "AquaPower 200." These boats are reasonably priced but have a lot of power, so they can be used for everything from a leisure outing on the lake to some high-intensity water skiing. This commercial will air on local television stations and should focus on families who enjoy taking their boat out for all levels of recreation.

Open and print the storyboard layout file **IG 7-1.pdf** from the location where you store your Data Files. Each frame of the story-board has two parts: the larger top rectangle is where you draw an image representing a segment of your commercial. The smaller rectangle is where you write in any dialog or indicate what sounds or music are playing during this time sequence. Also note the amount of time for each segment.

Print out seven to ten copies of the storyboard and use your markers to sketch two completely different commercial concepts for this new line of powerboats, using the design elements and concepts discussed in this chapter. Keep your sketches rough and simple; these are like thumbnails—you're only working on

concepts right now. Remember that the commercial has to be 30 seconds long, so as you draw out each frame, play it through in your mind. Then use a watch to read the complete storyboard aloud, pausing for musical and sound effects breaks. If the read-through takes longer than 30 seconds, you will have to cut out or shorten some of your frames; if the frames take less than 30 seconds you need to add more material.

One Step Beyond

Choose your best concept and redo it with color, and this time spend more time with your sketches to make them look more accurate. When you are done, mount these storyboards to 20" × 15" presentation board as if you were presenting them to a client.

Two Steps Beyond

Repeat what you did in One Step Beyond but create your sketches on the computer. Name your file **AquaPower**. Print each frame and carefully cut and paste them into the storyboard. When you are done, mount these storyboards on presentation board to present to a client.

Design a Web site that promotes your new Web design company, **"Your Name" Web Design**. Research other Web design company sites; see how they use the elements and principles discussed in this chapter to create their site. Look at the different pages and information they present and decide what information on those sites would match what you want to show on your company site.

Using markers and marker paper, design the layouts of your pages using the elements and principles you learned in the chapter. Also do a site layout showing how many pages your site will contain and how each page will connect to the other pages. Keep working on your layouts until you come up with a satisfactory design. A possible solution is shown in Figure 7-16.

FIGURE 7-16

Possible Web site solutions

Figure 7-17 shows two examples of real-world digital media projects created by designers. Look carefully at each project, and write a summary of how each project reflects the design elements and principles described in this chapter and in Chapter 1. (To view the Web page, connect to the Internet, go to www.course.com, navigate to the page for this book, click the Student Online Companion link, then click the link for this chapter.)

FIGURE 7-17

Designer-created projects

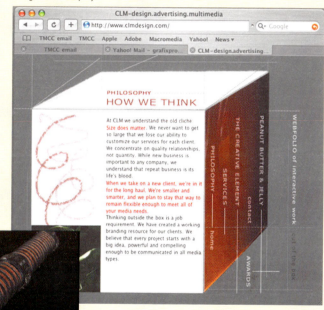

CLM Design
CLM Design Web site
clmdesign.com

Jason Allen Bronson
Blade Reflect Reference
Self-published
blueleafstudios.us

WEB DESIGN SOFTWARE

CHAPTER 8

WEB DESIGN SOFTWARE

Where It All Began

As you learned in Chapter 7, Tim Berners-Lee was instrumental in developing the technologies for the World Wide Web. Since 1989, the Web has exploded into a communications network made up of millions of Web sites supplying information on any topic imaginable and selling everything from discount car loans to prescription drugs to the latest music and movies. It seems like everyone has a Web site and every company has some sort of Web presence to promote itself and its products and services.

In the early days of the Web, developers created sites by typing programming code in

HTML (Hypertext Markup Language), the programming language that allows images and text to be seen on different computers around the world (see Figure 8-1). Anyone who learned this programming language could create a Web site. At that time, graphic designers knew little of this new communications network, and very few knew HTML. So most sites were created by programmers who had little understanding of design.

HTML versus WYSIWYG

Because the early sites were created by programmers, most of them were text-based, with little graphic content. But as the 1990s progressed, software companies

---

The importance of learning the code

Although applications such as Dreamweaver and GoLive have let nonprogrammers create Web sites, understanding HTML and other programming languages is still very useful. Web-development applications automatically create HTML code that works well in most situations; however, there are times when the designer has to go in and "adjust the code" to make a required effect work correctly. To keep pace with the ever-changing environment of the Web, anyone interested in Web design should learn HTML and other relevant programming languages, such as XHTML for Dreamweaver and XML for GoLive.

tried to simplify Web site development and make Web design as easy as page layout in print graphics. They released Web-development software that let users create Web pages in a WYSIWYG (What You See Is What You Get) environment. These applications would automatically generate the HTML code necessary to create a Web site. This was a difficult process because HTML is not a graphics language like PostScript, so the early WYSIWYG applications were very limiting due to the way HTML works (or doesn't work) with text and graphics.

In 1997, Macromedia launched its entry into the WYSIWYG Web design software market with Dreamweaver. Although similar in many ways to the earlier WYSIWYG applications, Dreamweaver adopted a more advanced version of the HTML code, **DHTML** (Dynamic Hypertext Markup Language). DHTML made some commands and procedures easier to use for the nonprogrammer. At the same time that Macromedia introduced Dreamweaver, a company called GoLive Systems launched CyberStudio, a competing product with similar capabilities. GoLive Systems was bought out by Adobe in 1999, which re-released CyberStudio as Adobe GoLive.

Web Design Matures

Both Dreamweaver and GoLive (see Figure 8-2) have evolved into more powerful, full-featured applications. Macromedia has added dynamic features to Dreamweaver that increase its formatting capabilities and has designed the software to work seamlessly with its other Web-based products. Adobe has added features to GoLive and has adopted XML (Extensible Markup Language) as its foundation. It has also integrated GoLive with Adobe's other graphics applications.

Today designers and programmers use WYSIWYG Web design applications such as Dreamweaver and GoLive to create and produce Web sites quickly and efficiently. Both are powerful applications that can create sites with a high degree of dynamic and interactive content, without requiring designers to learn HTML code.

FIGURE 8-1

HTML code

```
1   <!DOCTYPE HTML PUBLIC "-//W3C//DTD HTML 4.01 Transitional//EN"
2   "http://www.w3.org/TR/html4/loose.dtd">
3   <html>
4   <head>
5   <title>Untitled Document</title>
6   <meta http-equiv="Content-Type" content="text/html; charset=iso-8859-1">
7   </head>
8
9   <body>
10  <table width="600" height="300" border="0">
11    <tr>
12      <td width="200" height="150"><div align="center"><img src="assets/printing-press.gif"
13      <td width="200" height="150" align="center" valign="middle"><img src="assets/printing-
14      <td width="200" height="150" align="center" valign="middle"><img src="assets/printing-
15    </tr>
16    <tr>
17      <td width="200" height="100" align="center" valign="middle">Is the Internet <br>
18      the new printed medium? </td>
19      <td width="200" height="100" align="center" valign="middle">Is the Internet <br>
20  the new printed medium?</td>
21      <td width="200" height="100" align="center" valign="middle">Is the Internet <br>
22  the new printed medium?</td>
23    </tr>
24  </table>
25  </body>
26  </html>
27
```

FIGURE 8-2

Dreamweaver and GoLive

DREAMWEAVER AND GOLIVE: AN OVERVIEW

What You'll Learn

In this lesson, you will learn the major features of Dreamweaver and GoLive.

Macromedia Dreamweaver

Dreamweaver is a powerful Web site development tool that lets programmers and designers produce graphically rich Web content. Its WYSIWYG interface makes designing Web pages as easy as using page layout software. It also has a dual-window layout that lets users work with and modify the HTML code and see the changes on the page as they work.

Dreamweaver (shown in Figure 8-3) is easy to use at an introductory level. Basic tools are available at the top of the screen. A Properties panel at the bottom of the screen displays important information on any selected text, image, or object in your project. You can quickly apply hyperlinks to text and graphics. Also known as links, **hyperlinks** are special areas on a Web page that users can click to display other information. Graphics can have specific areas, called **image maps**, that act as links. You can crop, scale, sharpen, or adjust the brightness and contrast of imported

images in Dreamweaver. You can create many dynamic effects such as **rollover buttons** (where a button changes its appearance when a cursor moves over it), pop-up browser windows, and HTML-based animations. Dreamweaver also lets you upload and maintain Web sites without leaving the Dreamweaver application.

Dreamweaver has led the industry in adopting the latest Web-based technologies. The latest version, Dreamweaver MX 2004, features **Cascading Style Sheets (CSS)**, which allow Web designers to apply consistent style and layout to HTML elements throughout a Web site. Macromedia has also improved Dreamweaver's ability to display layouts more accurately within the application, so what you see in your screen layout more accurately reflects what you will see in a browser. Dreamweaver also ships with several layout templates to help less-experienced users create sophisticated layouts more quickly.

Adobe GoLive

Adobe GoLive has many features that both Web-savvy developers and WYSIWYG-based designers can use to create dynamic Web site content.

GoLive features include Smart Objects, which let you modify any image created in Photoshop or Illustrator in the original application and automatically update the image in GoLive. Using GoLive, you can crop and scale images without having to modify the original source file, and you can also generate and add links to a Web graphic from a PDF file. GoLive can rapidly translate an InDesign page layout into a Web document.

Like Dreamweaver, GoLive is also easy to work with at a basic level, letting you insert text and graphics quickly (see Figure 8-4). GoLive's Source Code Editor lets the viewer see the effects of HTML code (also called **source code**) changes right on the page. Links, tables, and other HTML-based concepts are easy to work with and easy to track through GoLive's various tools and palettes. GoLive also has increased support for CSS styles and the ability to create and modify CSS styles in one centralized palette.

FIGURE 8-3

Macromedia Dreamweaver

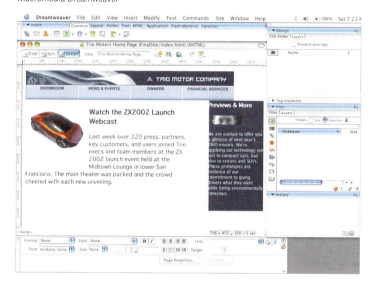

FIGURE 8-4

Adobe GoLive

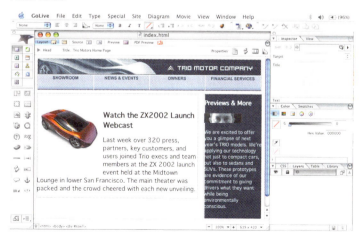

THERE HAS TO BE CONTENT

What You'll Learn

JPEG (Document, f▾   50 quality
6.44K
1 sec @56kbps

◄ ▷ ▷▎ 1 ◁▎ ▷▎ ✪   300 x 450   100% ▾

In this lesson, you will learn how text, images, and graphics are created for Web presentation.

Text and Type

Text and type are handled differently on the Web than they are in print graphics. In print graphics, the PostScript programming language lets you use thousands of different type styles and manipulate and edit type in many different ways.

But type in HTML is not as flexible. Because HTML was not conceived as a graphics language, it can't work with and re-create type like PostScript can. So although print graphics software can work with hundreds of different sizes of type, Web design software can work with only seven HTML-based sizes, which have names ranges from xx-small to xx-large (see Figure 8-5). (In previous versions of Dreamweaver, these sizes are numbered from 1 to 7, and had no relation to type sizes measured in points: 1 is xx-small, 7 is xx-large.)

In the past, Web design software could not apply different leadings to type; the vertical spacing between lines of type depended on the type size. The designer could not change this spacing except by using two techniques: pressing **[Enter]** (Windows) or **[return]** (Macintosh), which will add space depending on the size of type selected; the larger the type, the larger the space. Or, you could press **[Shift][Enter]** (Windows) or **[shift][return]** (Macintosh) to obtain a smaller additional space, again depending on the type size. CSS now allows for some control over leading.

DESIGNTIP   Dreamweaver sizes type differently

Because Dreamweaver MX 2004 uses CSS (cascading style sheets) coding as its foundation, it now sizes type in pixels in addition to the old HTML sizing. So in Dreamweaver, you can now choose from among sizes 9, 10, 12, 14, 16, 18, 24, and 36 pixel-high type, or you can type in any pixel size (see Figure 8-6).

HTML lets you set different type alignments, including left, center, right, and justified. But basic HTML does not let you set line length; if you set a paragraph of type and view the type in a Web browser window, the type will rewrap to the size of the window, as shown in Figure 8-7. So the wider the window, the longer the line length; the narrower the window, the shorter the line length.

The most difficult part of working on the Web is the lack of type styles to choose from. Because a Web page is viewed on millions of computers all over the world, it is highly unlikely that every computer that displays the page has the necessary fonts and font styles to display the type properly. And, as you learned in Chapter 4, most Macintosh computers use different font files than Windows computers. To address this issue, only a limited number of default font styles are used on the Web. Dreamweaver and GoLive use the default type styles shown in Figure 8-8.

FIGURE 8-5
HTML text sizes

FIGURE 8-6
HTML and CSS text sizes

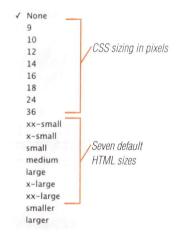

The default Web fonts are fairly generic. So how do designers use more creative font styles on the Web? They have to convert the type to a graphic that is imported into the Web page. When the type needs to be changed or modified, the designer has to go back to the original graphic software, modify the type, then reconvert the type into a graphic and replace the old type graphic with the new one. As you can see, designing text for an HTML-based Web page is a different process than designing text for a PostScript-based document for traditional printing.

Photography on the Web

Photographic images are common on the Web, and are easier to work with than traditional print graphics. The big advantage to working with photographic images on Web pages is the simple set of standards necessary to optimize these images. **Optimize** means to prepare images to be displayed quickly and correctly on the Web; you will hear this term a lot in Web graphics.

In print graphics, the goal is always to have a photographic image reproduce at the highest quality available. If doing so creates an enormous file, it is not a concern, as long as the file prints well. But in Web design the concern for quality must be balanced with the need for an image to be downloaded quickly. A graphic's **download speed**, or the time it takes for an image to transfer from a Web server to be displayed

Browser window adjusts line lengths

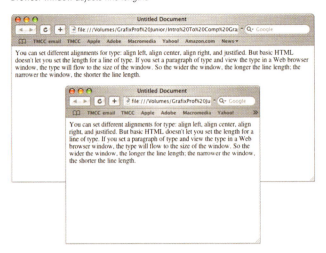

Default type styles

Macintosh	Windows
Times	Times New Roman
Times Italic	*Times New Roman Italic*
Times Bold	**Times New Roman Bold**
Times Bold Italic	***Times New Roman Bold Italic***
Helvetica	Arial
Helvetica Italic	*Arial Italic*
Helvetica Bold	**Arial Bold**
Helvetica Bold Italic	***Arial Bold Italic***
Courier	Courier New
Courier Italic	*Courier Italic*
Courier Bold	**Courier Bold**
Courier Bold Italic	***Courier Bold Italic***

on a user's computer, is directly affected by the size of the file on disk; the larger the file, the longer it takes to download. Optimizing a photographic image becomes a balancing act between getting the best possible quality with the smallest possible file size.

Most applications that optimize photographic images for the Web have a special feature that lets you compare the quality of the image against its upload speed; see the Fireworks 2-Up view in Figure 8-9. Here the original parrot.tif image was about 2.2 megabytes in size at 200 dpi resolution, much too large to be used on the Web. But the image on the right has been optimized so it is now only 6.5 kilobytes in size (over 338 times smaller). And over a traditional 56kbs modem this Web image would upload in merely one second. Although there is some loss of detail, the image quality will be acceptable for viewing on a computer monitor, so this would be a successful optimization.

Graphics on the Web

Almost all Web pages contain graphics, usually branding elements and navigational buttons. **Branding elements** are graphics on a page that identify a company, organization, or individual the Web site represents. Most sites include a **banner** (also called a **masthead**) at the top of the page with the company or organization name and logo. **Navigation buttons** are

FIGURE 8-9
2-Up optimize view

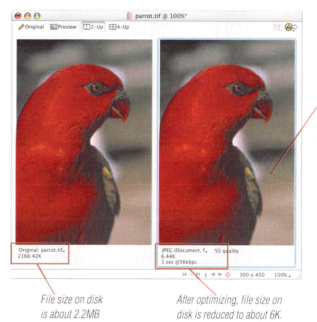

Image dimensions appear to be the same in Fireworks; will appear smaller in Web design software

File size on disk is about 2.2MB

After optimizing, file size on disk is reduced to about 6K.

The Web uses a different measurement system

There is a difference between file size on disk and the size of an image on the screen. When discussing image size on screen, Web developers do not work in inches and points as they do in print graphics. Because Web pages are viewed on a monitor, everything is measured in pixels (short for picture elements, which are small dots; you learned about pixels in Chapter 3). There are 72 pixels per inch on an average computer monitor, and the average viewing size of a Web page is 800 pixels wide × 600 pixels high. So when you size images for the Web, design them to work within this 800 pixel × 600 pixel area. This helps to keep images small in size. In the parrot image shown in Figure 8-9, the original file size was 600 pixels × 900 pixels, a huge image size that would have filled up an entire Web page. The parrot was scaled down to 200 pixels x 300 pixels, a much more manageable size for the Web. But this size would be small for a print graphic, only 2.75" × 3.165" in size.

type, graphics, or (more frequently) a combination of type and graphics, that the viewer clicks to move from page to page in a Web site (see Figure 8-10).

You can create banners, navigation buttons, and many other types of Web graphics just as you would create print graphics. But, like photographic images, Web graphics have to be optimized so they upload quickly.

Another way Web graphics differ from print graphics is that Web graphics can be **interactive**, meaning that the viewer of the Web site can click a graphic to display a different part of the page or a different page altogether. Navigational buttons are some of the most basic interactive elements on a Web site and add visual interest as well.

Many Web graphics today include movement to create dynamic presentations. Most of the animation effects you see on the Web

are created using Macromedia Flash. You will learn more about Flash in Chapter 9 of this book.

Content Creation Software

So what software can you use to create and optimize graphics and photographic images? Generally the same vector-draw and image manipulation software that you learned about in Chapters 2 and 3. Both Adobe Illustrator and Macromedia

FIGURE 8-10
Banner and navigational buttons

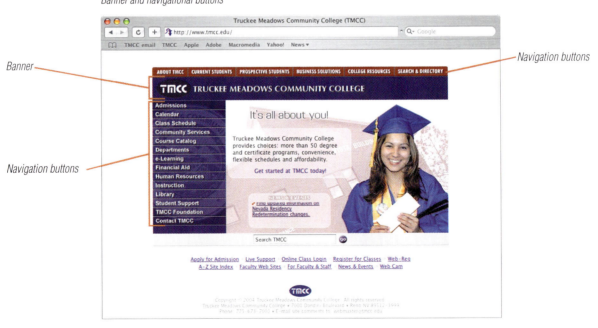

Banner

Navigation buttons

Navigation buttons

FreeHand can create and optimize a wide variety of graphics for the Web. Both integrate smoothly with their partner Web design software—Illustrator with GoLive and FreeHand with Dreamweaver.

You can use Photoshop to optimize almost any graphic or photographic image for the Web. Photoshop is sold with a companion software application called Adobe ImageReady that lets you create, view, and optimize graphics for the Web. And you can switch seamlessly between ImageReady and Photoshop while working on the same image.

Macromedia has also developed a product specifically for creating and optimizing Web graphics and images. The Fireworks application is an interesting hybrid of vector-draw and image manipulation software (see Figure 8-11). Fireworks lets you choose from a variety of vector-based and bitmapped-based tools. The array of vector tools is not as powerful as those in Illustrator or FreeHand, but for many types of Web-based graphics they are perfectly adequate. Like ImageReady, Fireworks can optimize photographic images, and even has a few of the image manipulation tools and filters found in Photoshop.

Creating content is the core of Web design, and should be done with thought and planning. Content creation often takes more time than the actual layout and production of the Web pages themselves. So be sure to allow adequate time for content creation in your site development schedule.

FIGURE 8-11

Macromedia Fireworks

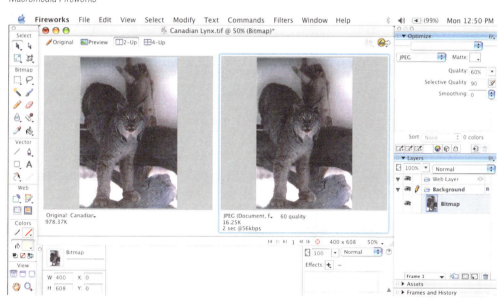

START THE SITE DEVELOPMENT PROCESS

What You'll Learn

In this lesson, you will learn how to start a Web site project.

Planning the Site

As in print graphics, it is best to work through a series of preliminary ideas before you dive into Web development software. Some Web designers sketch out different ideas using markers and pencils to give the client a visual representation of their ideas. Others will use applications such as Photoshop, FreeHand, or Illustrator to sketch out their proposed design, including color and layout of images, type, and navigational elements. Having the page layouts figured out before you start to use Dreamweaver or GoLive can speed up your production process dramatically.

Web designers also create preliminary sketches of the site layout, as discussed in Chapter 7. The site layout shows the number of pages required to create an effective presentation of the Web site content, and will also show how the different pages are connected to each other. You can create these site layouts using markers or a variety of applications.

DESIGNTIP Don't move that content!

It's important to understand that once you have placed content in the assets folder (discussed on page 282), you should not move the files around. Both Dreamweaver and GoLive are very particular about where content is stored, and if you move these files, both applications will lose track of them and you will get a broken link symbol (a red X) on your Web page. So keep track of the graphics and images you optimize, be sure to put them in the correct folder.

Set Up the Site Folders

As in previous chapters, you will learn about two different applications, in this case Dreamweaver and GoLive, at the same time. To help distinguish between the two, the Dreamweaver concept, tool, or command will be listed first, followed by the GoLive version in parentheses.

Before you can start to work on a Web site, you have to set up a **site folder** that will contain all the site content files. You must create this folder before developing any content, because when you set up a new site in the software, both Dreamweaver and GoLive ask you to designate a local root folder (which is another name for the site folder). The **local root folder** is the folder that the application searches to find and display all site content. If you skip this step, both applications will warn you that the site has not been established, and any work you do will not function properly. You can name your local root folder anything you like; in Figure 8-12 this folder is named local root folder.

FIGURE 8-12
Local root folder setup

local root folder

assets

FIGURE 8-13
Setting up a site in Dreamweaver

Your site names will differ

Web design software requires a similar folder to keep track of graphics. Inside the local root folder you create a subfolder to hold all of the optimized images and graphics to be used in the Web site. This default image folder is usually called assets, images, or graphics; you tell the application its name at the same time you designate the local root folder.

Establish the Site

You launch Dreamweaver and GoLive the same way you launch the other programs in this book: by using the Dock or Applications folder (Macintosh) or the Programs or All Programs menu (Windows). The steps you use to establish a new site are similar in Dreamweaver and GoLive but have some important differences:

Dreamweaver—To establish a new site in Dreamweaver, you click **Site** on the menu bar and then click **Manage Site**. The Manage Sites dialog box opens, as shown in Figure 8-13. Click **New**, click **Site**, and then the Site Definition dialog box appears. Dreamweaver lets you select a Basic mode or an Advanced mode (Advanced mode is shown here); either way you will need to provide the following information:

- The **site name**—This can be anything you want; it is simply the name Dreamweaver will use to track the site internally.

FIGURE 8-14

Defining a site in Dreamweaver

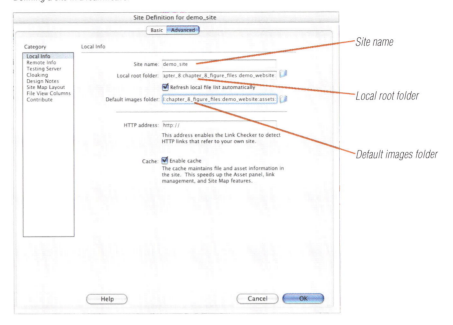

Site name

Local root folder

Default images folder

FIGURE 8-15

New site added in Dreamweaver

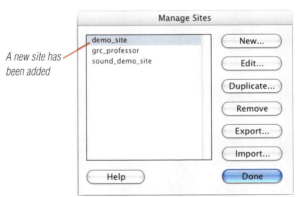

A new site has been added

- The **local root folder**—This is the folder you created earlier, before creating the site. Here you direct Dreamweaver to the site folder and designate it as the local root folder.
- The **default images folder**—This is the folder that will contain all of the graphics used in this Web site. You direct Dreamweaver to the assets folder you created earlier.

Once you have supplied this information, click **OK** and your site will appear in the Manage Sites dialog box list (see Figures 8-14 and 8-15).

GoLive—To establish a new site in GoLive, click **File** on the menu bar and then click **New Site**. The GoLive Site Wizard appears; this Wizard is a series of dialog boxes that walk you through the process of creating a new site. You click the **Single-User** button and then click **Next** (see Figure 8-16). You then choose **Blank Site** in the Options for a Local Site, and then click **Next** (see Figure 8-17). Here you type in the name for your site, which not only names the site but also names the local root folder. Click **Next** (see Figure 8-18). Your entries in the

FIGURE 8-16
GoLive Site Wizard

FIGURE 8-17
GoLive Options for a Local Sites dialog box

Specifying the New Site's Location dialog box tell GoLive where to put the local root folder on your computer; GoLive automatically creates the local root folder in the location you specify. Click **Finish** to complete the new site setup (see Figure 8-19).

Create New Pages for the Site

Each page of a Web site is a separate HTML document, indicated by the file extension **.htm (.html)**. To create a new page in Dreamweaver, click **File** on the menu bar, then click **New**; the New Document dialog box appears (see Figure 8-20). **Category: Basic page** and **Basic page: HTML** are the default options. When you click **Create**, a blank page appears with the insertion point in the upper-left corner. In GoLive, click **File**, then click **New Page**, and a new page appears.

GoLive Naming the New Site dialog box

GoLive Site Wizard

Naming the New Site

Specify the name for your new site here. GoLive uses the name for the site file and the site's enclosing folder.

Site Name   demo_site

Cancel   < Back   Next >

FIGURE 8-19
GoLive New Site Location dialog box

GoLive Site Wizard

Specifying the New Site's Location

Choose where you want GoLive to place the new blank site files and folders and set URL Handling preferences for the new site.

Click Browse to select the location:

/Users/db/Documents/demo_site/

Browse...

Click Advanced to specify the URL character encoding and checking for case-sensitive URLs. (URL encoding can be changed later in the application preferences but case sensitivity checking cannot be changed later.)

Advanced...

Cancel   < Back   Finish

Before you actually begin laying out a new page, save the document: Click **File** on the menu bar and then click **Save (Save As)**. If you are creating your site's **home page**, the main navigational page and usually the first page that appears when users go to a Web site, you should name the file **index.htm**. This is the name that most Internet service providers have designated as the page a browser should look for when accessing a Web site. You can use any name for the other pages in your site. When naming pages, use all lowercase letters and underscores instead of spaces. This ensures that both newer and older servers will be able to recognize your page names.

FIGURE 8-20

Dreamweaver New Document dialog box

INPUT TYPE AND IMAGES

What You'll Learn

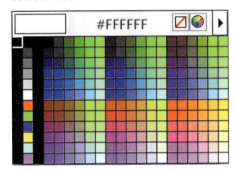

In this lesson, you will learn more about adding type and graphics and how to modify them in Dreaweaver and GoLive.

Inserting and Modifying Text

As with software for print media, you can enter text directly in Dreamweaver and GoLive, or you can enter it using a word-processing application or almost any graphics software, then copy and paste it directly into either application. The second option lets you bring text into your Web page that you created elsewhere without having to retype it in the Web design program.

As you learned earlier in this chapter, HTML does not offer a lot of choices for entering Web page text. But once you have entered type, you can modify it using the following commands in Dreamweaver's Properties panel or GoLive's Type menu, as shown in Figure 8-21.

Font—The Font command gives you a choice of fonts; in Dreamweaver this includes Times (Macintosh)/Times New Roman (Windows), Helvetica/Arial, and Courier/Courier New. As you can see from the list in Figure 8-21, three fonts that are supported by newer computers and browsers are also available: Georgia, Verdana, and Geneva. Choose the font set you want your Web site to look for on a user's computer when it opens the site.

DESIGNTIP   Where did my formatting go?

When you paste type into a Web design application, it is immediately converted into HTML-based text. This strips any PostScript-based text formatting out of the type so that it comes into the Web page without any customized leading, spacing, or type styles. So don't be alarmed when this happens; it's just the way HTML handles text.

In GoLive, fonts are listed in sets; these include a Helvetica set (including Helvetica, Geneva, and Arial), a Serif set (including Times, Times New Roman, and Georgia), a Monospace set (including Courier and Courier New), a Trebuchet set, a Verdana set (which are additional sans serif fonts), and a Cursive set (including Zapf Chancery and Comic Sans MS).

Size—The type sizes available depend on which application you are using. Dreamweaver lists the newer **CSS-based sizings** first, then the more traditional **HTML-based sizings**. In the HTML-based sizings, the Smaller and Larger commands let you reduce or enlarge the type one size at a time; if your type was sized Large and you selected Smaller, it would change the type size to the next smaller size on the list, which is Medium. The None choice lets the browser choose which type size to use. This option is not recommended—even though it makes your type more compatible with any browser, the browser may choose a size that does not work with your layout. GoLive lists the traditional HTML numberings of 1 through 7.

Color—Your type can be any one of the 216 Web-safe colors shown in Figure 8-22. **Web-safe colors** are a series of RGB-based colors that appear the same on any computer using any browser. These colors are designated by a **hexidecimal system**, which uses three pairs of letters and/or numbers in a six-character name to represent the makeup of that color. Black is 000000, white is FFFFFF, a teal color is 009966, and an orange color is FF9900. (The # sign that appears before the hexidecimal value is not part of the color designation.)

Bold and Italic—You can make type bold (by clicking the B button), italic (by clicking the I button), or bold italic (by clicking both the B and I buttons).

Alignment—Type can align left, center, and right; Dreamweaver also has justified alignment available.

Formatting—HTML text has its own unique formatting. You can create an **unordered list (bulleted list)**, with each text group having a round bullet, or an **ordered list (numbered list)**, with each text group having a number assigned in

FIGURE 8-22
Web-safe colors

*Hexadecimal value
for black*

*Black color
selected*

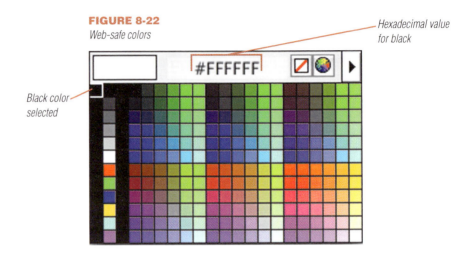

#FFFFFF

ascending order (see Figure 8-23). You can also apply a **text indent (increase list level)** by clicking an indent button. This indents the text a set distance on the left and right margins at the same time; the indent increment is determined by the software. Clicking the button a second time indents the text the same distance again; clicking three times indents the text three times the indent increment, and so forth. The **text outdent (decrease list level) button** reverses the process; if the text is indented twice and you click text outdent once, it will reduce the indent by one set amount.

Link—You can convert any text to a hyperlink, also called a **text link**, which you've probably seen on Web pages, to help users navigate to different Web locations. Text links appear in a different color and are often underlined.

Inserting and Modifying Graphics

Once you have optimized images and graphics, you can insert them into your Web page. In Dreamweaver, click **Insert** on the menu bar, then click **Image**. In GoLive, double-click the **Image button** to insert an

FIGURE 8-23
Ordered and unordered lists

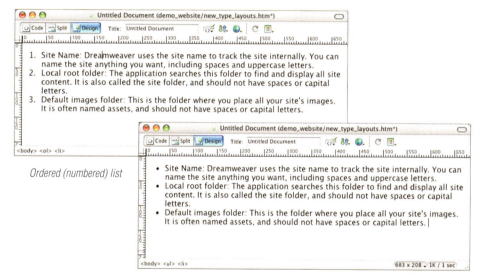

Ordered (numbered) list

Unordered (bulleted) list

image placeholder, then go to the Inspector palette and in the Source section click the **Browse button**. In both applications, you will then need to navigate to your assets folder, select the image you want, and then click **Choose (Open)**. The image will appear on your page. The default image alignment in HTML is on the left side of the page, as shown in Figure 8-24.

This is where HTML diverges from Postscript, because there are only three positions on the page where you can place a graphic: on the left, in the center, or on the right of the page (see Figure 8-25). HTML does not have the capability to position a graphic wherever you want on the page, which is a limiting factor in any Web design.

Graphics can also be scaled to different sizes in Dreamweaver and GoLive. However, you should avoid scaling graphics for several reasons: 1) some older versions of Web browsers can't work with scaled images, and the layout of your Web page can be altered when the graphic is not

FIGURE 8-24
Default HTML graphic placement

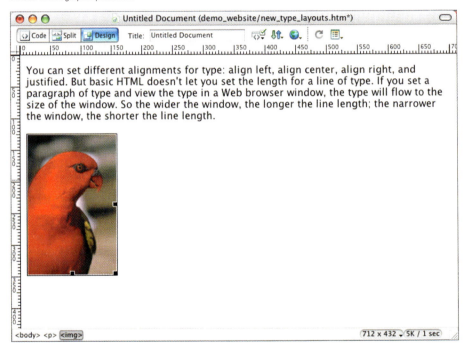

scaled; 2) images won't preview properly depending on whether the image is being scaled larger or smaller (you will learn about previewing Web pages later in this chapter; 3) even if a large image is scaled down in Dreamweaver or GoLive, it still has the same file size and will download more slowly than if the image were scaled before being placed in either application. So it is best to scale your images when they are being optimized and then place them in your Web page. If the same image is being used several times at different sizes throughout your site, then you should optimize multiple versions, scaling each one to the size you need.

As you can see, working with graphics in the HTML environment has some significant limitations, which can make it difficult to realize parts of your creative vision. But there are alternatives that can help you create visually compelling sites, as you will learn in the next section.

FIGURE 8-25

Graphic placement options in HTML

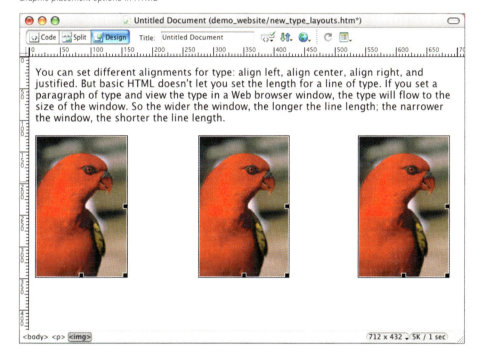

NAVIGATION AND LINKING

What You'll Learn

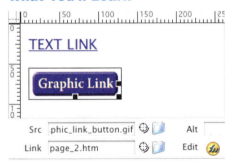

 In this lesson, you will learn how to set up navigation within a site and link site elements both internally and externally.

Setting Up Your Site's Navigation

Links are an important component of any Web site; they let you move within and between the pages of your Web site and connect to other Web sites on the Internet. Both Dreamweaver and GoLive make linking easy.

The links you create within a Web site can be either text links or graphics links. To create a text link, you select the type with the text pointer, then go to the **Properties panel (Inspector palette)**. In the Link box, type in the name of the page to link to (see Figure 8-26, where the linked page is page_2.htm). Press **[Enter]** (Windows) or

Absolute versus relative links

There are two types of links: relative and absolute. A **relative link** links to a location inside your own Web site; an **absolute link** connects to an exact location on the Web. The link type determines how much information you need to include in creating the link. For example, suppose you were developing a Web site with a home page (index.htm) and a second page named this_is_great.htm. If you created a link from the home page to the second page, this would be a relative link and you would have to specify only the name of the document, this_is_great.htm. An absolute link must include the protocol that's being used, such as **http://www.adobe.com** or **http://www.macromedia.com**.

[return] (Macintosh) and the text will change color and become underlined. When you preview the page in a browser, you will be able to click the link to display the new page.

You create a **graphics link** in almost the same way as a text link. Insert a graphic into a Web page, then click the graphic to select it. Go to the **Properties panel (Inspector palette)** and, in the Link box, type the name of the page to link to (see Figure 8-27; as before this example is now linked to page_2.htm). You can make any graphic into a link. Figure 8-27 shows a button graphic with text added.

Web site links can be either **internal links** (which link to the same page or site) or **external links**, which link to other Web sites.

Linking to Other Web Sites

Creating external links to link to other Web sites is just as easy as creating internal links to the same page or site. The only difference in creating an external link is that the link name is usually more complex, especially if you want to link to a page that's deep inside another Web site. The location you type in

FIGURE 8-26
Internal link

FIGURE 8-27
Graphic link

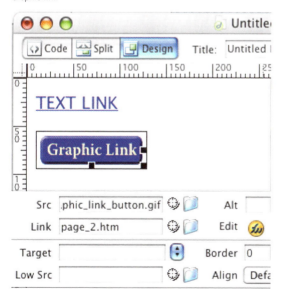

has to be exact—any typing errors will cause the link to not work properly. (For this reason, many people prefer to copy external link addresses from their Web browsers.) Figure 8-28 shows an example of a link to another Web site.

Linking Within the Same Page

Often you will want to create links that display different parts of the same Web page. These links are very common in pages with a lot of information that requires scrolling to view. For example, on a long Web page, you might want to include several links called "Back to Top" that, when the user clicks them, returns the top of the page into view, without the user having to scroll there.

To create these links, you first create **anchors**, which are named locations you insert at the places you want the browser to jump to. Then you create text links (such as "Back to Top") and connect them to the appropriate anchors. When the user clicks a link you created using an anchor, the page area that you designated appears.

To insert a link using an anchor in Dreamweaver, click to place the insertion point in the location you want the user to jump to. Click **Insert** on the menu bar, then click **Named Anchor**. In the Named Anchor dialog box, type a name for the anchor (use a distinctive name, with no

FIGURE 8-28
External link

spaces; see Figure 8-29), and then click **OK**. The anchor appears as a small anchor symbol in the location you choose (which will be invisible to the user). Next, select the text you want to create the link from (e.g. "BACK TO TOP"), then drag the **Point to File** symbol from the Properties panel over the anchor symbol on the page to create the link. Figure 8-30 shows two pages; the first contains a "BACK TO TOP" link which, when clicked, displays the top of the page shown in the accompanying figure.

To insert an anchor in GoLive, drag the anchor icon from the Objects palette to the destination on the page where you want the anchor. Select the anchor marker, and then enter a name in the Name/ID text box in the Anchor Inspector. Next, select the text to link from (e.g. "BACK TO TOP"). In the Link Inspector, enter the anchor name preceded by a pound symbol, such as "#back_to_top," and press **[Enter]** (PC) or **[Return]** (Mac).

Another way to use anchors is to create a list of topics at the top of a Web page, insert anchors where each of these topics appears on the page, and then link each topic in the list to an anchor. For example, the list of topics at the top of the page could be "Introduction, Section 1, Section 2, etc." Then, the anchors can be created at the points on the page containing these titles. This technique lets users to jump to the topic they are most interested in instead of scrolling to try to find the topic.

FIGURE 8-29

Inserting an anchor

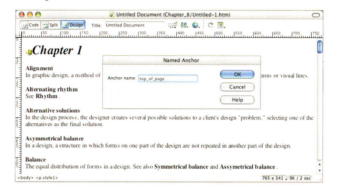

FIGURE 8-30

Linking on the same page

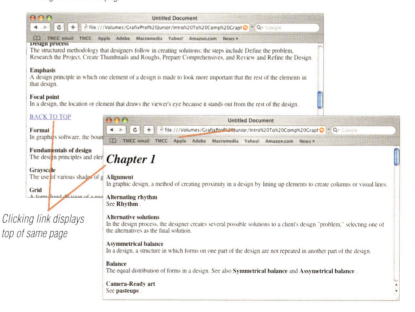

Clicking link displays top of same page

LAYOUT CONTROL WITH TABLES

What You'll Learn

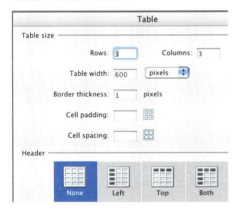

 In this lesson, you will learn how to create tables and how to use them to help control the layout of your Web site.

HTML and Tables

As you have seen, Web pages have very basic layout controls. Type can be on the left, center, or right sides of the page, and the same is true of graphics. So how do Web designers make Web pages look "designed?"

In HTML you can use tables to help organize and lay out your Web pages. A **table** in an HTML document is a grid of rows and columns, just like a table in a word processing document. An example of a table is shown in Figure 8-31. You can insert a table in any part of a Web page; your tables can be any size with any number of rows and columns. And the great thing about tables is they are HTML-based, so any Web browser can view a tables-based Web site.

Creating Tables

To add a table in Dreamweaver, you click **Insert** on the menu bar and then click **Table**. The Table dialog box opens, where you can select various properties of a table (see Figure 8-32). In GoLive, you double-click the **Table tool** in the Basic toolbar; a default table appears on your page. You then click **Window** on the menu bar, click **Table** and the Table palette will appear as shown in Figure 8-32. In both the Table dialog box and the Table palette you can modify the following:

Rows and Columns—Tables are divided into a series of blocks called **cells**. Each cell represents the intersection of a row and a column. The number of cells depends on the number of rows and columns in the table. Figure 8-31 shows a table three rows tall by two columns wide, which creates six cells.

Table width—You can set a table's width in two ways. You can specify a set number of pixels, which means that however large the viewer makes the browser window, the table will remain the same width. The second way is to make the table a percentage of the window's width, which means that the table will adjust its width based on the size of the browser window. So if the width of the table were set at 50%, the table would always occupy half the width of the browser window. The problem with using a percentage width is the information in your table will have to adjust every time the table width changes, which can greatly affect your page layout.

Border thickness—Any table can have a border around it, which can be different thicknesses. This thickness appears as a middle-gray, beveled border around the outside of the table. You can adjust this border's color or thickness. If you set the

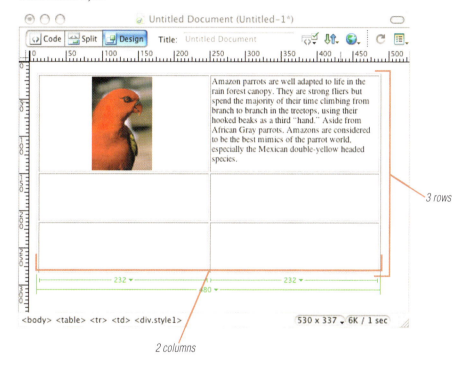

FIGURE 8-31
A table used for layout

3 rows

2 columns

thickness to 0, the border becomes invisible. This is a great way to use a table as a layout tool without the viewer knowing you are using a table (see Figure 8-33). Many Web sites use tables that are invisible to the viewer.

Cell padding—Padding creates a space within each cell that pushes the information in the cell away from the table border. This allows you to add a visual frame around your information instead of having it push up against the border of the table and/or cell.

Cell spacing—The space between each cell in a table is called **cell spacing**. When you add border thickness to a table, it applies only to the outside of the table, not to the spaces inside the table, between each of the cells. Cell spacing adjusts this space.

Using Tables as a Layout Tool

Once you get the feel for creating tables, you can then develop an understanding of how tables can be used to add more variety to your page layouts. Each table cell can contain different information, and each

FIGURE 8-32
Table dialog box and Table palette

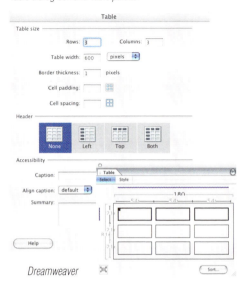

Dreamweaver

GoLive

FIGURE 8-33
Table with and without borders

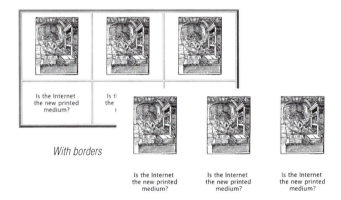

With borders

Without borders

row or column of cells can have a specific height or width assigned to it. Any information you place in a cell can be horizontally positioned left, center, or right within the cell, and can have a vertical position of top, middle, or bottom in the cell (see Figure 8-34).

Cells can also be merged (or split) to create different types of layouts. In Figure 8-35, the top row of cells has been merged, allowing space for one long headline over three columns of information. Merging and splitting cells can help enhance the layout of a Web site and provide more visual interest.

FIGURE 8-34
Different cell alignments

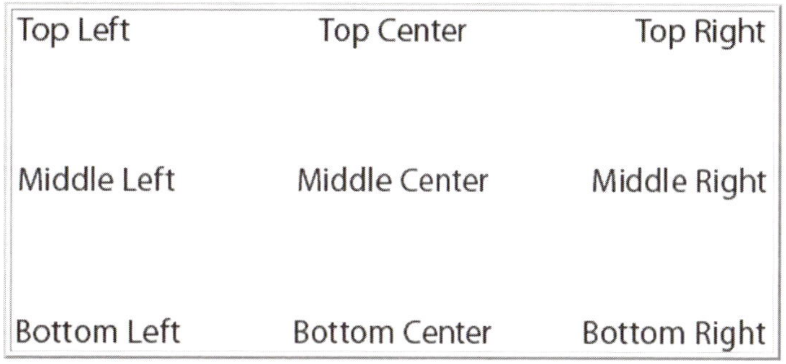

Top Left	Top Center	Top Right
Middle Left	Middle Center	Middle Right
Bottom Left	Bottom Center	Bottom Right

FIGURE 8-35
Merged cells

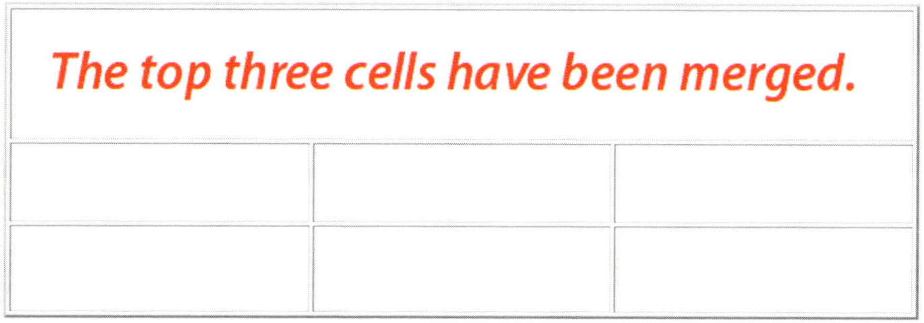

The top three cells have been merged.		

PREVIEWING YOUR WEB SITE

What You'll Learn

In this lesson, you will learn how to preview your Web site in different browsers.

Available Browsers

As you work on your Web site, you will want to check on your progress. But unlike print graphics, where you print out your work as it progresses, Web pages are not meant to be printed. Instead, to check on your work you need to **preview** your pages in several Web browsers. Both Dreamweaver and GoLive allow you to review your work as you go with a simple keyboard command in the browser of your choice.

There are several Web browsers being used on the Internet. The current favorite is **Internet Explorer**, created by Microsoft. It is the browser most people working on Windows computers use. There is a version of Internet Explorer for Macintosh computers, but it was discontinued when Apple Computer decided to release its own Web browser, **Safari**. Many Macintosh users now use Safari, although a number continue to use Internet Explorer, and some also use the third major browser, Netscape. **Netscape** once had the lion's share of the

browser market, but lost ground during the 1990s to Internet Explorer. Netscape is currently owned by America OnLine (AOL), so it still has enough market share to give it consideration when developing a site. In addition, some people use other browsers like Opera and Mozilla Firefox, but not enough to be considered (see Figure 8-36).

Previewing in the Browser

Why do you need to preview in more than one browser when designing a Web site? Because standards have not been set for how browsers should view HTML files, and each browser will display the same information a little differently. Web information will also preview differently on a Macintosh computer and a Windows computer. One difference between the two platforms is that the type preview for HTML-based type on a Windows computer is always a little larger than on a Macintosh computer. But because there are so many more Windows computers than Macintosh computers, it is always best to design your type to view properly on a Windows computer, knowing it will view a little smaller on a Macintosh. You can avoid this problem by using CSS-based type, because CSS uses specific pixel sizes for type.

So what's the best solution? Unfortunately, most Web designers cannot afford to have both a Windows computer and a Macintosh computer to preview their work. But any Web designer can have all three major browsers, Internet Explorer, Safari, and Netscape, installed on their computer. Both Dreamweaver and GoLive let you specify multiple browsers when you preview work in progress. This will give you a better idea of how your site looks in each browser so you can make any necessary adjustments.

FIGURE 8-36

Three major browsers

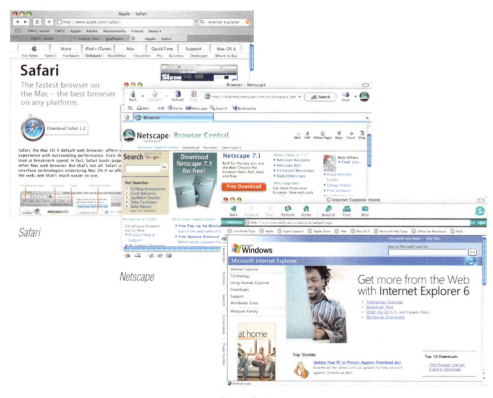

Safari

Netscape

Internet Explorer

Web design has come a long way since 1989. Hand-coding has been replaced by powerful WYSIWYG-based Web design applications such as Dreamweaver and GoLive. Both let you bring in text and graphics and create layouts in an HTML-based environment, and though understanding HTML is important, Web pages can be created in either application with little knowledge of HTML. By adding navigation and linking, you can design and produce entire Web sites with multiple Web pages rapidly. Adding tables lets you create Web pages with strong, dynamic layouts that can be viewed successfully in any of the major Web browsers. (To view the Web pages shown below, connect to the Internet, go to www.course.com, navigate to the page for this book, click the Student Online Companion link, then click the link for this chapter.)

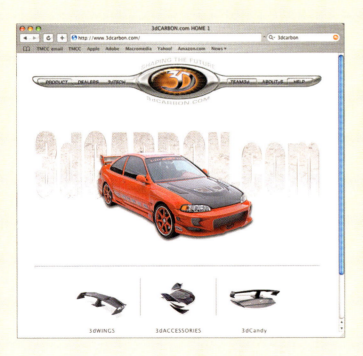

KEY TERMS AND CONCEPTS

absolute link

assets folder

banner

border thickness

branding elements

browser

buttons

cell

cell padding

cell spacing

column

content creation

CSS (cascading style sheets)

CSS-based sizings

default images folder

DHTML (Dynamic Hypertext)

download speed

external link

graphics link

hexidecimal system

homepage

.htm (.html)

HTML (Hypertext Markup Language)

HTML-based sizings

hyperlinks

image maps

index.htm

interactive

internal link

Internet Explorer

local root folder

masthead

navigation buttons

Netscape

optimize

ordered list (numbered list)

pixels (picture elements)

preview

relative link

rollover buttons

row

Safari

site folder

source code

table

table width

text indent (increase block indent)

text link

text outdent (decrease block indent)

unordered list (bulleted list)

upload speed

Web browser

Web-safe colors

WYSIWYG (What You See Is What You Get)

1. Why is Web design software called WYSIWYG and what are its benefits?

_____

_____

_____

2. How is the size of type measured in HTML?

_____

3. List three styles of type available in HTML on a Windows computer:

_____

_____

_____

4. What does optimize mean?

_____

_____

_____

5. Why is download speed important?

_____

_____

_____

6. What are navigation buttons?

_____

_____

_____

7. What is an interactive graphic?

_____

_____

8. Why is establishing a local root folder important?

_____

_____

_____

9. What subfolder must be created inside the local root folder before you start to produce a Web site?

_____

_____

10. What is the name usually assigned to the file that will be a Web site's home page?

_____

11. What are Web-safe colors?

12. What is the difference between an internal link and an external link?

13. In a table, what are cells?

14. How can tables be used to improve the layout of a Web page?

15. Name three Web browsers:

16. What is the difference between relative and absolute links?

As a Web designer for Fast Downloads Web Design company, you have been assigned to design a Web site for Andrew Jackson Middle School. The school would like a home page that reflects the name Andrew Jackson and a history of the seventh president of the United States.

Go on the Web and research school Web sites. See how they are designed, and also notice how the sites use navigation to move from page to page. Using markers and marker paper, draw 8" wide x 6" tall rectangles on your paper, reflecting a standard format for a Web page. Design three different visual concepts for a home page, each one with its own layout, graphics, and navigational structure. Use the design elements and principles discussed in Chapters 1 and 7 to create three exciting concepts.

Take your best concept and create a home page using Dreamweaver or GoLive. Be sure to optimize any images in the correct size, file format, and color model so they will upload quickly and view accurately. Use a content creation application to design branding elements that invite the viewer into the Web site,

as well as a set of navigation buttons. For text, try to use HTML text as much as you can so the site is easy to update. Design banners in content creation software and optimize them for your site if you choose. Be sure to preview your work in at least two different browsers so you know it will view properly.

One Step Beyond

Create three additional pages for the school's Web site. Produce a page that shows the school staff, a page that discusses the school's sports teams, and a page that discusses the computer technologies the students use. Use the same branding elements and navigational buttons as the home page. Link these additional pages to the home page to create a fully functional Web site.

Two Steps Beyond

On the site's home page, add at least three external links to other school Web sites, or to other Web sites that talk about Andrew Jackson.

One of your clients, The Running Pair, has asked you to develop a Web site for their company. They have received contracts from several athletic shoe manufacturers to sell their shoes online and want you to create a Web site for this purpose.

Research Web sites that sell athletic shoes, and develop a layout for a four-page site. Design and produce branding elements and navigational buttons for a home page that introduces the company and what the company is selling. Then produce three additional pages, each one advertising a different brand of athletic shoes. Get pictures of at least three different shoe models from each manufacturer, optimize them, and organize them in a table so the viewer has a good idea what each model is and how one model is different from the others. (If you are selecting text or graphics from the Web, read the site's "fine print" to make sure you are not violating any copyright restrictions.)

One Step Beyond

On each of the product pages, include an external link to the manufacturer's Web site.

Two Steps Beyond

Add a fifth page to the Web site and create an order form. Research order forms on the Web and use a table to organize the information effectively.

Produce a Web site that promotes your new Web design company, **"Your Name" Web Design**. Research other Web design company sites and use similar types of information to create a site for your own company.

Use either Dreamweaver or GoLive to produce the site. Create a banner and navigational buttons, and optimize any images that you want to put into this site. Create internal links and include at least three external links to other designers' Web sites that you would like to be connected to (see Figure 8-37 for an example of a Web designer's sites). (To view the Web page shown below, connect to the Internet, go to www.course.com, navigate to the page for this book, click the Student Online Companion link, then click the link for this chapter.)

FIGURE 8-37
Possible Web site solution

Figure 8-38 shows two examples of real-world Web design projects. Look carefully at each project, and write a critique of how the basic elements and concepts of design discussed in previous chapters are used within the limitations of HTML. (To view the Web pages shown below, connect to the Internet, go to www.course.com, navigate to the page for this book, click the Student Online Companion link, then click the link for this chapter.)

FIGURE 8-38
Possible Web site solutions

Diane Brody
BioProcess Web site
www.brodymarketing.com

Diane Brody
Vericol Web site
www.brodymarketing.com

WEB ANIMATION SOFTWARE

WEB ANIMATION SOFTWARE

From Static to Dynamic

In the early 1990s, Web pages were static. Text and pictures had to be designed within the strict limitations of HTML, which gave little opportunity to add movement and sound. But by 1995, new file formats and applications began changing the Web into a showcase for dynamic content.

The first use of movement on the Web came with the development of animated GIF files. **GIF animations** are a series of graphic images that are displayed one right after the other, like a simple cartoon (see Figure 9-1). To create a GIF animation, you first create a series of images, using any graphics application. Then you combine the images into a single GIF animation file, which requires special software that places the images in a set of frames. Each frame is then played in the correct order, creating a simple animation. GIF animations are ideal for Web pages because the files are very small, which means they can be downloaded quickly; also, they can be viewed by any browser without the need for extra software.

Along Came Flash

In 1995, a small company called FutureWave Software developed a product specifically for producing Web-based animations. Originally based on a vector-draw application called SmartSketch, this new application required Web browsers to use a separate animation player application. FutureWave's first attempt at creating an animation player used the Java

Keep your eye on the message

Although Flash can create almost any animation effect you can imagine, it's easy to create a project that overwhelms the eye and causes the viewer to lose sight of the message. Good design, whether for print or digital media, should communicate the client's message first and foremost; any effects or animations should help to support that message. So have fun in Flash and other graphics applications, but be sure to keep the message and good design in mind at all times.

programming language. **Java** can create compact applications that users can run in conjunction with a Web browser. But it was painfully slow in downloading and running animations, so the company decided to use the Netscape browser to play animations. Netscape had just released its Application Programming Interface (API), which let programmers easily create applications to extend Netscape's capabilities. API enabled FutureWave to develop an animation player with good performance.

With their animation-player problems solved, FutureWave released the newly named FutureSplash Animator application in May 1996. Within three months several large companies, including Microsoft and Disney, adopted the application to create dynamic content for their Web sites. This caught the eye of Macromedia, who in December of 1996 bought out FutureWave Software and re-released FutureSplash Animator as Macromedia Flash 1.0.

The Web Goes Wild

Flash was originally developed as a simple Web drawing and animation application. But as it evolved, Flash became the first Web animation software able to use vector art instead of bitmapped art. Because vector art is much smaller in file size and is resolution independent, you can scale any Flash image to a larger size without loss of quality. Because it used vector art, Flash could create animations that downloaded and ran faster than any others developed at that time, and Flash animations proliferated across the Web.

Macromedia Flash Player, the small, freely downloadable application that plays animation files, has also become very popular; every major Web browser has adopted the Flash Player as a standard application for viewing animations on the Web. This has allowed Flash to become the dominant Web animation creation software in the industry, with more than 500,000 Flash developers and more than 325 million Web users now viewing this diverse array of interactive content with the Flash Player.

FIGURE 9-1
GIF animation

Action 1

Action 2

Action 3

Action 4

FIGURE 9-2
Macromedia Flash

FLASH: AN OVERVIEW

What You'll Learn

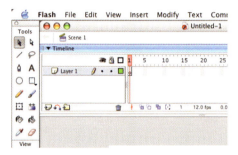

In this lesson, you will learn the major features of Macromedia Flash.

Macromedia Flash

Macromedia Flash is the leading Web animation software in the industry. From its beginnings as a simple animation application, it has grown to become a complete package for developing highly interactive Web sites. Flash can be useful for all levels of users; even those with little or no Web animation experience can quickly learn to create simple but effective Web animations and interactive Web sites.

The Flash graphics tools contain a wide range of vector-based shapes, including customizable polygon, circle, line, and curve tools with stroke and fill settings. You can control the position, scale, rotation, and skew using one tool. Flash also has a variety of paint tools and lets you trace bitmapped images to create vector shapes.

Flash can control text using formatting controls such as size, kerning, tracking, justification, and color. You can even apply CSS (Cascading Style Sheets) to makes type more consistent throughout a project. You can also share styles with Dreamweaver.

Flash lets you control animation timing, using effects such as stop-motion, and automatically fills in intermediary frames between animation actions, a process known as tweening. A timeline lets you create content quickly with multiple layers and layer folders, allowing you to organize multiple or similar layers into a single folder. Flash also features Timeline Effects, which let you create, duplicate, and modify common or repetitive timeline animations without having to re-create each one from scratch. A variety of other effects lets you create dynamic visuals, including Blur, Drop Shadow, Expand, and Explode.

Flash supports many external graphics formats and can now work with PDFs and Illustrator EPS formats. You can also import video clips (including AVI and Quicktime formats) and manipulate, rotate, skew, mask, scale, and animate video content directly in Flash. Flash supports many audio formats and lets you control and sync the audio within your project. You can create simple animations or complete, interactive Web sites that can be delivered through the Flash proprietary file format. This format produces small, compact files that can be optimized for both narrow and broadband Web connections. And finally, Flash content can be viewed on Windows, Macintosh, and Unix operating systems, as well as on the Web, PDAs, and even cell phones.

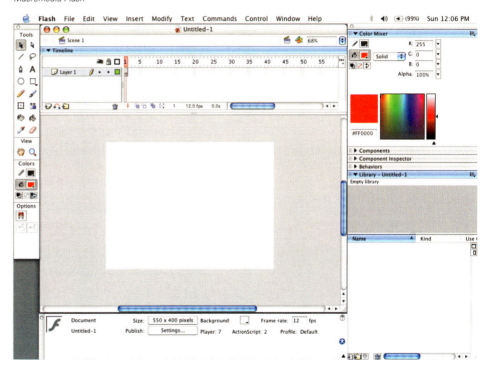

FIGURE 9-3
Macromedia Flash

OPEN AND SAVE FILES

What You'll Learn

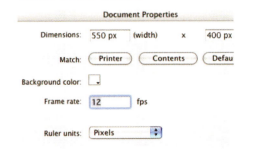

Document Properties

Dimensions: 550 px (width) x 400 px

Match: (Printer) (Contents) (Defau

Background color:

Frame rate: 12 fps

Ruler units: Pixels

In this lesson, you will learn how to create new projects in Flash.

Creating a New Project

You launch Flash the same way you launch the other programs in this book: by using the Dock or Applications folder (Macintosh) or the Programs or All Programs menu (Windows). When you launch Flash, a new document with an empty stage appears on your screen. The **stage** is the Flash work area; the Properties panel appears below it, as shown in Figure 9-4. This panel is the same as the Properties panels in other Macromedia products: it displays information for the element you are working on. In this example, the Properties panel shows the attributes of the stage and certain project defaults.

To dig deeper, on the Properties panel, click the button to the right of Size, which shows the default stage size of 550 x 400 pixels.

This opens the Document Properties dialog box shown in Figure 9-5, which contains the same information that appeared in the Properties panel. Here you can set the size of your document (which is the size of the stage), set the stage background color, adjust the **frame rate** at which your project will run (this is measured in **fps, frames per second**, as the speed Flash will display your project), and set the ruler measurement system you can use to measure elements in your project. Flash can use inches, inches (decimal), points, centimeters, millimeters, and pixels.

QUICKTIP

Measuring for the Web means using pixels instead of inches, so you'll need to get used to measuring in pixels. Recall that 72 pixels equals 1 inch.

Once you have selected the parameters of your project, save your file in a project folder. Flash lets you choose only one file format, **.fla**, the Flash working file format. You can also choose between saving the file as a Flash MX 2004 or a Flash MX document. Due to significant changes in the application between MX 2004 and MX, you have to "save down" to the earlier version for the file to work properly in Flash MX; you cannot modify Flash MX 2004 files in Flash MX.

FIGURE 9-4

The stage and the properties panel

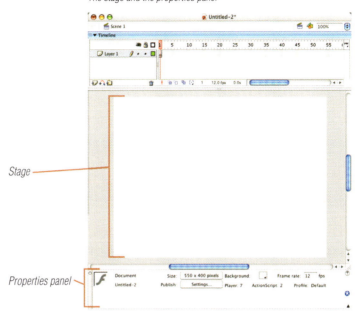

Stage

Properties panel

FIGURE 9-5

Document Properties dialog box

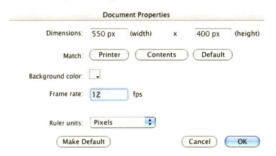

DEVELOP GRAPHICS AND TEXT

What You'll Learn

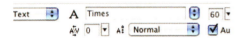

 In this lesson, you will work with the tools and commands in Flash that create and modify graphics and text.

Graphics Tools and Commands

Flash has a wide variety of graphics creation tools to produce vector-based images for your projects. The **Toolbox** (shown in Figure 9-6) displays these tools, as well as variations (called **modes**) to each tool if they are available. For example, when you select the Brush tool, you can select from several painting modes, including Paint Normal, Paint Fills, Paint Behind, Paint Selection, and Paint Inside, and you can change the size and shape of the brush.

Selection and Subselection tools—These tools let you select complete shapes so you can move or modify them. The Subselection tool lets you select a portion of a shape.

Line tool—Use this tool to create straight lines at any angle, in thicknesses of .1 pixel to 10 pixels. Hold down [Shift] to draw horizontal, vertical, and 45°-angle lines.

Lasso tool—This Lasso works the same as the Lasso tool in Photoshop; click-and-drag to select an area.

Pen tool—The Pen tool works the same as the Pen tool in Illustrator; use it to create unique lines and shapes.

Text tool—Use the Text tool to create text blocks and modify them using the Properties panel.

Oval tool—This tool makes any type of oval or circle. You can also apply strokes and fills to them.

Rectangle/PolyStar tools—The Rectangle tool makes any type of rectangle or square, to which you can apply strokes and fills. The PolyStar tool makes polygon and star shapes.

Pencil tool—You can use the Pencil tool to create a variety of lines. Flash offers three Pencil tool options: Straighten, which automatically straightens any lines you draw; Smooth, which attempts to smooth your lines; and Ink, which leaves your lines exactly as you drew them. Figure 9-7 shows a circle drawn with the Pencil tool and with each option applied.

Brush tool—The Brush tool lets you make shapes with fill only, without a stroke. You can adjust the size and style of the brush.

Free Transform tool—Use this tool to modify any object. You can scale, rotate, flip or skew; by holding down [Shift] you can modify an object proportionally.

Fill Transform tool—This tool lets you change the direction, size, or center point of a gradient fill.

Ink Bottle tool—This tool changes the width or color of a stroke, or adds a stroke to a shape that has none.

Paint Bucket tool—This tool adds a fill inside a shape that has none, or changes the color of a fill.

Eyedropper tool—Use this tool to copy a fill or stroke and apply it to another object.

Eraser tool—This tool removes any object or part of an object from the stage.

FIGURE 9-6

Flash Toolbox

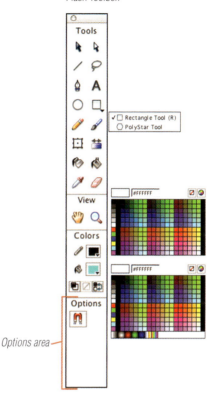

Options area

FIGURE 9-7

Different Pencil tool options

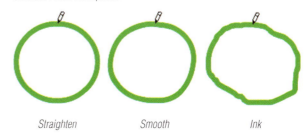

Straighten   Smooth   Ink

Creating Basic Graphics

Drawing with Flash tools is similar to drawing in other graphics applications, but there are a couple of differences that you need to know. Flash graphics can have a stroke and a fill that can become separate objects. The top part of Figure 9-8 shows a circle drawn using the Oval tool with a black stroke and a purple fill. The same circle is shown at the bottom; the stroke was selected with the Selection tool and separated from the fill. This technique is handy if you want to animate the stroke and the fill independently from each other.

You can also use the Selection tool to modify the shape of any graphic. In other vector-draw applications, the Selection tool lets you change only the scale or proportion of a graphic, not its shape. And, as in other vector-draw applications, the Subselection tool in Flash can select individual anchor points and handles to modify a graphic's shape. So Flash gives you two different techniques to reach the same solution!

FIGURE 9-8
Stroke and fill

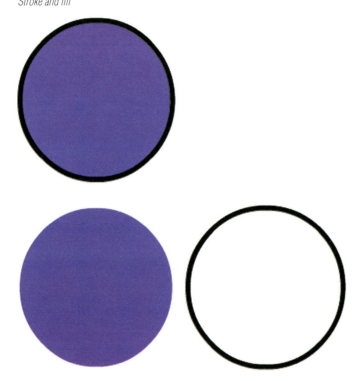

Entering Type

Flash lets you work with many of the typographic tools and commands you have used in other graphics applications. The Text tool lets you create an insertion point to start a new text box. As you type, the text box expands to display all of your type (see Figure 9-9). You can make text boxes larger than the type in them, or you can double-click the text box handle to make the box shrink to match the size of the text. A **defined text box** exactly matches the height and width of the text it encloses.

The text options available in the Properties Panel follow. Figure 9-10 shows a collapsed Properties panel for text. The panel can be expanded to show more text options, but the collapsed panel gives you enough options to use the program at an introductory level.

Text Type menu—This menu lets you select from three types of text behavior: static text, dynamic text, or input text. Each behavior creates different effects; in this chapter you will focus on **static text**, which is text with no specific behavior effect applied.

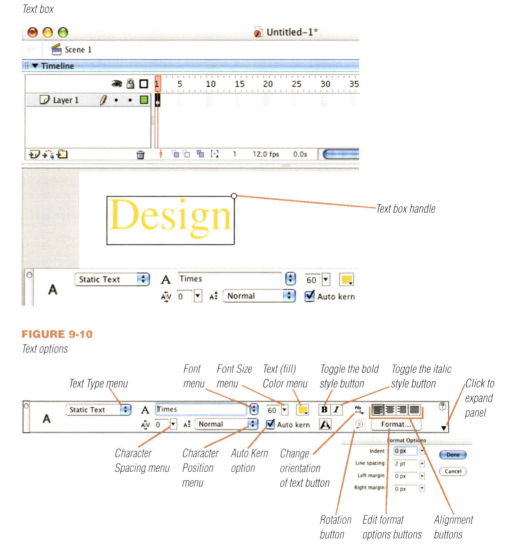

FIGURE 9-9

Text box

Text box handle

FIGURE 9-10

Text options

Font menu—This menu displays the fonts available on your computer. As you scroll through the different fonts, Flash displays a preview of each font, instead of just the name of the font, making font selection easier.

Font Size menu—This menu lets you set the type size in points.

Text (fill) color menu—This menu lets you apply any of the 216 Web-safe colors to type.

Toggle the bold style and Toggle the italic style buttons—These buttons make selected type bold, italic, or bold italic.

Change orientation of text button—This option changes the direction of text in a text box. Choose from Horizontal; Vertical, Left to Right; and Vertical, Right to Left (see Figure 9-11).

Alignment buttons—These buttons control the alignment of text in a text box; choose from Align Left, Align Center, Align Right, and Justified.

Character spacing menu—This option adjusts the spacing between letters and between words in selected text.

Character position menu—This menu provides the three settings that determine the position of characters in relation to other text. The Normal setting aligns the type along the baseline. (The **baseline** is the imaginary line where the bottom of the majority of letters aligns, not including letters with **descenders,** which are the

FIGURE 9-11
Text direction

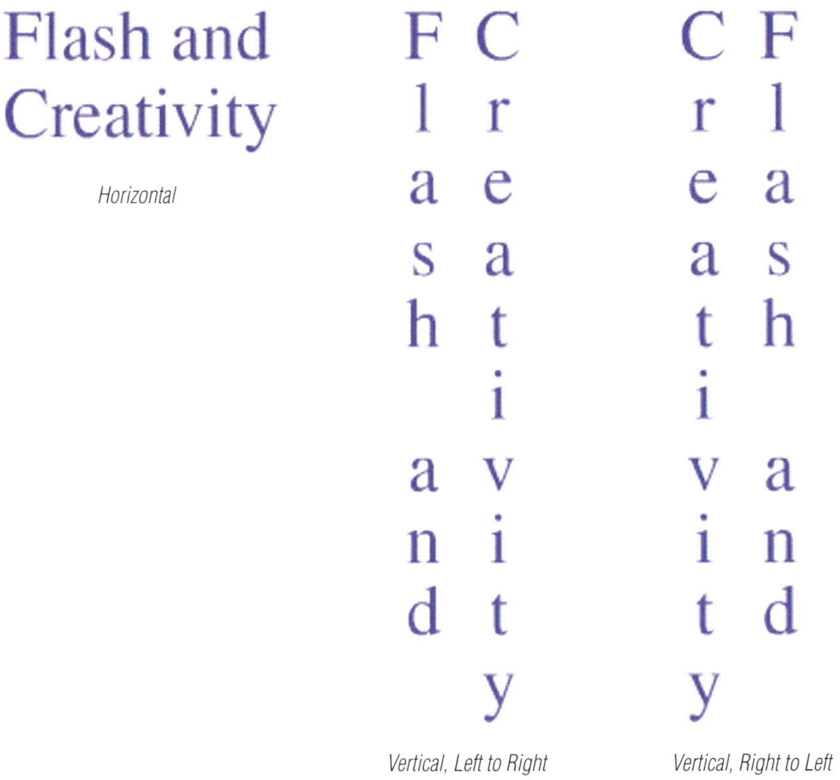

Flash and
Creativity

Horizontal

F C
l r
a e
s a
h t
  i
a v
n i
d t
  y

Vertical, Left to Right

C F
r l
e a
a s
t h
i
v a
i n
t d
y

Vertical, Right to Left

parts of lowercase (small) letters that go below the baseline.) **Superscript** makes the character smaller and shifts it above the baseline and **Subscript** makes the character smaller and shifts it below the baseline.

Auto Kern option—This option automatically adjusts the space between letters in a word to make the spacing appear more even to the eye.

Rotation button—The Rotation button adjusts how vertical type is displayed in a text box (see Figure 9-12).

Edit format options button—This button displays a pop-up window with options for formatting text blocks. These options include: Indent, which controls how much the first line in a paragraph will indent from the left margin; Line Spacing, which adjusts the leading between lines of type; Left margin, which indents the left side of a column of type; and Right margin, which indents the right side of a column of type.

FIGURE 9-12
Vertical text rotation

CONCEPT 4

MAKE SYMBOLS AND INSTANCES

What You'll Learn

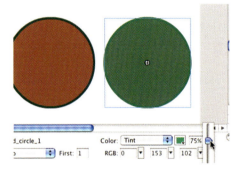

 In this lesson, you will learn how to create, work with, and modify symbols and instances.

The Importance of Symbols

Although you can animate graphics and text, you cannot directly modify them to create many of the effects you are about to learn. So, to give yourself all of the animation power Flash has available, you should convert all graphics and text into symbols.

Symbols are an important concept; they form the foundation of Flash animation on the Web. A **symbol** is a representation of a graphic that can be used over and over again. A symbol can represent a simple or a complex graphic. Symbols are also

smaller in size than the original graphic, so using symbols lets Flash files remain small. Each symbol is stored in the Flash library and can be reused. Each of these duplicates of a symbol is called an **instance**, and every instance adds very little to the file size of a Flash animation.

Here is an example of how this concept works: Suppose you want to create an animation of a boat moving from left to right across your monitor (see Figure 9-13). A very simple Flash project may take 50 versions of the boat to make it appear to be moving. That would require 50

Naming symbols

The current version of Flash (MX 2004) requires a specific naming convention for symbols. Do not use spaces; either delete them altogether or use underscores (_) instead. Avoid special characters (~!@#$%^&*?) and forward slashes (/). Always start a symbol name with a lowercase letter, and don't put dots (.) in the name. Also, try to use a descriptive name so it's easy to reference a specific symbol in your Library.

different boat drawings, each one requiring a certain file size. If someone wanted to view the animation on the Web, each of the 50 versions would have to be downloaded, one at a time—an unwieldy and time-consuming task. But in Flash you can create one drawing of the boat and convert that drawing to a symbol. The symbol would be smaller in size than the original drawing, and you could use 50 instances of the boat symbol to create motion. Each instance would be many times smaller than each individual boat drawing, and when someone views your animation, only the one symbol would need to be downloaded.

Creating and Storing Symbols

You can convert any graphic or text created in Flash into a symbol; you can also convert any graphic or bitmapped image created in another program. To start, you select a graphic, piece of text, or image on the stage. Click **Window** on the menu bar and make sure your Library panel is open.

FIGURE 9-13
Graphics versus symbols

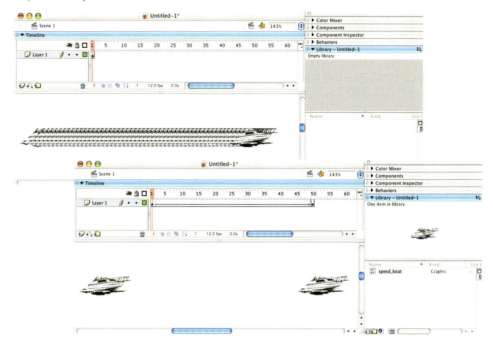

DESIGNTIP Behaviors in Flash

The majority of symbols you create in Flash will be graphic symbols. But Flash also lets you create Button symbols, which make navigational buttons for your project, or Movie clip symbols, which are self-contained mini-animations or video presentations that you can embed into your Flash project.

Figure 9-14 shows an empty Library; the **Library** is where you store your symbols.

Click-and-drag the selected graphic or text to the white area in the lower half of the Library panel. The Convert to Symbol dialog box opens as shown in Figure 9-15. Here you name the symbol, choose a **behavior** for the symbol, and designate where Flash will show a Registration point, which helps align your symbol on the Stage.

Click **OK** and the graphic will be added to your Library as a symbol. Figure 9-16 shows how the Library panel displays the name of the symbol in the bottom half of the panel, and a preview of the symbol in the top half. This symbol is now a permanent part of your Flash project, and you can click the symbol preview and drag as many instances of the symbol onto the stage as you like. To delete a symbol from your Library, click the name of the symbol

FIGURE 9-14
Library

FIGURE 9-16
Library panel with symbol added

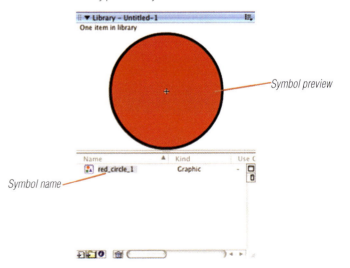

Symbol preview

Symbol name

FIGURE 9-15
Convert to Symbol dialog box

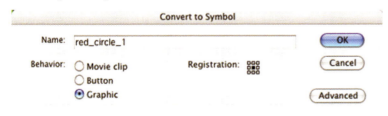

in the bottom half of the Library panel, click the **Trash icon** in the bottom-left corner of the Library panel, and then confirm the deletion in the dialog box. This deletes the symbol and all its instances.

Editing Your Symbols

Once you have created a symbol and set instances of the symbol on the stage, how can you edit the symbol? Go to the symbol listing in the Library and double-click the icon to the left of a symbol's name (see Figure 9-17). The stage changes; you are now editing the symbol rather than working on the main stage of your Flash project. The Information Bar at the top of the stage window shows Scene 1 (indicating the current contents of the stage), and the name of your symbol appears to the right of the scene number, indicating that you are in the symbol editing area.

This editing area lets you modify your symbol; any changes you make here will change every instance of the symbol on the stage. You can change the stroke color, weight, and style; or the fill color; or use the Free Transform tool to scale, rotate, or skew the symbol. As you modify the symbol, you will see your changes appear in the symbol preview in the Library panel. Once you have completed your changes, click Scene 1 in the Information Bar (see Figure 9-18) to return to the stage.

FIGURE 9-17

Editing a symbol

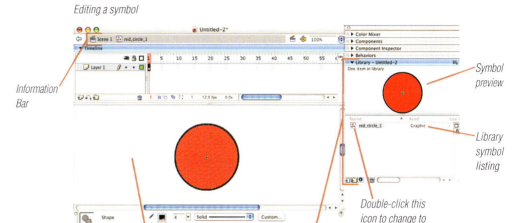

Information Bar

Symbol preview

Library symbol listing

Double-click this icon to change to the edit symbol area

Editing area

Library panel

FIGURE 9-18

Returning to the Stage

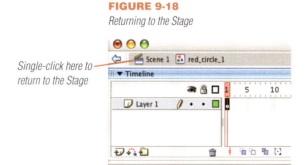

Single-click here to return to the Stage

Editing Instances on the Stage

You can also modify instances individually, without modifying the symbol itself. When you select an instance on the stage, the Properties panel displays a Color menu that lets you modify four characteristics of an instance: Brightness, Tint, Alpha, and Advanced adjustments. Click the **Color menu** and then click **Brightness**. This lets you select a slider and change how light or dark your instance appears. Moving the slider up from 0% makes the instance brighter, until at 100% it turns completely white. Move the slider down to make the instance darker, until at –100% it turns completely black (see Figure 9-19).

Click the **Color menu list arrow** and then click **Tint**. This lets you choose any of the 216 Web-safe colors and use it to **tint**, or color, an instance, using a slider. You can select 0% tint, which applies no change to the instance color. As you slide upward, the tint changes to the color you selected (see Figure 9-20), until at 100% the instance is completely tinted to that color. Click the menu again and then click Alpha. **Alpha** changes the transparency of the instance. Using the slider, you can select 100%, which is completely opaque, through higher levels of transparency until you reach 0%, which is a completely transparent (invisible) instance (see Figure 9-21).

FIGURE 9-19

Adjusting the brightness

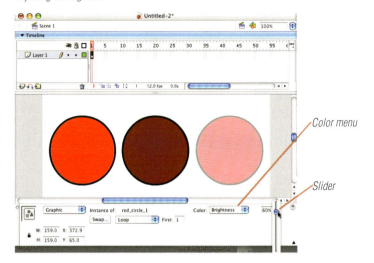

Color menu

Slider

FIGURE 9-20

Adjusting the tint

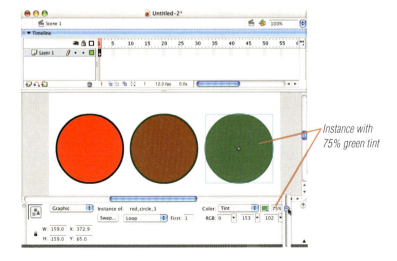

Instance with 75% green tint

When you select **Advanced** in the Color menu, you can click the **Settings button** to open the Advanced Effect dialog box (see Figure 9-22), which lets you change the Tint and Alpha at the same time. If you change an instance and then decide you want to remove these changes, you can select None on the Color menu, which removes any changes you made.

FIGURE 9-21
Adjusting the Alpha

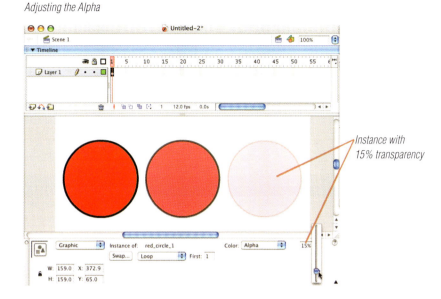

Instance with 15% transparency

FIGURE 9-22
Advanced adjustments

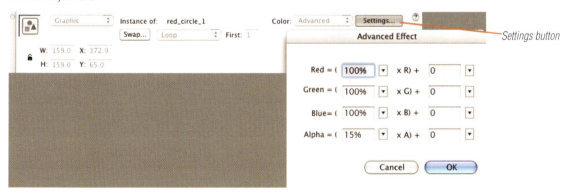

Settings button

WORK ON THE TIMELINE

What You'll Learn

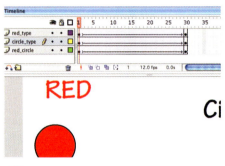

In this lesson, you will learn how to create layers and animate on the Timeline.

Working with Layers

Once you have created symbols, you can move them to the stage and start animating them. Flash uses a Timeline to help you develop animations throughout a project. The **Timeline**, shown in Figure 9-23, displays the structure of your Flash project. The left section lists the different layers on the timeline. A **layer** on the Flash timeline is similar to layers in a Photoshop file; each element of your animation will occupy its own layer. Clicking a layer in the Timeline selects that layer, and any modifications you make will affect that layer only. Double-clicking a layer name highlights it, letting you change the name to a new one.

To the right of the layer name are three columns that let you turn the visibility of the layer on and off, lock the layer so no modifications can be made to any graphics on that layer, and select a highlight color. The **highlight color** is the color of the bounding box around a graphic when you select it; this lets you color-code each layer so you can see which graphic is on which layer.

Below the layer names are two additional icons you will use frequently. The Insert Layer icon on the lower-left lets you add more layers to your timeline. The Delete Layer icon on the lower-right lets you

Hand-drawn animation

Before computers, animations were created by hand, frame by frame. Companies like Disney hired talented artists to work in their animation departments. The senior artists, known as lead animators, would draw or paint the main frames of an animation sequence, called keyframes. (Sound familiar?) The lead animator would then hand off the keyframes to a group of junior animators, who would then paint all of the required "in-between" frames. These frames would create the animation effect, and the process became known as tweening.

delete any layer that you have highlighted in the timeline. You can add or delete layers at any time. *Remember that if you delete a layer, all of the graphics on that layer will also be deleted.*

Frames and Keyframes

The right section of the timeline contains the frames you use to animate your graphics. A **frame** is an area that can contain a graphic, with the number of frames governing the duration of your project. The Flash default rate for running a project is 12 fps (frames per second). For example, if you have a project with 60 frames, the project will run for 5 seconds. If the project contains 540 frames, it will run for 45 seconds. The frame numbers appear in a list at the top of the timeline.

When you create a new layer in Flash, that layer has its own set of frames on the timeline. To add animation to the timeline, you have to insert special frames, called keyframes. A **keyframe** is a specific frame along the timeline in which you designate an event to occur. This event can be the start of an animation effect, the end of that effect, or some type of change in that effect. Figure 9-24, for example, shows a simple

FIGURE 9-23
Timeline

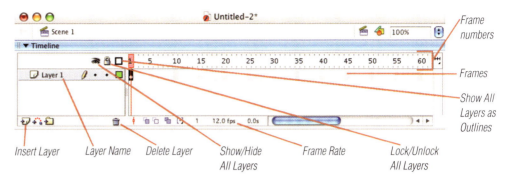

Insert Layer   Layer Name   Delete Layer   Show/Hide All Layers   Frame Rate   Lock/Unlock All Layers

Frame numbers

Frames

Show All Layers as Outlines

FIGURE 9-24
Using keyframes—Part 1

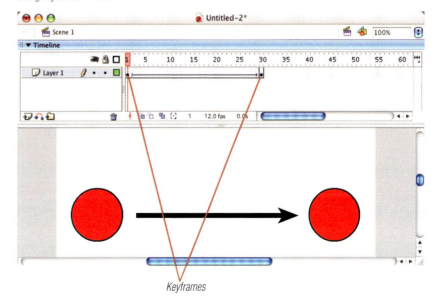

Keyframes

animation where a graphic moves from left to right across the stage. There are two keyframes on this timeline. The first timeline shows where the animation starts, and where the graphic is on the stage as it starts to move. The second keyframe shows where the movement will stop and where the graphic will be on the stage when it stops. So the graphic will move in a straight line across the stage.

A second example, shown in Figure 9-25, shows the same graphic, but it contains three keyframes on the timeline. This additional keyframe is necessary because the graphic moves from left to right, but then changes direction and moves up the stage. This direction change requires an additional keyframe. A third example (Figure 9-26) is similar to the first example: The graphic moves in a straight line from left to right, but halfway across the stage, the graphic starts to get larger as it moves. This size change requires an additional keyframe.

As you decide how you want each graphic in your project to be animated, you create the number of keyframes required along each timeline. You can also position a keyframe anywhere along the timeline, which lets you specify when a graphic will

FIGURE 9-25

Using keyframes—Part 2

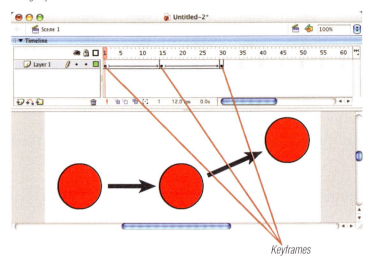

Keyframes

FIGURE 9-26

Using keyframes—Part 3

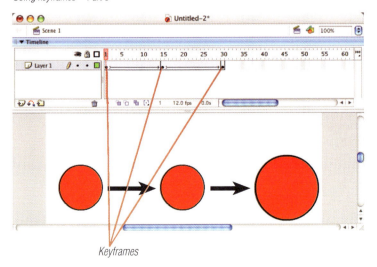

Keyframes

start or stop its effect(s) during the animation. It could start at the beginning, 10 seconds into the project, or near the end of the project. The distance between each keyframe is also an important consideration; this distance designates the duration of each effect and the overall duration of each layer on the timeline.

Tweening Between Keyframes

In hand-drawn animations, every frame had to be created to produce the desired animation effect. But in Flash you need to create only the keyframes, and Flash creates the required in-between frames. This automatic addition of frames is called **tweening**, and it makes creating simple animations much easier. To start, you must have an instance of a symbol on the stage on its own layer. The timeline will show a keyframe on Frame 1 (see Figure 9-27), which is where you start to construct an animation.

FIGURE 9-27
Starting a tween

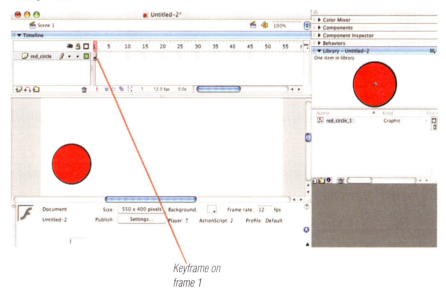

Keyframe on
frame 1

Using the Selection tool, move the pointer down the timeline until it is over Frame 30, and then click to select that frame. Click **Insert** on the menu bar, point to **Timeline**, and then click **Keyframe**. A new keyframe appears on Frame 30. Flash also duplicates your graphic into all of the frames between the two keyframes. You can view all of these duplicates by dragging the **Playhead** back and forth on the timeline (see Figure 9-28).

Click the keyframe on Frame 1 on the timeline; on the Properties panel, click the **Tween** list arrow (see Figure 9-29), and then select **Motion**. A **motion tween** lets you apply most types of animated effects. A black arrow appears on the timeline between the first and the second keyframes, indicating that a tween has been applied. Now go back and select the second keyframe on Frame 30. Using the Selection tool, drag the graphic from the left side of the stage to the right. Because you have applied a tween, Flash automatically adjusts the position of the graphic on each individual frame to make the graphic appear like it's moving from left to right. To preview this tween, click **Control** on the menu bar and then click **Play**. The graphic should now move from the left to the right of the stage.

FIGURE 9-28
Playhead

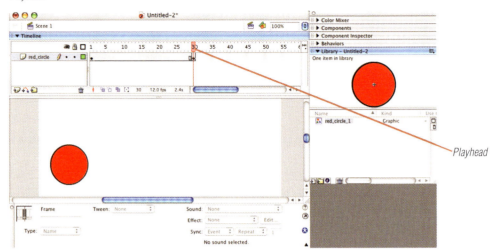

Playhead

FIGURE 9-29
Adding a motion tween

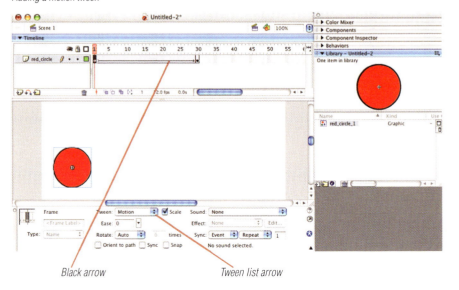

Black arrow

Tween list arrow

You can create more complex animations by adding more keyframes to the timeline. Each keyframe lets you do something different to the graphic, whether it is changing the direction of the motion; making your graphic larger, smaller, rotating or skewing it; or any combination of effects that can occur together, such as scaling, rotating and skewing at the same time. You can also use the Brightness, Tint, and Alpha effects you learned about earlier to give graphics additional animated effects.

To take your Flash animations to the next level, you can put more than one graphic into your project. You'll need to create a new layer for each graphic you want to animate. In Figure 9-30, the graphic and each word has its own timeline, with its own set of keyframes and effects, but when you play the animation, the objects all work together as one cohesive project.

FIGURE 9-30

Multiple layers on the timeline

Red Type layer

Circle Type layer

Red Circle layer

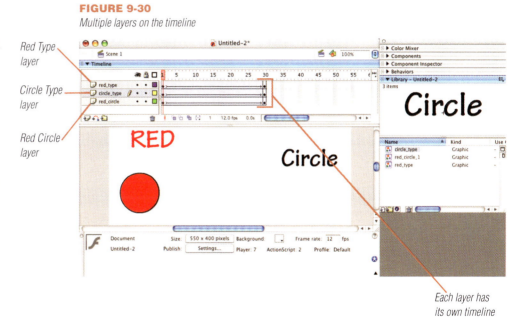

Each layer has its own timeline

EXPORT AND VIEW FILES

What You'll Learn

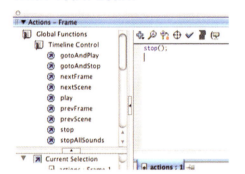

 In this lesson, you will learn how to export your Flash project so it can be viewed on the Web.

Previewing Files as You Work

As you develop your project, Flash lets you preview your work in three ways. You learned about the first two earlier in the chapter: You can drag the Playhead across the timeline, or you can click Play on the Control menu. The advantage of the second technique is that it plays your project at the speed (fps) you set. The third technique is to click the **Control menu** and then click **Test Movie**. This creates a temporary Flash movie file that previews your animation in a separate window. This method is the most accurate way to view your project; it shows the stage at its actual size, and if you have images going off the stage, they disappear from the movie preview window.

Stopping the Animation

As you preview your file, you will notice that when your movie plays in the Test Movie mode, your animation keeps repeating. To make your animation stop after the first play-through, you have to add a **stop action**, which you do by adding an ActionScript behavior. **ActionScript** is the Flash programming language, just as HTML is the programming language of Dreamweaver and GoLive. To become proficient in Flash and create more advanced and complex projects, you'll need to learn ActionScript, but at this introductory level you'll need to learn only how to add one simple ActionScript behavior. First return to the Flash stage by clicking the tab at the top of the window.

To add a stop action at the end of an animation, first select the last keyframe of an animation. On the Properties panel, click the **Edit the action script for this object button** (see Figure 9-31). The Actions panel appears, as shown in Figure 9-32. In the top-left section of the panel are a series of preprogrammed **actions** you can apply to your animation, such as play or stop. Click the **Global Functions folder** and then click the **Timeline Control folder**. If necessary, scroll down until you see the "stop" action, and then double-click **stop**. You will see a stop command added to the list on the right as stop();. Close the Actions panel, and you will see a stylized letter "a" has been added to the keyframe. This is the stop action, and if you play your movie you will see that the animation will now stop after one play.

If you have more than one animation layer, it's best to create a separate layer and title it "action," then add the stop action to that layer's timeline, instead of adding a stop action to the end of every layer's timeline.

FIGURE 9-31
Edit the action script for this object

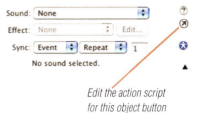

Edit the action script
for this object button

FIGURE 9-32
Actions panel

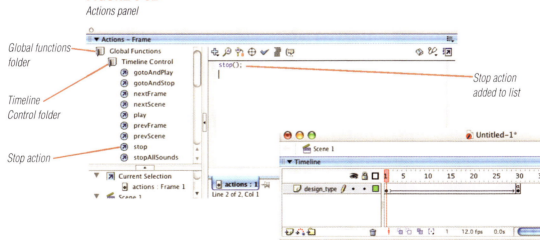

Global functions folder

Timeline Control folder

Stop action

Stop action added to list

Exporting to a Flash Movie

As you create your Flash project, you work in the Flash native file format, which has the file extension .fla. But to use your project on the Web, you have to export the file into a **Flash Movie format**. To do this, click **File** on the menu bar, point to **Export**, and then click **Export Movie.** The Export Movie dialog box opens (see Figure 9-33). Here you name the file and specify a save location and file format. Flash can export to several different formats, but by far the most common is the Flash Movie format, which has a **.swf** extension.

FIGURE 9-33

Export Movie dialog box

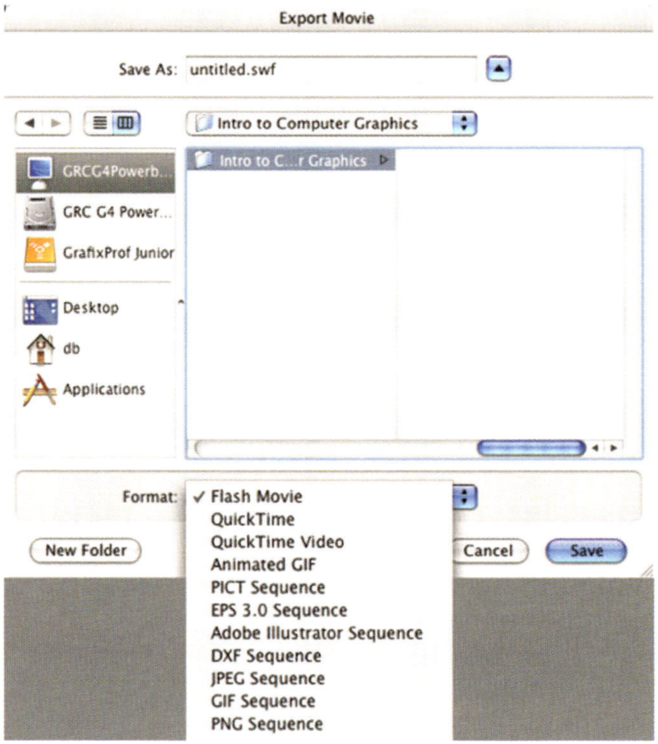

Click **Save,** and the Export Flash Player dialog box appears (see Figure 9-34), which lets you export down to earlier versions of the Flash Player and set certain parameters for your movie file. If you're using Flash at an introductory level, there is no need to change any of these settings, so click **OK.** Your file will be exported to the file format you chose. You can now import the .swf file as a part of a layout with other objects on a Dreamweaver or GoLive Web page, or you can import only the .swf file so that it appears to be an entire Web page on its own.

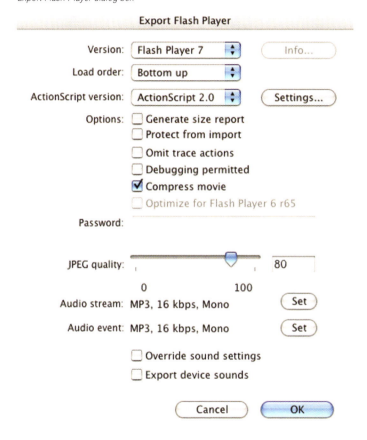

The addition of animation has created a new dimension to Web design. Flash is the leading application for creating Web animations from the simple to the complex. Flash lets you create a wide range of graphics and text, all of which can be converted to symbols and animated. The use of symbols and instances allows Flash files to remain small, making download speeds on the Web very fast. The timeline in Flash lets you create multiple animations, all in the same project. By working with keyframes and tweening, you can produce a wide array of animated effects. You can export any Flash project to the Flash Player format, the most common and widely used animation format on the Web. To view the animations shown below, connect to the Internet, go to www.course.com, navigate to the page for this book, click the Student Online Companion link, then click the link for this chapter.

KEY TERMS AND CONCEPTS

actions
ActionScript
Alpha
baseline
behavior
Brightness
defined text box
descenders
Flash Movie format
.fla
frame
frame rate
frames per second (fps)
GIF animations
Highlight color
instance
Java
keyframe
layer

Library
Macromedia Flash Player
modes
motion tween
play
Playhead
stage
static text
stop action
subscript
superscript
.swf
symbol
Test Movie
Timeline
Tint
Toolbox
tweening

1. What is a GIF animation?

   _____

   _____

   _____

2. Flash was the first Web animation software able to use what type of art?

   _____

3. When you open a new Flash document, what working area appears first on your screen?

   _____

4. How is the frame rate in Flash measured?

   _____

   _____

5. What three options are available when you use the Pencil tool?

   _____

   _____

   _____

6. What is a defined text box?

   _____

   _____

7. What is a symbol?

   _____

   _____

8. How is an instance different from a symbol?

   _____

   _____

9. What is the Library used for?

   _____

   _____

10. Name three ways you can modify an instance in the Color menu.

    _____

    _____

    _____

11. What designates the duration of an animation on the timeline?

    _____

    _____

    _____

12. What is a keyframe?

    _____

    _____

    _____

13. What is tweening?

_____

_____

_____

14. Name three ways you can preview an animation in Flash.

_____

_____

_____

15. What is ActionScript?

_____

_____

_____

16. What is the difference between the .fla format and the .swf format?

_____

_____

_____

The Building Blocks Preschool wants you to create a Flash animation for their Web site. They would like you to use the three basic design shapes—a circle, a square, and a triangle—and animate them so they move across the screen. Create a new document in Flash, and make the stage 600 pixels × 100 pixels. Use the Flash graphics tools to create a circle, a square, and a triangle. Convert each to a symbol and place each on its own layer. Animate each of the shapes to create a fun animation. Save your file as **building_blocks_1.fla**.

One Step Beyond

Add the words "Building Blocks Preschool" as a symbol, and animate the words along with the three shapes. Save this version as **building_blocks_2.fla**.

Two Steps Beyond

Separate each of the three words, make each a symbol, and place each on its own layer so you can animate each word individually. Save this version as **building_blocks_3.fla**. When you are finished, export your file as a Flash Player file, naming it building_blocks_3.swf.

As the Web designer for Graphics Unlimited, you have been asked to design a Web animation for a local skateboard company, Radical Wonders. Create a new Flash document that is 650 pixels × 250 pixels, and then draw three to five skateboards with some cool, contemporary designs on them. Use Flash to animate the skateboards to do some "radical" tricks. Save your file as **radical_wonders_1.fla**.

One Step Beyond

Add the words "Radical Wonders" in your project, making each letter a separate symbol, and animate each of the letters individually. Save this version as **radical_wonders_2.fla**.

Two Steps Beyond

Add a background color and additional graphics that match the young-skateboarder audience for this animation. Be as "wild and crazy" as you can. Save this version as **radical_wonders_3.fla**. When you are finished, export your file as a Flash Player file, naming it radical_wonders_3.swf.

Produce three animated Web banner ads that each promote a different holiday. Choose any three holidays and create your new documents at 468 pixels × 60 pixels, a standard Web banner ad size. Create graphics and copy that promote some aspect of each holiday, using appropriate type styles and color. Save your files as **holiday_one.fla**, **holiday_two.fla**, and **holiday_three.fla**, then export them to .swf files and view them using Flash Player. (To view the files below, connect to the Internet, go to www.course.com, navigate to the page for this book, click the Student Online Companion link, then click the link for this chapter.)

FIGURE 9-35

Possible Flash solutions

Figure 9-36 shows three examples of real-world Flash projects on Web pages. Look carefully at each project, and write a critique of how each project uses design and animation successfully. (To view the Web pages, connect to the Internet, go to www.course.com, navigate to the page for this book, click the Student Online Companion link, then click the link for this chapter.)

FIGURE 9-36

Examples of work done in Flash

Robert Hodgin
Flight 404 Web site
www.flight404.com

Jordan Dossett
Antharia Web site
www.antharia.com

David Trawin, Mickey
Delorenzo, and Diana Neary
Basic Function Web site
www.basicfunction.com

DIGITAL VIDEO SOFTWARE

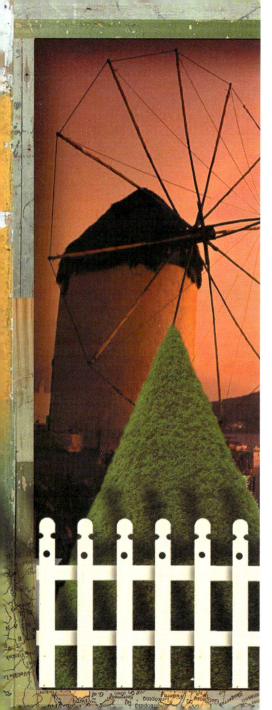

DIGITAL VIDEO SOFTWARE

The Joy of Film

You may remember creating your own simple "moving" pictures in school, drawing multiple copies of a stick figure, each one on a corner of your class notebook, with arms and legs in different positions in each version. Then you would bend the corner of the pages back just a little and flip through the pages... and your stick figure would suddenly come alive, running along to an unknown destination.

At the end of the 19th century, a few enterprising individuals decided that the concept of moving pictures could make money, and they developed nickelodeon machines like the one shown in Figure 10-1. For a nickel it would run a short flip book of still pictures showing a horse running, people swimming, or other everyday scenes. These nickelodeons were huge hits at amusement parks and fairs across the country.

The next step in the development of moving pictures was film. There are two teams of inventors that are generally credited with making the major advances in this area: The first team was the famous American inventor Thomas Alva Edison and his

talented British assistant, Kennedy Laurie Dickson. Their work, spearheaded by Dickson in Edison's West Orange, New Jersey, laboratory, produced the **Kinetoscope** in 1891. This device allowed a viewer to look through a small lens opening and view a strip of film moving continuously over a light source. The second team of inventors was Auguste and Louis Lumière, who many call the "founders of modern film." They created their own device, the **Cinematographe**, which was a combination movie camera and projector. This device was much more compact and lightweight than the Kinetoscope, and set the standard for similar devices developed over the next two decades.

These inventions eventually led to the development of the motion picture industry throughout the world. Two important films were produced during the first two decades of the 20th century: Edwin S. Porter's *The Great Train Robbery* (1903), which was the first film that used a storyline instead of simple everyday actions, and D. W. Griffith's *Birth of a Nation*, a shockingly racist and controversial film that many film scholars consider to be the most important film in American cinema history. Three hours long, it contained many new movie effects and technical innovations, including intercutting scenes from different storylines and the use of multiple locations, that were used for years after (see Figure 10-2).

Film Goes Digital

Over the years, moviemakers around the world have used film as a form of artistic expression, creating masterpieces that have become a part of our cultural history. But film production has always been a long, painstaking, and expensive process that relies on exposing and developing film and building the finished work through editing during a long post-production period. The 1950s saw the development of **video tape**, a digital recording medium which was a lower-quality, lower-cost alternative to high-quality movie film. Video tape permitted the recording of action and sound that could be played back immediately—without the need for chemical processing—making it ideal for live broadcasts and live news coverage. However, film had an advantage over video tape because it has a wider **dynamic range**, meaning it can capture a larger amount of information at higher quality, leading to the perception that film was more artistically valuable than video.

But like other technologies in visual communications, film has moved into the digital arena. Computers have created a more flexible and dynamic environment for editing and viewing video productions. New desktop applications make video creation and production available to anyone at almost any price level. In the early days of computer video applications, film producers had to start with traditional film and use specialized equipment to convert the film into digital files. But today there are hundreds of digital video cameras that can plug into any desktop computer using a **FireWire** connection, which allows for the transfer of digital images at very fast speeds. Digital video cameras are becoming more sophisticated and capture images at much higher quality than ever before.

FIGURE 10-2
A classic American film

By the early 1990s, digital video technology had become so widely accepted by video filmmakers and the general public that the motion picture industry had to catch up. In 2002, George Lucas released *Star Wars: Episode II*, the first feature-length motion picture using all digital cameras.

Two very similar video-editing applications are leading the rapid growth of desktop digital video: Apple Final Cut Express and Adobe Premiere. First introduced in 1991, Premiere is the veteran, whereas Final Cut Express was released early in 2003 (see Figure 10-3). Both applications are **nondestructive** (meaning they won't destroy the original video files) and **nonlinear** (meaning you can edit the content in any order you want), and can help you create professional-level video productions.

FIGURE 10-3

Apple Final Cut Express and Adobe Premiere

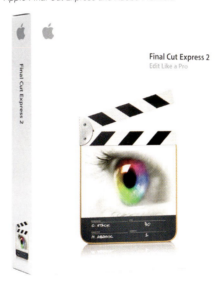

FINAL CUT EXPRESS AND PREMIERE: AN OVERVIEW

What You'll Learn

In this lesson, you will learn about the major features of Final Cut Express and Premiere.

Final Cut Express

Based on Apple's popular Final Cut Pro (which is used by professional film production companies), Final Cut Express (shown in Figure 10-4) is a full-featured digital video and audio editing and production application. Although it does not have all of the features of Final Cut Pro, Express lets you produce high-quality projects comparable to work done by professional editors.

Final Cut Express lets you plug your digital video camcorder directly into the FireWire port of your Macintosh computer. In the application's Capture Window, you specify whether you want to capture the entire video clip, or you can move through the clip and select only the parts you want to capture. Once you have placed a video clip in your Final Cut Express project, you can add numerous effects and filters without affecting the original source files, unlike film-based editing, in which you literally cut and splice film strips to create a production. Final Cut Express also supports nonlinear

editing. While film-based editing requires you to run through your entire film to find and edit the clips you want, Final Cut Express lets you access any video clip in any order you want, again without worrying about modifying your source files.

Final Cut Express provides you with a full range of professional editing tools. You also get more than 200 transitions and effects, and a computer with a fast processor can preview your edited files in real time. In addition, Final Cut Express lets you create professional-quality titling and titling effects. An additional titling option called Boris Calligraphy, lets you create unique 2-D and 3-D type effects.

Compositing (assembling images into the final video) is easy in Final Cut Express, with the tools you need to create up to 99 layers of video, graphics, and titles all at the same time. You can also work with up to 99 layers of audio tracks—using transitions, adjusting volume levels, and applying a three-band equalizer to craft the audio to your liking. Final Cut Express also has a built-in color-correction tool that can edit video clips shot under different lighting conditions so they all look the same. And you can export your finished video projects directly onto high-quality DVD disks.

Adobe Premiere

Adobe Premiere (see Figure 10-5) is the original nonlinear video editing application for desktop computers. It comes in two packages: Premiere Pro and Premiere Elements, a version with reduced features. Real-time video and audio editing tools and techniques let you create complex and powerful video presentations.

Premiere can capture and store video directly from any FireWire-equipped digital video camcorder. You can create multiple Timelines and manage them in the Timeline window. Powerful editing tools include razor, rolling edit, range select, cross fade, and transparency and motion adjustment. Numerous built-in transitions, filters, and special effects give you a high degree of creative control. Premiere also contains Adobe Title Designer, an advanced titling feature that lets you create many different types of titles and graphic effects. You can stretch, squeeze, distort, and slant type, and add animated effects such as rolling titles and crawls.

Advanced color-correction techniques also are available; you can adjust hue, saturation, and lightness, and also replace color to make different video clips match each other. Audio enhancements include precise audio editing for specific frames and sequences, and the ability to record live voice-over narration directly to your audio timeline.

Premiere also works closely with Adobe's other video production applications, including After Effects, Photoshop, Encore, and Audition. Premiere can import from and export to all major industry video formats, including delivering HD (high definition) content for video and television.

FIGURE 10-4
Apple Final Cut Express

FIGURE 10-5
Adobe Premiere

OPEN AND SAVE A PROJECT

What You'll Learn

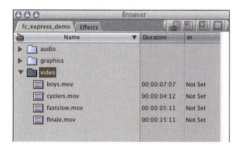

 In this lesson, you will learn how to create new projects in digital video applications.

Organizing Your Content

Before you start working in a digital video application, it's always best to organize your content. Depending on the complexity of the video you want to produce, you will have a number of source files that you will need to access, so you should collect them in one location. This collection of files is known as a **project**. The project will contain files that are known as clips. A **clip** can be a video, still photo, audio, or graphics file. A clip is not the source file itself, but a reference to the source file that you can modify without affecting the original source file. This is why both Final Cut Express and

Premiere are called nondestructive video editors: the source files remain intact throughout the editing process.

As you may have already guessed, video projects can become very complex, with dozens or even hundreds of clips. To help you organize a project's clips, both applications let you create folders within the project called **bins**. Figure 10-6 shows a project with the clips divided into three bins: audio, graphics, and video. Final Cut Express stores bins and clips in the Browser window; Premiere uses the Project window.

Create your story concepts first

Creating a video is like telling a story. As you learned in Chapter 7, storytelling is an important skill for those who want to get into the video and film industries. Before you create your video, use storyboards to help you determine the images you will need to shoot, and the dialog, music, sounds and effects you want to be part of your production. Like all planning, storyboards will help save you time and money; you then will focus your energy on obtaining only the material you need.

Creating a New Project

You launch Final Cut Express and Premiere the same way you launch the other programs in this book: by using the Dock or Application folder (Macintosh) or the Programs or All Programs menu (Windows). After you launch either program, you begin by specifying the **Project Settings**. These match up the input device and output file specifications based on broadcast industry standards for video. The two main standards are NTSC and PAL. **NTSC** (National Television System Committee) is the broadcast standard for the United States and North America. **PAL** (Phase Alternating Line) is the standard for Europe and many other parts of the world. Consider where you plan to distribute your video and select the appropriate standard. Figure 10-7 shows the Final Cut Express Easy Setup dialog box and the Premiere Load Project Settings dialog box where you can select a standard.

In this chapter, for any commands or buttons that are different between the two applications, the Final Cut Express term is listed first, with Premiere's terminology listed next, in parentheses.

When you select your project settings and click **Setup** (**OK**), both applications open several palettes (look back at Figures 10-4 and 10-5). You then save your project; as with other graphics applications, it's important to save your project in a project folder so you can track your work, and always save your work as you go. To save your project, click **File** on the menu bar and then click **Save Project** (**Save**), naming your project and selecting the folder where you want to store it.

FIGURE 10-6

Project, bins, and clips

Project name

Bins

Clips

Project name

Bins

Clips

Final Cut Express Browser window

FIGURE 10-7

New Project Settings

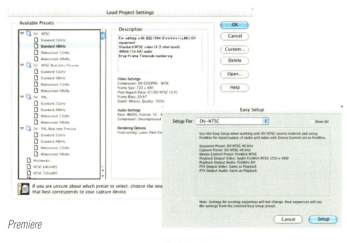

Premiere

Final Cut Expresss

BRING CLIPS INTO A PROJECT

What You'll Learn

In this lesson, you will learn how to bring clips into a video project.

Identifying Source Material

You can obtain source material in three ways:

1. You can create your own video images using a video camera. While this method is inexpensive and lets you capture exactly the material you want, it also takes time, especially if you don't have very much video or film experience. Also, you may not be able to shoot the exact footage you want; for example you may want to shoot a beach scene in Hawaii, but unless you can afford to fly there, you won't be able to get the shots you want.

2. You can use video material from an individual, company, or licensing agency that shoots video for companies and agencies and sells unused footage. You will have to get written permission and pay them a fee. Because their work is highly professional, it can be very expensive, up into the thousands of dollars. But you will probably be able to get footage that's quite close to what you want.

3. You can use **stock video**, which are collections of prerecorded videos on various subjects. Stock video is available in CD or DVD collections or online

Don't forget to consider copyrights!

Before you start collecting clips, it's important to understand that there are limits on the material you can use. Video, audio, and graphic content created by other individuals or companies have usually been protected by **copyright** laws intended to limit unauthorized use of intellectual property. Because of these laws, you can't record a television broadcast or a scene from your favorite movie and drop it into your video project without first getting permission. The same is true of music and graphics, especially company logos and similar graphic images.

through stock photography companies. With the rise in desktop video production, you now can purchase video clips in CD or DVD collections. Stock video fees are lower than those you would pay for an individual company's video. But be sure to read the "fine print" with any collection, which outlines permitted uses for the clips.

Bring in Video Directly from a Camera

Both Final Cut Express and Premiere let you connect directly to a digital video camcorder and download the video from the camera to your computer. To do this, click **File** on the menu bar and then click **Capture** (**Capture/Movie Capture**). As you can see in Figure 10-8, the Capture palette has a preview window on the left, which lets you play the video directly from the camera. Both applications let you import either the entire video or just portions of it, which can help control the size of your video files. You then can store the video files on your computer's hard drive or some other storage device that you can easily access once you start your production.

Video capture

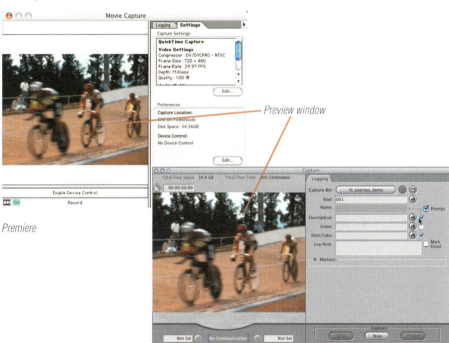

Preview window

Premiere

Final Cut Expresss

Import Video Files

Once you have captured video files from a camera or organized existing files and stored them on your computer, both Final Cut Express and Premiere let you import them into the program as clips: Click **File** on the menu bar, and then click **Import**. As you can see in Figure 10-9, both applications let you import individual files or import folders; you can use the folders as bins to organize your clips.

Audio File Formats

Both applications let you import audio files into your video project just as you would with a video file. Creating a separate bin for your audio files will help keep them organized. There are many different audio file formats that both Final Cut Express and Premiere can import, including .avi, .mov, .aiff, and .wav formats. Final Cut Express also supports the .cda format, which is the format used by the music industry for standard audio CDs. (Again, get permission if you want to use copyrighted recorded music.) To use this format in Premiere, you have to purchase an audio utility application that can convert the .cda format into one of the formats Premiere does recognize, then import the file into Premiere.

FIGURE 10-9

Import files and folders

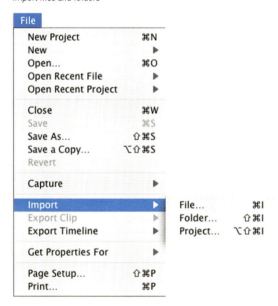

Premiere

Final Cut Expresss

Graphics File Formats

Although Final Cut Express and Premiere can be used to create graphics, the tools and commands available are very basic. Most video producers use applications such as Photoshop, FreeHand, Illustrator, CorelDRAW, and Fireworks to create project graphics. Final Cut Express and Premiere can work with a variety of graphics formats, including .psd, .ai, .gif, .jpg, .pict, .tga, and .tif. You also can import pre-existing graphics into Final Cut Express and Premiere, but make sure you do not use copyrighted graphics without obtaining permission. Figure 10-10 shows a graphic in Premiere that uses gradients.

FIGURE 10-10
Gradients in Premiere

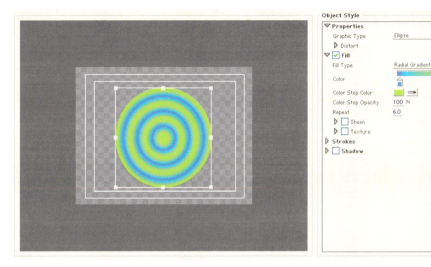

FIGURE 10-10
Gradients in Premiere

Video file size

Video files are extremely large compared to traditional print graphics or Web-based images. The average digital video occupies 3.6 MB of disk space per second of video time. This would mean a one-minute video file would be 3.6 MB/sec × 60 seconds = 216 MB of hard drive space. A 10-minute video would be 3.6 MB/sec × 60 seconds × 10 minutes = 2.16 GB of hard drive space. So you can see how quickly your hard drive would fill up after only a couple of video projects. Video producers often have to add a large amount of hard drive capacity to work on and store their video productions.

WORK WITH CLIPS ON THE TIMELINE

What You'll Learn

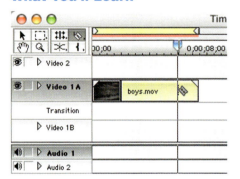

In this lesson, you will learn how to bring your clips into the Timeline and work with them.

Timeline Basics

The **Timeline** is where you do the majority of work in a video project. You bring clips into the Timeline, position and size them, and then add effects and controls. Figure 10-11 shows the Premiere and Final Cut Express Timelines, which work similarly. Figure 10-12 shows that the Premiere Timeline is divided into a video section at the top and an audio section at the bottom. Along the top of the Timeline is the length of time the project is running, also called the **duration**. The Timeline in this figure has two video tracks and three audio tracks. Both Final Cut Express and Premiere can handle up to 99 video and audio tracks per project.

There are two different ways you can edit clips on the Timeline: single-track editing and A/B editing, shown in Figure 10-13. In **single-track editing**, the video clips and the transitions that move from one clip to another are laid out in one continuous line

on one track (Video 1) from left to right. In **A/B editing**, there are three subtracks within the one main track (Video 1); the top and bottom subtracks are for video clips, which can be laid out in a staggered fashion. The transitions are positioned on their own subtrack, matching the space where the clips overlap each other on the Timeline. The two formats work the same and provide the same results, but some editors prefer one over the other. This chapter uses the A/B track method to demonstrate work on the Timeline.

Dragging Clips to the Timeline

To start working on the Timeline, go to the Browser (Project) window, click a clip to select it, and then click-and-drag the clip onto the Timeline. In Figure 10-14 the boys.mov clip has been dragged onto the Video 1A track on the Timeline. You can drag any additional clips to the Timeline in any order you wish. Both Final Cut Express and Premiere have a

FIGURE 10-11

Timelines

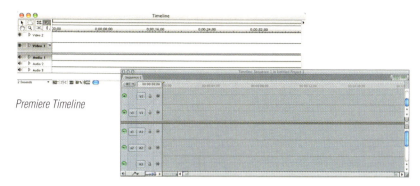

Premiere Timeline

Final Cut Express Timeline

FIGURE 10-12

Sections of a Premiere Timeline

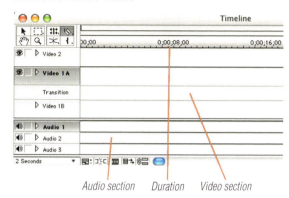

Audio section   Duration   Video section

FIGURE 10-13

Single-track and A/B editing

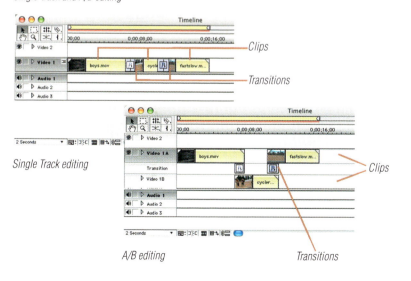

Clips

Transitions

Single Track editing

Clips

A/B editing

Transitions

FIGURE 10-14

Moving a clip onto the Timeline

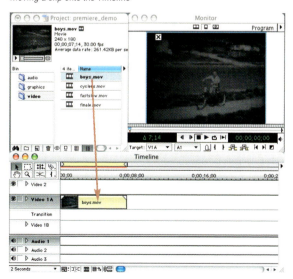

Concept 4   Work with Clips on the Timeline

Selection tool (Figure 10-15) that lets you select the clip and move it anywhere along the track. To delete a clip from the track, select it and then press **[Delete]**. When you delete a clip the original is still in your project bin; you can always drag it back on to the Timeline.

Editing Your Clips

Now that you have a clip on the Timeline, you can edit it to suit the needs of your video presentation. You can cut a clip into different pieces or copy the clip (or parts of it) as many times as you want. To cut your clip into pieces, you use the Razor Blade (Razor) tool, shown in Figure 10-15. You can determine where to cut your clip by running the Playhead back and forth across your clip until you find the spot to cut. The **Playhead** is located in the same area of your Timeline as the time listings.

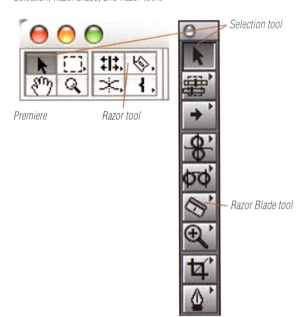

FIGURE 10-15
Selection, Razor Blade, and Razor tools

Selection tool

Premiere

Razor tool

Razor Blade tool

Final Cut Express

Adding titles

Titles are text and graphics you can add to your video file, and they can add a new level of communication to your videos. You might use titles to include credits, commentary, or historical background. In Premiere, you create titles using Adobe Title Designer, a separate application. To start the Title Designer program, click the **Create Item button** in the Premiere Project window, and then use the Selection, Text, Pen, and Shape tools to create title content. Any titles you create are saved with a .prtl file extension. When you save a title, Premiere adds it to the Project window of your current Premiere project. Final Cut Express uses a special area within the application called the Text Generator to create titles. You can open this area using the Effects tab of the Browser palette.

The left side of Figure 10-16 shows the Playhead being moved so that one section of the video clip, showing a boy riding a bicycle, is played in the Monitor window. The **Monitor** is like a small television screen, allowing you to preview any clip along your project's Timeline. On the right side of Figure 10-16, the Playhead has been moved slightly, showing that the video suddenly changes to a different boy riding a bicycle. Notice that the Playhead extends a black line down into the track area of the Timeline. This lets you line up your cut with the Razor Blade (Razor) tool accurately. Figure 10-17 shows the video being cut; each piece can now be moved and positioned anywhere along the track, moved to another track, or deleted from the track.

FIGURE 10-16

Moving the Playhead

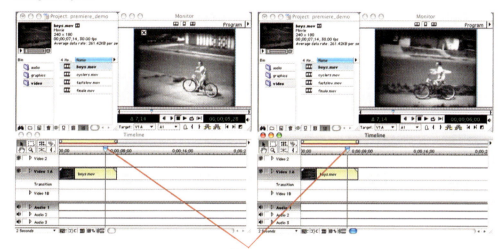

Playhead

FIGURE 10-17

Clip being cut

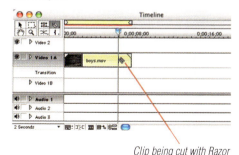

Clip being cut with Razor Blade (Razor) tool

DESIGNTIP   Creating a rough cut

Before you get too involved with editing and adding more involved effects, consider creating a **rough cut**. This is a preliminary version of your project that has the video clips positioned on the Timeline in the proper order, but with little else added. A rough cut lets you see how your story is coming and if you need to make large-scale changes in the story before you spend time creating special effects.

DEVELOP TRANSITIONS

What You'll Learn

 In this lesson, you will learn how to add and modify transitions on the Timeline.

Adding Transitions

As you add video clips to your project, you will need to decide what transitions you want to use between the clips. If you position one clip to start as soon as the first clip ends, the viewer will see a sudden change from one clip to the next. **Transitions** are effects that allow for a visual change from one video clip to another video clip in your project. Both Final Cut Express and Premiere have a library of transitions you can use anywhere in your project.

Adding Transitions to the Timeline

Final Cut Express lists transitions in the Effects panel in the Browser window;

Premiere lists them in the Transitions panel (see Figure 10-18). There are many transitions to choose from. As you work in either application, you will become more familiar with how each transition works. Figure 10-19 shows some of the more popular transitions.

You determine the length of a transition by the amount of overlap of the video clip on Track 1A and the video clip on Track 1B. The more overlap, the longer the transition between the two clips; less overlap creates a shorter transition. To add a transition, click-and-drag the transition from the Effects (Transitions) panel onto the Transition track. The transition then will occupy the overlap space, as shown in Figure 10-20.

> **DESIGN TIP** **Don't overdo transitions**
>
> Although transitions can add a lot of visual interest to a video production, you must be careful not to add too many transitions to your project. You want your audience to focus on the content of your production; too many transitions can distract the viewer and create a choppy video that's hard to follow. Think carefully about each transition and how each transition fits your overall artistic vision.

Modifying Transitions

As you work on your project, you may decide to change the transition duration between two video clips. To do this, you adjust the overlap distance between the two clips on the Timeline. Select the transition with the Selection tool, move the pointer over either end of the transition, and then click-and-drag to lengthen or shorten the transition.

FIGURE 10-18

Transitions and Effects panels

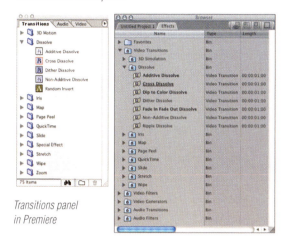

*Transitions panel
in Premiere*

Effects panel in Final Cut Express

FIGURE 10-19

Different transitions

Cross Dissolve

Iris Diamond

Page Peel

Band Slide

FIGURE 10-20

Adding a transition

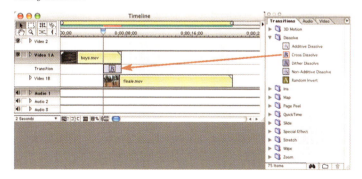

Each transition also has its own settings that you can adjust by double-clicking the transition icon on the Timeline, which opens the Cross Dissolve Settings dialog box for that transition, shown in Figure 10-21. In the transition dialog box, you can adjust how quickly or slowly the transition dissolves out of the first video clip, or how quickly the transition dissolves into the second video clip.

Previewing Your Work

As you add transitions to your Timeline, you will notice that as you move the Playhead, your transitions don't play in the monitor. Although saving your file saves other changes you make outside the Timeline, it does not save work you do on the Timeline. To view your Timeline changes in the monitor, you first have to **render the Timeline.**

FIGURE 10-21
Transitions settings

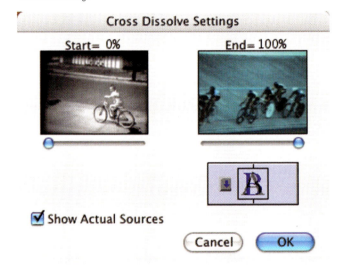

DESIGNTIP   **Render in small chunks**

As you progress through your production you will find that rendering large portions of your Timeline takes a lot of time. Consider rendering after you have completed a few changes in your project so you don't have to wait a long time for your project to render.

Figure 10-22 shows a Timeline at the top with a red bar going across, indicating that work has been done that needs to be rendered. The Timeline at the bottom of Figure 10-22 shows a green bar going across the Timeline, indicating that the Timeline has been rendered. In Final Cut Express, you click **Sequence** on the menu bar, and then click **Render** or **Render all**. In Premiere, you click **Timeline** on the menu bar, and then click **Render Work area**. The amount of time the rendering process takes depends on the amount of work on the Timeline you are rendering and the speed of your computer. Figure 10-23 shows a rendering in progress in Final Cut Express and Premiere. Once your Timeline has been rendered, you can preview your transitions.

FIGURE 10-22
Unrendered and rendered Timelines

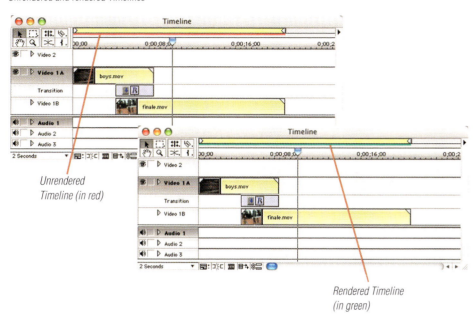

Unrendered Timeline (in red)

Rendered Timeline (in green)

FIGURE 10-23
Rendering a Timeline

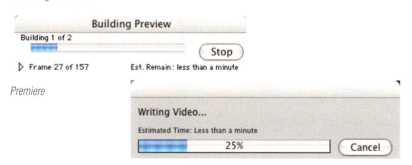

Premiere

Final Cut Express

WORK WITH SOUND

What You'll Learn

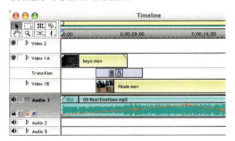

In this lesson, you will learn how to add and modify sound in your digital video project.

Adding Sounds to the Timeline

The process of adding sound to your project is very similar to adding video. First you need to add the **audio** (sound) files to your collection of resource files for the project; creating a bin just for audio files can help you keep track of them. On your project's Timeline, there are tracks dedicated to audio. They are separated from the video tracks and appear at the bottom of the Timeline. To add an audio clip, drag the clip from the Browser (Project) window onto the Timeline, as shown in Figure 10-24.

Editing an Audio Clip

Once you've placed an audio clip on the Timeline, you can move it anywhere along the Timeline using the Selection tool. By dragging the Playhead back and forth you can hear the audio and decide what parts of the audio clip you want to use. To use only part of the audio clip, cut it using the Razor Blade (Razor) tool. You can cut the audio segments any way you want, as well as copy or delete individual segments.

You can also adjust the volume of any audio clip on the Timeline. This technique, called **rubber banding**, lets you fine-tune your audio. First expand the audio clip view by clicking on the triangle to the left of the Audio 1 title (see Figure 10-25). This lets you access the rubber band controls, which appear as one continuous red line running through the middle of the audio track, as shown in Figure 10-25. You add **anchor points** to the rubber band that let you control a clip's volume at certain locations: Use the Selection tool and click along the rubber band (see Figure 10-26). Then drag each anchor point up or down along the audio clip, which increases or decreases the audio clip's volume. Figure 10-27 shows an audio clip that starts silent, slowly builds in volume, then fades down to a quieter volume. You also can put two audio clips on different tracks, and by overlapping the two clips and using rubber banding you can fade out one audio clip and fade in a second one, creating a gradual transition from one sound to another.

FIGURE 10-24

Adding an audio clip

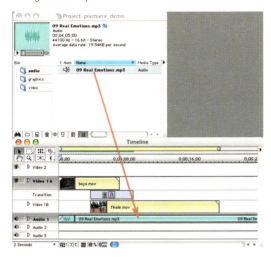

FIGURE 10-25

Expanded audio clip with rubber band

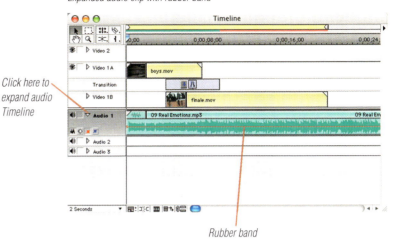

Click here to expand audio Timeline

Rubber band

FIGURE 10-26

Adding anchor points to a rubber band

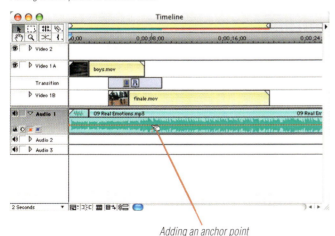

Adding an anchor point

FIGURE 10-27

Changing volume of an audio clip

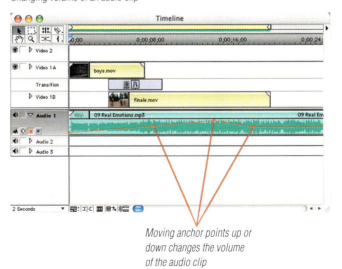

Moving anchor points up or down changes the volume of the audio clip

EXPORT FILES FOR CD AND MONITOR PRESENTATIONS

What You'll Learn

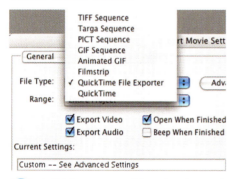

 In this lesson, you will learn how to export your video project so it can be viewed on CD or on a monitor.

Exporting Your Video Project

Once your project is completed, you will do a final rendering of the entire project, which finalizes all your edits and transitions and makes your project ready to export. When you **export** your project, the application takes all the edited video and audio clips, along with all of the transitions and effects you've added, and puts them together into one seamless video file.

To export a project in Premiere, click **File** on the menu bar, click **Export Timeline**, and then click **Movie**. In Final Cut Express, click **File** on the menu bar, click **Export**, and then click **Quicktime Movie**

(to export directly to a Quicktime format) or click Using Quicktime Conversion (to export to Quicktime or to other formats). When you select Using Quicktime Format, the Save dialog box in Figure 10-28 opens. In Premiere, the Export Movie dialog box appears; you then can click the **Settings button** and the dialog box shown in Figure 10-29 opens. Both dialog boxes let you choose several formats to which you can export your project. By far the most popular format is **Quicktime**, a movie file format commonly used for CD presentations as well as on the Web. For CD presentations you can burn the Quicktime

---

Working project versus exported video

As you are creating your project, you will be dealing with a working file that keeps track of all of your source files, clips, and edits. When you export your project it will become one seamless movie, with all of your work pulled together into one complete file. You cannot modify your exported movie; if you want to make any changes to your movie you have to go back to the original working file, make the changes there, then render and export your project again.

movie file of your project onto a CD; anyone viewing your movie only needs to have the Quicktime movie player installed in their computer. Quicktime movie files also can be embedded into Web pages and viewed over the Web. Final Cut Express also can export to an MPEG-4 format, which is another popular Web video format, and Premiere can export to a GIF animation format, another format used on the Web.

Both applications let you export your project to video tape, so it can be played on traditional tape-based video devices, such as VHS or other formats. This process requires you to have the necessary equipment, like a video tape camcorder or a VHS video tape recorder/player and the proper plugs and adapters, to connect to your computer so you can record to video tape. If you do have the correct setup you can click **File** on the menu bar, and then click **Print to Video** (Final Cut Express) or click **File** on the menu bar, click **Export Timeline**, and then click **Print to Video** (Premiere), and you can transfer your project to video tape media.

FIGURE 10-28
Final Cut Express Export dialog box

FIGURE 10-29
Premiere Export Movie Settings dialog box

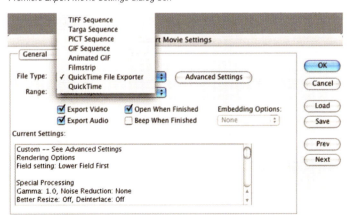

Professionally produced movies have been with us for more than 100 years, but the development of digital video on personal computers has made moving pictures available for anyone to use. Whether you have video on tape or on a digital camcorder, Final Cut Express and Premiere can take your work and produce video projects from the simple to the complex. You can bring in video, audio, still images, and graphics and organize them using bins. Then you can move them onto the Timeline and manipulate them, without affecting the original source files. You also can use an array of transitions to create unique changes between video clips, and cut, copy, and position clips anywhere within a project. You then can add, cut, and position audio clips and adjust the clips to create a unique musical soundtrack, sound effects, and transitions. When you are finished developing a video file, you can export it to CD or for Web presentations; you also can put it on a standard video tape. (To view the site shown below, connect to the Internet, go to www.course.com, navigate to the page for this book, click the Student Online Companion link, then click the link for this chapter.)

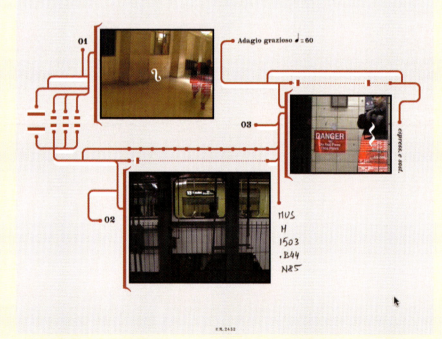

A/B editing
anchor points
audio
bins
Cinematographe
clip
compositing
copyright
duration
dynamic range
export
FireWire
Kinetoscope
monitor
nondestructive
nonlinear

NTSC
PAL
Playhead
project
Project Settings
Quicktime
render the Timeline
rough cut
rubber banding
single-track editing
stock photography
stock video
Timeline
titles
transitions
video tape

1. What is a nickelodeon machine?

   _____

   _____

   _____

2. What machine did Thomas Alva Edison and Kennedy Laurie Dickson develop?

   _____

3. Which two people are considered the "founders of modern film?"

   _____

   _____

4. Name two important American films created during the first two decades of the 20th century?

   _____

   _____

5. What is the dynamic range of film?

   _____

   _____

   _____

6. What is a project in Final Cut Express and Premiere?

   _____

   _____

   _____

7. What is a clip?

   _____

   _____

8. What is a bin?

   _____

   _____

9. What are the two main broadcast industry standards for input device and output file specifications?

   _____

   _____

10. How much hard drive space would a 30-minute video file take up?

   _____

   _____

   _____

11. What is stock video?

   _____

   _____

   _____

12. What is the difference between single-track and A/B editing?

_____

_____

_____

13. How do you cut video clips into pieces on the Timeline?

_____

_____

14. What does the Playhead do?

_____

_____

_____

15. What are transitions?

_____

_____

_____

16. Why do you have to render the Timeline?

_____

_____

_____

17. What is rubber banding?

_____

_____

_____

Cawabunga Surf Shop wants you to create a 30-second video for their company. They have provided you with one audio and five video clips. The video files IG 10-1.mov, IG 10-2.mov, IG 10-3.mov, IG 10-4.mov, IG 10-5.mov, and the audio file IG 10-6.mp3 are located where the Data Files are stored for this chapter. You also will need to open and print the file IG 10-7.pdf, a storyboard layout. Review the files and create a storyboard of your proposed video, showing which clips you will use, in what order you will use them, and whether you will be cutting any of the clips into smaller portions.

One Step Beyond

Create a new project in your digital video application, bringing all six files into your project. Re-create your storyboard on the Timeline using the five video clips. View the assembled clips as a rough cut, and then add transitions to make your project flow from one clip to the next. Save this version as **cawabunga_video_1**.

Two Steps Beyond

Add the audio file to your Timeline, cutting and positioning your music to go along with and enhance the video. Save this version as **cawabunga_video_2**.

Paul Revere Junior High School has hired you to produce a one-minute video promoting their music programs. They can provide you with five video files for you to use. Use the files IG 10-8.mov, IG 10-9.mov, IG 10-10.mov, IG 10-11.mov, and IG 10-12.mov, in the location where your Data Files are stored. Review the files and create a storyboard of your proposed video using file IG 10-7.pdf. Show which clips you will use, in what order you will use them, and whether you will be cutting any of the clips into smaller portions.

One Step Beyond

Create a new project in your digital video application, bringing all five video files into your project. Attempt to re-create your storyboard on the Timeline using the video clips, creating a presentation that promotes their music program. Add transitions to your project as well. Save this version as **revere_video_1**.

Two Steps Beyond

Find one or two songs that you think would work well for this video. Import the file or files into your project, then add the audio clip(s) to your Timeline, cutting and positioning your music to go along with and enhance the video. Save this version as **revere_video_2**.

You want to create a 3-minute video about an environmental issue. It can be anything from noise pollution to water purity to deforestation or overpopulation.

1. Develop a storyboard that will help you determine the theme and approach, as well as the footage you will need.
2. Go out with a digital video camcorder and shoot the video footage that you want to include.
3. Find prerecorded sounds or music that supports the environmental theme and video footage you have chosen. (If you have a microphone that connects to your computer, consider recording a sound file to provide a brief narration, then import the file into your project.)
4. Bring all of your video and audio clips into your digital video application and create a three-minute video presentation, using your video images and sound to express and bring attention to your chosen issue. Save your project as **environment_video** and export the file as a Quicktime movie, naming that file **environment_video.mov**. See Figure 10-30 for a possible solution.

(The movie file shown below is included in the Chapter 10 folder in the location where you store your Data Files.)

FIGURE 10-30
Possible digital video solution

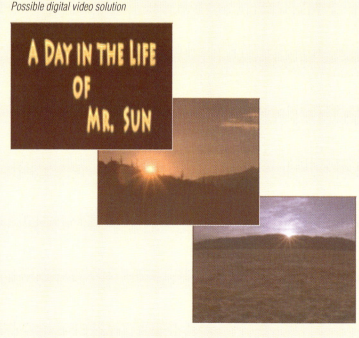

Figure 10-31 shows two examples of real-world digital video projects presented on Web pages. Look carefully at each project, and write a critique of how each project uses design and motion successfully. (To view the sites shown below, connect to the Internet, go to www.course.com, navigate to the page for this book, click the Student Online Companion link, then click the link for this chapter.)

FIGURE 10-31
Possible digital video solutions

Tubatomic Studio
The Beautiful Mistake Player
The Beautiful Mistake EP and the
Tubatomic Studio Web site
www.tubatomic.com

The Subservient Chicken
The Barbarian Group
for Burger King
www.barbariangroup/com

CHAPTER 11

MULTIMEDIA SOFTWARE

MULTIMEDIA SOFTWARE

Bringing Disciplines Together

The term **multimedia** refers to the use of two or more media to make a visual presentation. In fine art this has usually described the combination of different materials, such as using oil paint and real pine needles to create a forest scene, merging the illusion of the painting with the reality of actual forest material. A **collage**, a combination of various objects and materials pasted onto a flat surface, is a good example of a fine arts-based multimedia work.

Today the definition of multimedia has expanded to include the combination of art and technology to produce new visual concepts. Randall Packer and Ken Jordan's book *Multimedia: From Wagner to Virtual Reality*, traces the beginnings of this type of multimedia back to the famous German composer Richard Wagner (see Figure 11-1). They state that as early as 1849, Wagner believed that the future of music, and of all of the arts, lay in the "collective art-work," a combining of all of the arts into a synthesis known as the *Gesamtkunstwerk*, the total artwork.

To this end, Wagner opened the Festspielhaus Theater in Bayreuth, Germany, in 1876. This famous theater had many technical innovations, including the darkening of the theater during performances, an orchestra pit, surround-sound reverberance, and an amphitheater-style seating arrangement that forced the audience's view to the stage. Packer and Jordan believe this "virtual" world approach made Wagner the true pioneer of today's concepts of multimedia.

Combining Visuals with Technology

The most significant advances in multimedia occurred during the second half of the 20th century with the development of the computer. In the 1960s, artists started to explore how visual creativity could be combined with the power of electronic technology. They began to use computers to combine text, graphics, video, animation, and sound in an integrated way. The ability to work with different media elements within one electronic "project" requires a programming language that can track these elements, determine the order of presentation, and manage how each element will be presented, which depends on whether the element is a piece of text, a graphic, a video, an animation, or a sound.

The first application with multimedia capabilities was **HyperCard**, a relatively simple application developed by Bill Atkinson in 1987 (see Figure 11-2). Apple Computer provided HyperCard free with every Macintosh computer they sold. The application was easy to use and was an instant success. HyperCard creates a collection, or **stack**, of electronic cards that can contain fields of information. These fields can include backgrounds (of color or images), pictures, text, and buttons that can be programmed to jump from one card to another. HyperCard's programming language, **HyperTalk**, was easy to learn because it used plain English instead of complex programming codes and commands. For example, if you wanted to find all of the cards that contained the words "fine art", you would simply type *find "fine art"*. HyperCard was used as a presentation program, similar to an electronic slide show, that could be projected onto a screen and presented to an audience. It was also used to create computer games and educational presentations.

FIGURE 11-1
Richard Wagner

A program similar to HyperCard is Microsoft's popular **PowerPoint** application. Like HyperCard, PowerPoint also works on the concept of an electronic slide show, with each slide being able to contain text, graphics, video, and sound. Originally developed for business users, PowerPoint now has many personal and professional uses. Developed and released in early 1987 by a small software company called Forethought, PowerPoint 1.0 was a black-and-white application that ran only on Macintosh computers. In late 1987, Forethought was bought out by Microsoft, which released a Windows version in 1988. Since then, PowerPoint has been sold as part of Microsoft's popular Microsoft Office suite of business applications, which has made it the world's most widely used presentation application.

FIGURE 11-2

Simple HyperCard presentation

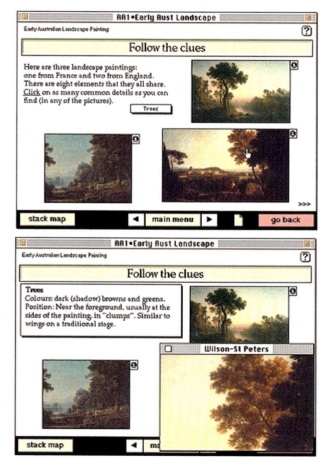

The Development of Director

In 1985, a small company named MacroMind developed an application called VideoWorks. Running only on the Macintosh computer, it was a simple animation program that let you create animated movies. MacroMind renamed the application Director in 1988. Director 1.0 introduced full-color graphics and high-quality sound, along with its own programming language called **Lingo**, which was much more powerful than its competitor, HyperTalk. By 1995, MacroMind had become Macromedia, and more than 70% of all multimedia CD titles were produced using Director. In 1996, Macromedia added the **Shockwave Player**, a browser plug-in that allows Director movies to be played over the Internet, expanding a designer's ability to create interactive content for any Web site. Today, Director (see Figure 11-3) has became the dominant application for integrating different digital media into one presentation.

FIGURE 11-3
Macromedia Director

DIRECTOR: AN OVERVIEW

What You'll Learn

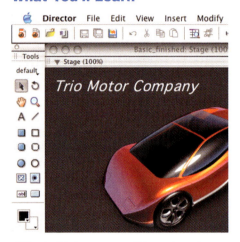

In this lesson, you will learn about the major features of Macromedia Director.

How Macromedia Director Is Used

Macromedia Director has become the application of choice for professional developers who create electronic multi-media presentations and applications. Director-based presentations, called **movies**, can provide content for an almost unlimited number of uses, including online and CD-based games, product and sales pieces, computer-based education, corporate demonstrations, corporate reporting, and training. Director movies can then be distributed on CDs and DVDs, freestanding information centers (called **kiosks**), and more.

Director Tools and Features

Director (shown in Figure 11-4) has a complete set of tools you can use to create text and graphic content from scratch. This content can become part of a collection of images in a Director movie. You can also include elements from other applications, including drawn and photographic images, video, audio and music, animations, and 3-D images. Any of these elements can be animated in Director, and then synchronized to sound, music, or video. Director uses both Lingo and JavaScript to let advanced users program almost any interactive effect imaginable.

For less-experienced users, Director has many preprogrammed behaviors and actions to add interactivity to your movie. You can create 3-D text and other 3-D elements, as well as import images from other 3-D modeling applications. You can also import Flash animation movie files and play them in your Director movie file.

Director can export your movie to a standalone "projector" file, which you can burn to CD or DVD and play back on any computer without requiring Director. You can export the same movie to a Shockwave format file for viewing on the Web. Director also provides accessibility features for users with hearing or visual impairments.

FIGURE 11-4
Macromedia Director

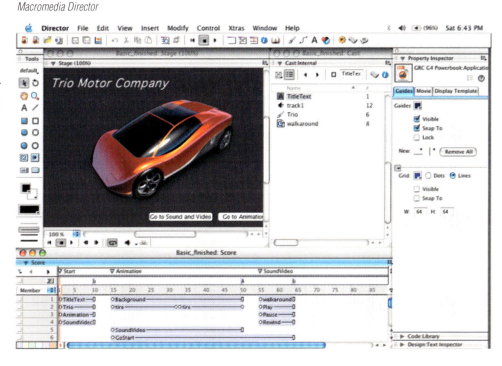

CREATE A NEW MOVIE

What You'll Learn

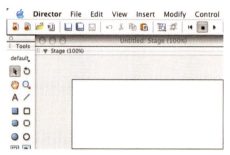

In this lesson, you will learn how to create a new movie file in Director.

Getting Your Content Together

As you create your movie, you will add many different files. The power of Director is its ability to work with so many external file formats. The file formats that Director can import are listed in Table 11-1.

Creating a New Movie

To create a new movie, launch Director, click **File** on the menu bar, point to **New**, and then click **Movie**. Your screen will look similar to that shown in Figure 11-5. (If your screen does not display the Stage,

Cast, or Score, click **Window** on the menu bar, point to **Panel Sets**, then click **Director 8**.) The Property Inspector displays information on any selected object in your movie. Figure 11-6 shows the properties for a new movie project.

You can modify several **movie properties** in the Property Inspector on the Movie tab, including the size of the **stage** (the work area background), the number of **channels** (individual timelines for each element), the stage color, and the **palette** (color model) to be used in your movie.

TABLE 11-1: Importable file formats

Text files	ASCII, RTF, HTML, scripts in Lingo and JavaScript
Still images	Photoshop 3.0 or later, TIFF, PICT, BMP, GIF, JPEG, PNG, Targa, LRG (xRes), and MacPaint
Animation and multimedia	Animated GIFs, Flash movies (.swf), and Director movies (.dir)
Video	Quicktime 2 or later, AVI, RealMedia, Windows Media, and DVD
Sound	AIFF, WAV (compressed and uncompressed), MP3, Shockwave Audio, and AU

You can also specify whether you want to use RGB or Index color. **Index color** is based on an RGB color model but contains only 256 colors, making it perfect for use on the Web. **Preferred 3-D Renderer** lets you choose the best 3-D rendering method for imported 3-D graphics for the computer hardware you are using. The About and Copyright areas let you identify your movie when it is being played, and Font Map lets you save a listing of the fonts used in your movie, so the correct fonts can be accessed whether your movie is played on a Macintosh or a Windows system.

The size of the stage is an important consideration; the size you choose will depend on the size of the monitor or display your movie will be shown on. Be sure to verify this information before you start building your movie. If your movie is going on the Web, then standard sizes for banner ads and Web sites (like 800 pixels × 600 pixels) would be appropriate. Once you have selected the properties for your movie, you can save it into the appropriate location on your computer. Director movie files have a .dir file extension.

FIGURE 11-5

Director desktop

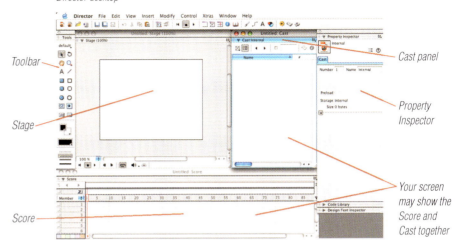

Toolbar

Stage

Score

Cast panel

Property Inspector

Your screen may show the Score and Cast together

FIGURE 11-6

Properties for a new movie

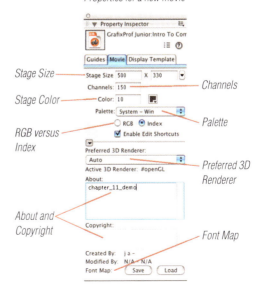

Stage Size

Stage Color

RGB versus Index

About and Copyright

Channels

Palette

Preferred 3D Renderer

Font Map

CREATE GRAPHICS AND TEXT

What You'll Learn

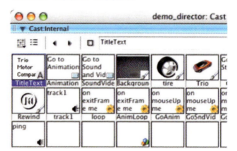

 In this lesson, you will learn how to use the various graphics and text tools in Director.

Everything Is a Sprite

As you create new graphics or text in Director, you will start to develop a collection of images and text for your movie. These images are collected in a cast, as shown in Figure 11-7. A **cast**, similar to a Library in Flash, is the storage location where you assemble all the components you want to use in your movie. A **cast member** is an image or piece of text; to add a cast member to your movie, drag it over the stage. Each cast member can be used over and over again in your movie. Every time you drag a cast member onto the stage, it then becomes a sprite. A **sprite** works the same as an instance in Flash: It is a reference back to the original cast member. You can create as many sprites of the same cast member as you want, and each sprite can have its own set of properties on the stage.

You will learn more about the cast, cast members, and sprites later in this chapter. For now, it's important to at least understand the concept that every graphic or text that you create in Director becomes a cast member; when you use it, it becomes a sprite.

Graphics Tools

Director has several tools, shown in Figure 11-8, that let you create graphics:

Arrow tool—This is Director's selection tool. Use it to select, move, and resize sprites on the stage.

Rotate and Skew tool—Use this tool to rotate or skew any sprite.

Magnifying Glass tool—This tool lets you zoom in or out to get a closer or wider view of your work on the stage.

Line tool—This tool lets you create lines to which you can apply different thicknesses, colors, and styles.

Filled Rectangle, Filled Round Rectangle, and Filled Ellipse tools—Each shape you create with these tools will have a fill of whatever color or texture you apply to it, but no stroke.

Rectangle, Round Rectangle, and Ellipse tools—Each of these shapes will have a stroke of whatever color and thickness you apply to it, but no fill; it will be transparent.

Whenever you create a graphic in Director, the Property Inspector changes to show its properties. Figure 11-9 shows a red rectangle selected on the stage, with its properties displayed in the Property Inspector.

FIGURE 11-7

A cast

Cast members

FIGURE 11-8

Graphics tools

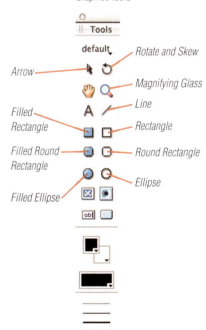

Text Tools

Director has three ways of handling text, depending on the effect you want in your movie. A Director movie can contain:

Regular text—This is the same type of text as in word processing or graphics software. Regular text you create in Director is easy to edit and format; you can resize it and it will still look smooth and clean. Director lets you apply only a few special effects to text, because text with special effects requires more time to download and view in your movie. Regular text can also be used as a link to a Web page.

Field text—This is low-resolution text that has one major benefit: It can be downloaded rapidly and viewed on older, slower computers without loss of speed. But field text is usable only at smaller sizes and has few formatting or effects options to choose from.

Bitmapped text—This is not text but a graphic of text. Because it is a bitmap, you can apply many different gradients, patterns, and effects such as rotate, skew, distort, and warp. But because it's a bitmap, you cannot make it larger in Director or it will start to get jagged edges. You can also use bitmapped text from other applications such as Photoshop, where you can apply more type effects than you can using bitmapped text created in Director.

FIGURE 11-9
Selected graphic and its properties

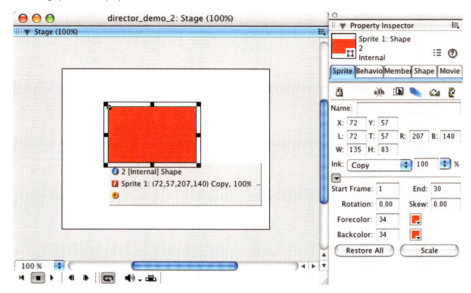

DESIGNTIP **Director can do vector shapes and more**

Hidden away in Director's Window menu is a panel called the Vector Shape panel. This panel lets you create and modify many types of vector graphics from within Director, using a Pen tool, and modify existing vector graphics you have imported from other applications. You can also specify gradient blends, as shown in Figure 11-10.

To work with text in Director, use the Text tool in the Toolbar and the Text Inspector panel. To open this panel, click **Window** on the menu bar, and then click **Text Inspector** (see Figure 11-11). Use the Text tool to create new text and the Arrow tool to select and modify text. The Text Inspector lets you change the text style and size; change text to bold, italic, or underlined; and change its alignment (left, center, right, or justified). You can also change the text color, adjust the kerning (spacing between letters) and the leading (vertical spacing between lines of type), and apply a link to a Web page.

Importing Graphics from Fireworks

Although you can create a variety of graphics in Director, many designers use Macromedia Fireworks because of its more complete range of graphic creation tools and effects, and Macromedia has made it easy to import Fireworks graphics into Director. Fireworks effects include drop shadows, glows, bevels, embosses, and more. Fireworks also works with layers, which let you organize your graphics and special effects on their own work areas. When you import a Fireworks file into Director, each layer becomes its own sprite, with its own Timeline, making it very easy to use Fireworks graphics in your movie.

FIGURE 11-10
Vector Shape panel

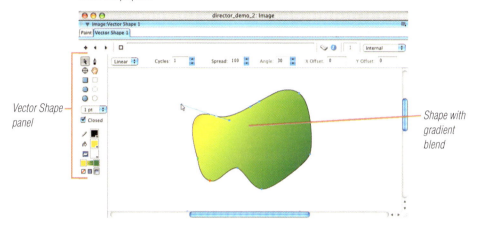

Vector Shape panel

Shape with gradient blend

FIGURE 11-11
Text tool and Text Inspector

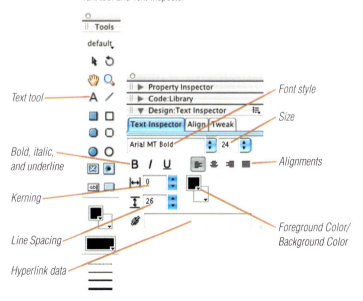

Text tool

Font style

Size

Bold, italic, and underline

Alignments

Kerning

Line Spacing

Foreground Color/ Background Color

Hyperlink data

BRING THE CAST MEMBERS TOGETHER

What You'll Learn

In this lesson, you will learn about developing and organizing a cast.

Bring in Cast Members

As you assemble your cast in the Cast panel, Director lets you view cast members in two ways: in List view or in Thumbnail view. To change views, click the **Cast View Style button** in the top-left corner of the Cast panel, as shown in Figure 11-12. Choose the view you are most comfortable with.

To add external files to your cast, click **File** on the menu bar, click **Import**, and the Import Files dialog box shown in Figure 11-13 opens. In the dialog box, navigate to the area on your computer where you store your external files, select each one, and then click **Add**, which moves the graphic's filename into the bottom window of the dialog box. Once you have added the files you want, click **Import** and your files will be brought in to the cast. The file's name becomes its name in the cast; Director deletes any file extensions. You can assign any graphic a different cast name at any time.

Director has a second way to bring external files into your movie cast: Click **Insert** on the menu bar, and then point to **Media Element**. This menu gives you more control over how you import an element into your Director movie. As you can see in Figure 11-14, selecting Flash Movie opens a dialog box with settings specific to a Flash movie file.

Organizing your source files

Selecting an internal or an external cast sets up how Director will handle the cast members within your movie, and whether Director will share this information with other movies. As with other digital media software, it's best to create a project folder for your movie, then create an images, graphics or assets folder and store your source files in an organized fashion. This makes it easier for you to access the correct files as you develop your own movie, and for others if you are sharing your files.

Cast Members Created in Director

When you import cast members into your Director movie, they are added to the cast and nowhere else. But when you create a cast member using Director's graphics and text tools, it is added to both the Cast panel and the **score** (Director's Timeline). Also, Director graphics are assigned a number; the first graphic you create is numbered 1, the next 2, and so on. This can start to get confusing if you create a large quantity of graphics within Director. So after you create each graphic, go back into the Cast panel and give each graphic a name by

FIGURE 11-12

Cast panel

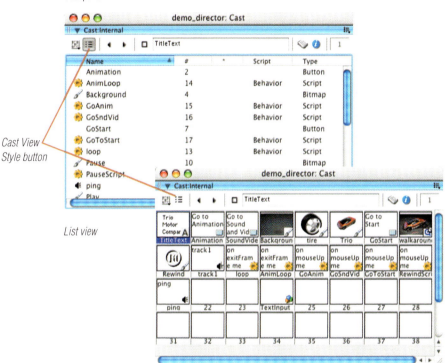

Cast View Style button

List view

Thumbnail view

FIGURE 11-13

Importing a new cast member

single-clicking to highlight the name, typing in a new name, and pressing **Enter** (PC) or **return** (MAC). Figure 11-15 shows three graphics in the Cast panel that were created with Director tools. The third graphic has been renamed, whereas the other two are still numbered.

Internal versus External Casts

When you create and save a new movie, Director automatically creates an internal cast. An **internal cast** is a cast that is specific to your movie; no other Director project can access an internal cast. Using an internal cast is fine if your cast is not too large or if you don't plan to share cast members with other movie files. But if your movie contains a large number of

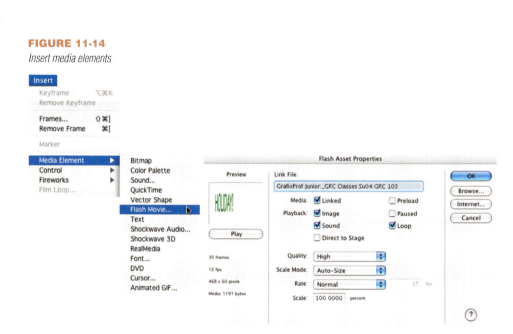

FIGURE 11-14

Insert media elements

cast members, you may want to create several **external casts**, each containing similar elements, such as a cast for bitmapped images, a cast for Flash movies, and a cast for text. Creating an external cast also lets you share cast members with other movie files, making repetitive elements such as fonts, sounds, or corporate graphics easier to access. Just remember that if you use an external cast, the cast files need to be organized in the same folder as your finished Director file when i plays so the application can find the necessary cast members. Figure 11-16 shows the New Cast dialog box where you can specify an internal or external cast.

FIGURE 11-15
Naming cast members

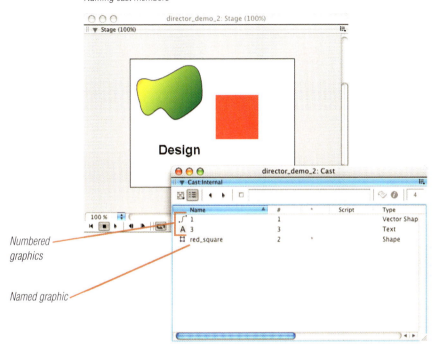

Numbered graphics

Named graphic

FIGURE 11-16
New Cast dialog box

Choose internal or external cast

WORK ON THE SCORE

What You'll Learn

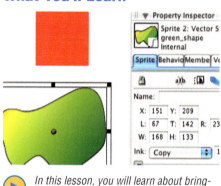

In this lesson, you will learn about bringing cast members onto the score and organizing your work.

Moving Cast Members onto the Score

The **Score panel** (also called the score) is the working area of Director where you add cast members to make them part of the movie as sprites, and is similar to Flash's layers and Timeline panel.

Each sprite in your Director movie will have a row on the score known as a channel. Each channel has its own **Timeline**, where you can position each of your sprites in its own space. Each vertical column on a Timeline is a **frame**, which represents a small segment of time. Figure 11-17 shows the various channels in Director; their functions are as follows:

Marker channel—used to label important sections of the score, and to jump from section to section of a movie.

Palette channel—specifies a change in color palettes to accomodate different monitors. Current versions of Director no longer use this channel; it exists in the software only to support files created in earlier versions of the software.

Transition channel—lets you add transition effects between different scenes in your movie. Director offers over 50 transitions.

Sound channels—two channels are available for adding sound effects, music, and voice tracks.

Script channel—used to add Lingo and JavaScript scripts, enabling users to interact with your movie.

Sprite channels—used to add your cast members to the score.

To add a sprite to the score, point to the cast member in the Cast panel, then drag it onto the appropriate channel in the score. As you can see in Figure 11-18, two cast members have been added to the score as sprites, and they also appear on the stage. By default, each sprite occupies 30 frames in the score, but you can change this number at any time.

Selecting and Modifying Sprites

Once a sprite is on the stage, you can position it anywhere you want using the Arrow tool. Click the sprite to select it; a selection bounding box appears around the sprite. You can also use the Arrow tool to scale a sprite to any size. Press **[Shift]**

FIGURE 11-17
Channels in the Score panel

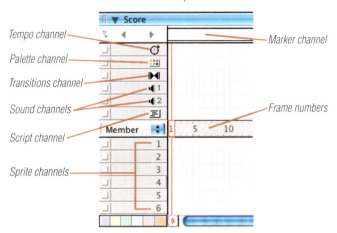

Tempo channel
Palette channel
Transitions channel
Sound channels
Script channel
Sprite channels
Marker channel
Frame numbers

FIGURE 11-18
Adding sprites to the score

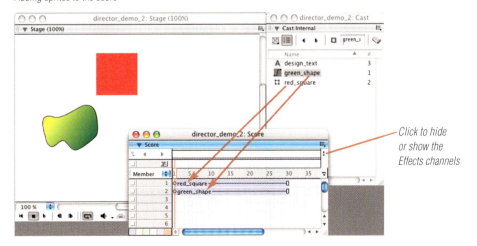

Click to hide or show the Effects channels

while you click-and-drag a corner bounding point to scale the sprite proportionally (see Figure 11-19). You can also use the Rotate and Skew tool to rotate and skew any sprite; these changes can also be made in the Property Inspector panel (see Figure 11-20). To make additional transformations, click **Modify** on the menu bar, point to **Transform**, and then select one of the options from the menu (see Figure 11-21).

Adjusting a Sprite's Timeline

As you learned earlier, a sprite, by default, takes up 30 frames on the score. But you can work with the sprite's Timeline to adjust the number of frames a sprite occupies, which determines where and for

Scaling a sprite

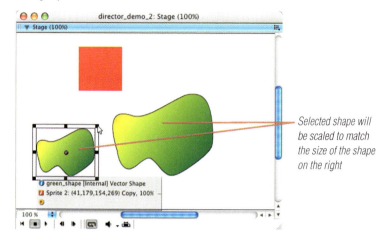

Selected shape will be scaled to match the size of the shape on the right

Sprite properties

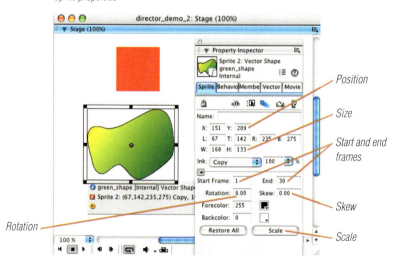

Position

Size

Start and end frames

Skew

Scale

Rotation

how long it will appear in the movie. In Figure 11-22, the sprite in Channel 1 occupies 20 frames on the Timeline. The sprite in Channel 2 occupies 40 frames, which means it will play twice as long as the sprite in Channel 1.

A sprite's location in your movie depends on the position of the **keyframe** (a location where you designate that an effect should begin, in this case, the first frame) and **end frame** (the last frame) of your sprite's Timeline. In Figure 11-23, the sprite in Channel 1 starts on Frame 1 and ends on Frame 19. The sprite in Channel 2 starts on Frame 20 and ends on Frame 32. This means these sprites will play sequentially during your movie. To make sprites play together on the stage, you simply overlap their Timelines.

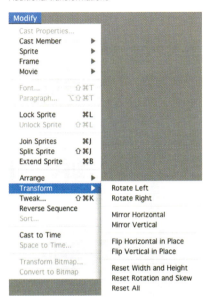

FIGURE 11-22
Length of Timelines

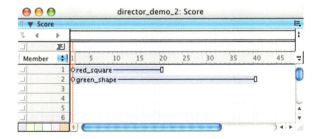

FIGURE 11-23
Sequential Timelines

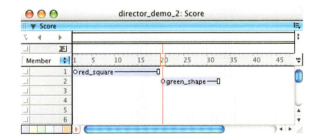

ADD ANIMATIONS AND BEHAVIORS

What You'll Learn

Dropdown List

Jump Back Button

Jump Forward Button

Jump to Marker Button

 In this lesson, you will work with Director's animation techniques and behaviors.

Setting Up Keyframes

If you look carefully at a sprite's Timeline, you will see that the first frame has a circle in it, indicating that it is a keyframe, and the last frame has a small rectangle in it, indicating that it is an end frame (see Figure 11-24). With only a keyframe on the first frame and an end frame on the last frame of a Timeline, your sprite will remain in the same position and will retain the same attributes, such as size and color, throughout the time allotted in your movie.

A keyframe can indicate the beginning of a sprite or the start of an animation effect, the end of that effect, or some type of change in that effect. To change a sprite's behavior (for example, to animate it), you convert the frame at the desired change location to a keyframe, shown in Figure 11-25. To do this, click any frame along a sprite's Timeline to select the frame, click **Insert** on the menu bar, and then click **Keyframe**. This converts the frame to a keyframe. By having two keyframes along the Timeline, you can now animate the sprite on the stage. To delete a keyframe, click the keyframe on the Timeline and then press **[Delete]**.

In Figure 11-25, the sprite on the last keyframe has been moved from the top of the stage to the bottom by first selecting the last keyframe on the Score, which also selects the shape on the stage, then by dragging the shape on the stage with the Selection tool. The sprite will now move from where it was positioned on the stage at the first keyframe to the new position on the stage at the last keyframe.

To view your animation, use the playback controls at the bottom of the stage. These controls work like other motion controls; there's a Play button and a Stop button.

You can add as many keyframes as you want along a sprite's Timeline, and each keyframe can have one or more effects applied to it. There are many types of effects you can create with Director animations. In Figure 11-26, three additional keyframes have been added to the Timeline, and the sprite appears to be bouncing up and down and slowly disappearing. Figure 11-27 shows a sprite with three keyframes; in the second keyframe, the sprite has been enlarged and rotated, and in the third keyframe, the sprite has been enlarged again and rotated.

FIGURE 11-24
Keyframe and end frame

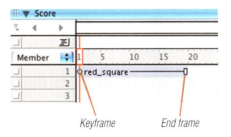

Keyframe   End frame

FIGURE 11-25
Adding a keyframe

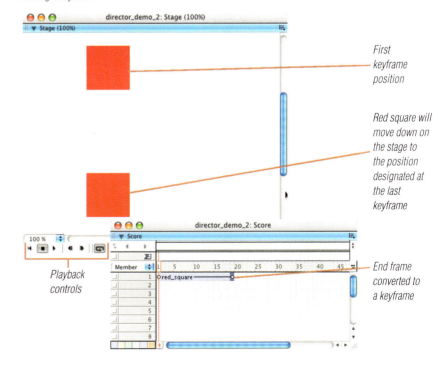

First keyframe position

Red square will move down on the stage to the position designated at the last keyframe

Playback controls

End frame converted to a keyframe

Adjusting a Sprite's Motion Path

As you move sprites on the stage, you will notice that a motion path appears. A **motion path** indicates the direction in which a sprite is moving between keyframes. The larger yellow circles with a black outline indicate keyframes, and the smaller black circles indicate the frames between the keyframes. These motion paths will always be straight, but you can modify the shape of a motion path. Use the Arrow tool to click-and-drag any keyframe's circle on the motion path to move it wherever you want on the stage. Your sprite will then follow the new path (see Figure 11-28).

Adjusting the Tempo

When Director plays back the score, it plays at a standard speed (or **tempo**) of 30 **fps** (**frames per second**). You can adjust the overall movie speed or the speed of any segment. To adjust the overall movie speed, click **Window** on the menu bar, click **Control Panel**, and then in the panel, adjust the setting in the fps text box, shown in Figure 11-29. To adjust the speed of a portion of your movie, use the Tempo

FIGURE 11-26
Adding keyframes

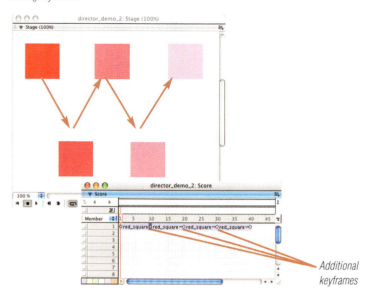

Additional keyframes

FIGURE 11-27
Keyframe effects

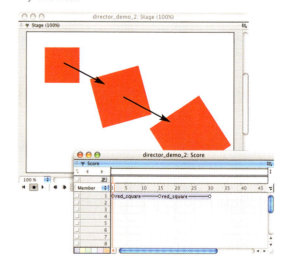

channel shown in Figure 11-30. Choose the frame on the score whose tempo you want to change. Click **Modify** on the menu bar, point to **Frame**, and then click **Tempo**. The Frame Properties: Tempo dialog box opens, where you can adjust the speed from 1 to 999 fps. You will probably never need the higher settings; most movies run at tempos between 10 to 30 fps.

As your movie plays, it will run until it reaches the frame on the Tempo channel whose tempo you adjusted. At that point, your movie will then switch to the new speed you set. You can add as many tempo changes as you like along the Tempo channel.

FIGURE 11-28

Sprite motion path

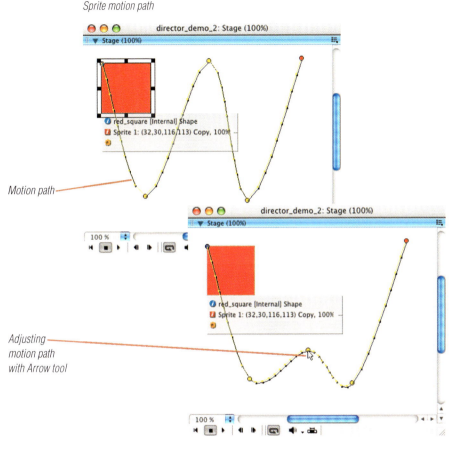

Motion path

Adjusting motion path with Arrow tool

FIGURE 11-29

Control panel

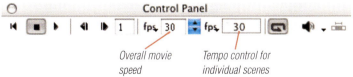

Overall movie speed

Tempo control for individual scenes

Adding Behaviors

Director uses two programming languages to create different behaviors: Lingo and JavaScript. But many Director users don't have the skills necessary to program a Director movie, so Director has a large group of preprogrammed **behaviors** that are stored in the Library palette (see Figure 11-31). These behaviors fall into seven different categories, including:

3-D—These behaviors add animation and interactivity to 3-D objects.

Accessibility—These behaviors help make a movie more accessible to people with physical impairments.

Animation—These include a wide range of behaviors that can make sprites move or change color automatically (without user interaction), let you add transitions between different movie scenes, or create an interactive behavior where the user performs an action and the sprite reacts to it in some way.

FIGURE 11-30

Tempo channel

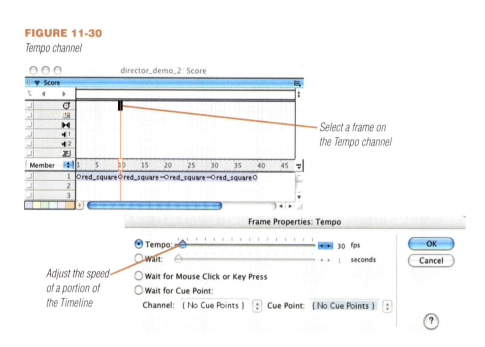

Select a frame on
the Tempo channel

Adjust the speed
of a portion of
the Timeline

Controls—These controls let you create menus and navigation buttons.

Internet—These behaviors let you create forms that can be filled out and submitted over the Internet; they can also configure a movie to be streamed over the Internet.

Media—These let you create control buttons for Flash, sound, RealMedia, and QuickTime files in your movie.

Navigation—These behaviors control the action of the Playhead, letting you jump to a specific frame.

As you can see, the range of behaviors is quite large, but they will add a lot of interactivity to your movie without requiring you to program the behavior using Lingo or JavaScript.

FIGURE 11-31
Library panel

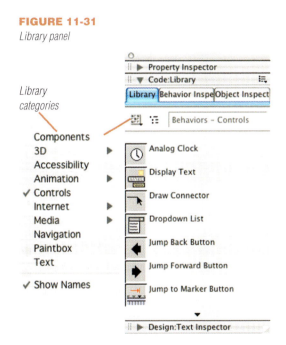

EXPORT FILES FOR CD AND WEB PRESENTATIONS

What You'll Learn

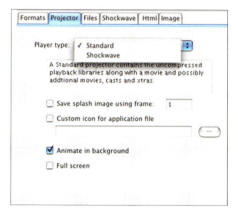

 In this lesson, you will learn how to export your movie file so it can be viewed on CD or on the Web.

Exporting Your Movie File to a Projector

When you produce a movie file using Director, the file can only be opened and played using the Director application. To let others view your movie, you will need to create a projector file. A **projector file** is a self-contained, self-running version of a Director movie that shows all the elements and actions you have created on the stage. Users viewing the projector file do not need any additional software to view the movie on their computers. You can distribute a projector file on any media, including e-mail, removable hard drives and flash memory media, CDs, and DVDs.

On a Windows computer, Director automatically creates a projector file that will run on any version of Windows, from Windows 98 and up. On a Macintosh computer, Director creates a projector file that runs on any version of Mac OS X.

To create a projector file, click **File** on the menu bar, and then click **Publish Settings**. The Publish Settings dialog box opens, as shown in Figure 11-32. Using the Formats tab of this dialog box, you can also create a projector file that will work in Windows or Macintosh computers running an older operating system (called Macintosh Classic in the dialog box). Click the **Projector tab** and make sure Player type is listed as **Standard,** to indicate that you want to create a projector file to be used on a CD or other non-Web format. Click **Publish** and the Save Movie dialog box opens. Name and save the file. Director creates a projector file from your movie and then opens a preview for your review.

Exporting Your Movie File to the Web

A Director movie on the Web can be as simple as an animated banner to as complex as an entire Web site. To make your movie playable on the Web, specify the Shockwave format, rather than the Standard format, on the Projector tab of the Publish Settings dialog box. This produces a much smaller file because the automatic player is not included in the file. The projector file instead relies on the Shockwave player installed in the user's browser application. If users do not have the Shockwave player installed, a dialog box appears that directs them to download the player, and then they can view the movie on their browser.

FIGURE 11-32
Publish Settings dialog box

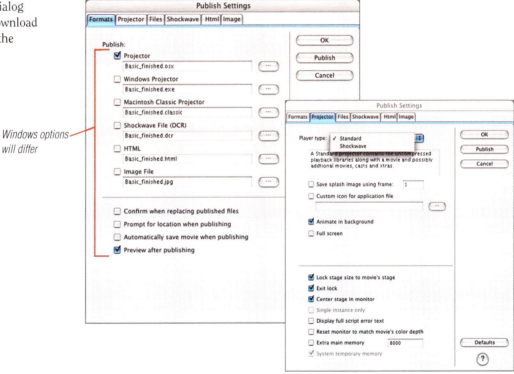

Windows options will differ

Multimedia has existed for more than 150 years, whether as the mixing of different artistic media or the integration of art with technology. Macromedia Director has become the standard desktop application for the development and distribution of multimedia projects. Director can create a wide variety of original graphics and text, and can also bring in files from other graphics, animation, video, and sound-based applications. Director's cast and score let you organize a complete multimedia movie, whether it contains a few elements or hundreds. You can also create a multitude of animated effects, and apply a range of behaviors to give your movie many levels of movement and interactivity. Director can also create movies for the visual and hearing impaired, and movie files can be exported as self-playing projector files for CD or DVD use, or into Shockwave files for Web movies. (To view the files below, look in the Chapter 11 folder in the location where you store your Data Files.)

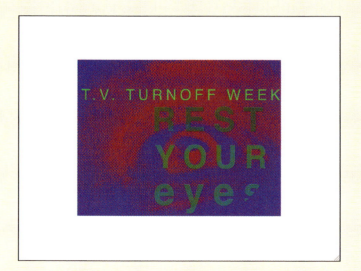

KEY TERMS AND CONCEPTS

behaviors
bitmapped text
cast
cast member
channel
collage
end frame
external cast
field text
fps
frame
frames per second
HyperCard
HyperTalk
index color
internal cast
JavaScript
keyframe
kiosk
Lingo

marker
motion path
movie
movie properties
multimedia
palette
PowerPoint
Preferred 3-D Renderer
Projector file
regular text
score
Score panel
Shockwave player
sprite
stack
stage
tempo
Timeline

1. What is multimedia?

   _____

   _____

   _____

2. What is a collage?

   _____

3. What was the first application with multimedia capabilities?

   _____

4. What browser plug-in is used to view Director files over the Internet?

   _____

5. Name four types of file formats that can be imported into Director:

   _____

   _____

   _____

   _____

6. When you import files into Director, where are these files stored so you can access them?

   _____

   _____

7. What is a sprite?

   _____

   _____

8. What are the three different ways of handling text in Director?

   _____

   _____

   _____

9. What are the two ways you can bring external files into your cast?

   _____

   _____

10. What is the difference between an internal and an external cast?

    _____

    _____

    _____

11. What is a movie's score?

    _____

    _____

    _____

12. The score is divided into separate spaces called what?

_____

13. What is a frame?

_____

_____

_____

14. When a sprite is added to the score, what is the default number of frames it will occupy on the Timeline?

_____

15. What is a keyframe?

_____

_____

_____

16. What are Director's two programming languages?

_____

_____

_____

17. What does a marker do?

_____

_____

_____

18. When exporting a Director file, what is the difference between Standard and a Shockwave player type?

_____

_____

_____

While working at Media Masters Studio, you receive a call from a client. Craftsman Construction wants you to create a simple animation that can be part of a CD catalog movie of their projects. They have provided a copy of their logo, which is made up of several basic shapes. They would like the basic shapes to appear from the edges of the screen, and take 15 seconds to come together, creating a form that matches the shape of their logo; they then want their actual logo to appear over the joined shapes.

Go to the location where you store your Data Files and copy the file IG 11-1.jpg to your hard drive. Create a new Director movie, make the size of the stage 500 × 400 pixels, and change the speed of your movie to 10 fps, which will let you put 150 frames in the score to create a 15-second animation. Bring the IG 11-1.jpg file into the cast, and then construct the shapes in the logo, each as a

separate sprite, making each one an animated object. Have all of the sprite's Timelines end at Frame 149, then bring the logo onto the stage and shorten the Timeline to cover just Frame 150, which is the end of the movie. Save your file as **craftsman_movie_1.dir**.

One Step Beyond

Increase the movie from 15 seconds to 30 seconds, adding animation effects to the logo. Save this version as **craftsman_movie_2.dir**.

Two Steps Beyond

Export your file as a Director projector file. Export this movie as **craftsman_movie_2**.

You are a digital artist at Valley Digital Hot Shop. One of your clients, Motorcycle Extreme, needs a quick multimedia movie that they can use in their video kiosks in their showroom. They have provided a video file and a logo file, and they want you to create a 30-second movie, which should start with the logo in an animated introduction, followed by a video of a radical motorcycle jump with the sun setting in the background.

Go to the location where you store your Data Files and copy the file IG 11-2.jpg and IG 11-3.mov to your hard drive. Create a new Director movie, making the stage size 640 × 480 pixels. Change the movie speed to 10 fps, which will let you work 300 frames in the score to create a 30-second animation. Bring in the IG 11-2 file and create an introductory animation using the logo and any other text and graphics you want to create in Director. Have this introductory sequence continue for 25 seconds, and then have the IG 11-3.mov movie file play for the final five seconds. Save your file as **motorextreme_movie_1.dir**.

One Step Beyond

Create an additional 10 to 15 seconds of animation after the video to advertise a motorcycle race that's coming up at the end of the month. Work with Director's graphics and text tools or create some graphics in another application and bring them into your movie. Save this version as **motorextreme_movie_2.dir**.

Two Steps Beyond

Export your file as a Director projector file. Export this movie as **motorextreme_movie_2**.

Create a digital portfolio of your graphics or any other artwork that you have produced. Save or export your files into formats that Director will recognize and import them into your movie's cast. Using markers and behaviors, create five separate pages in your movie, the first being a title page, the other four displaying your work. Design a visually consistent theme throughout, using as many animated effects as you like. Save your movie as **my_digital_portfolio.dir** and export the movie as both a projector file and a Shockwave file. See Figure 11-33 for an example. (To view the file below, look in the Chapter 11 folder in the location where you store your Data Files.)

FIGURE 11-33
Possible digital video solutions

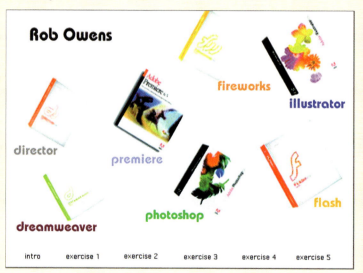

Figure 11-34 shows two examples of real-world multimedia projects. They are also included in the Data Files for Chapter 11 so you can view them on your computer. Look carefully at each project, and write a critique of how each project uses design and motion successfully.

FIGURE 11-34
Possible digital video solutions

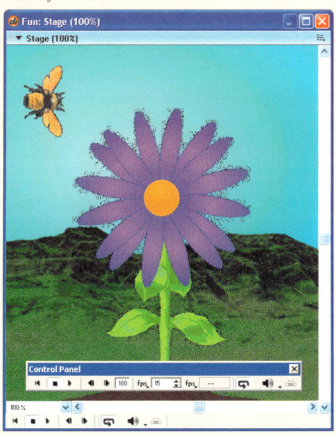

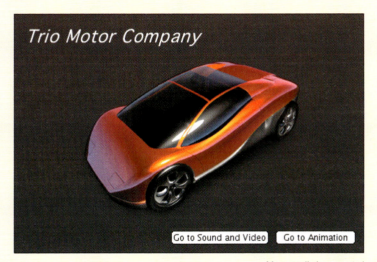

Macromedia Incorporated
Trio Motor Co.
www.macromedia.com

Steve Johnson
Macromedia Director MX 2003 - Design Professional
www.perspection.com

CONCEPTS OF 3-D DESIGN AND ANIMATION

421

CHAPTER 12

CONCEPTS OF 3-D DESIGN AND ANIMATION

A Rich History

Animation has its roots in the early 20th century when J. Stuart Blackton, a British vaudeville performer who performed high-speed "lightning sketches," met the American inventor Thomas Edison in 1895. For the next five years, they worked together on a film called *The Enchanted Drawing*. In this groundbreaking combination of live action and animation, an artist draws a man's head on a canvas. He then draws a wine glass and bottle and appears to pull them magically off the canvas, turning them into the real thing. The cartoon head frowns when the artist draws a hat and puts it on his own head, but smiles when the artist returns the hat, wine, and glass (see Figure 12-1).

The next advance in animation occurred in 1914. Winsor McKay was a successful cartoonist who had gained national recognition with his *Little Nemo in Slumberland* and *Dreams of the Rarebit Friend* cartoon strips. But his *Gertie the Dinosaur* became the first true animated cartoon. McKay created more than 10,000 drawings for this production, including all of the backgrounds (see Figure 12-2). McKay's work was incredibly time consuming; it took him a year to complete a five-minute animation. So as the cartoon industry expanded during the 1920s, animation became an assembly-line process, with film studios hiring dozens of artists to draw characters and backgrounds.

Two studios opened during the 1920s and rose to prominence over the next 30 years: Walt Disney Company and Warner Brothers. Walt Disney was the first to merge animation with sound in his 1928 cartoon *Steamboat Willie*, which introduced the world to Mickey Mouse. In 1937, his studio released *Snow White and the Seven Dwarfs,* the first full-length animated movie. Warner Brothers became home to the legendary cartoon creators

Chuck Jones, Tex Avery, and Friz Freleng. Warner Brothers released the first *Looney Tunes* cartoon in 1930, followed by the introduction of dozens of cartoon character standards, including Daffy Duck, Porky Pig, and Bugs Bunny.

Many consider the 1950s to be the last great decade of studio cartoons. As the television industry grew, many of the large animation studios closed, and even the Disney animation division seemed to fall into a creative rut during the '60s and '70s. But this slowly started to change, and in 1989 Disney released *The Little Mermaid*, which showed that the studio had not lost its creative spark. Over the next 15 years, films such as *Beauty and the Beast*, *The Lion King*, and *Tarzan* found critical acclaim and box office success around the world.

The Computer Takes Over

In the 1980s, several individuals and groups were looking to the computer as a way to create animations for the movie screen. John Lassiter left Disney Studios in 1984 when he found that the company had little interest in his computer animation work. Lassiter went to work for the computer graphics division of Lucasfilm, which was working on computer-generated

FIGURE 12-1
The Enchanted Drawing

special effects for the *Star Wars* movies. The division was sold to Steve Jobs, one of the founders of Apple Computer. Renamed Pixar, the group developed powerful new animation and rendering systems and software. Lassiter thrived in the environment, and in 1986 Pixar released *Luxo Jr.*, a short animation about a "child" lamp playing with a bouncing ball. This was the first computer-animated piece to be nominated for an Academy Award.

Since the creation of *Luxo Jr.*, 3-D computer animation has exploded, with animations being integrated into traditional hand-drawn productions. The first full-length computer-animated movie, *Toy Story*, was released in 1996 (see Figure 12-3). The growth of 3-D computer animation has also produced a growing job market that requires many of the skills discussed in this book.

3-D Animation Software

Today there are many applications that create 3-D objects and animations. For desktop computers, four applications have

FIGURE 12-2
Gertie the Dinosaur

become popular: Discreet 3D StudioMax, NewTek Lightwave 3-D, Alias Products Maya, and Maxon Cinema 4D. These products work in similar ways, and each can create complex 3-D models (visual representations of actual or imaginary objects) and animation sequences. This chapter provides examples from Cinema 4D to display some of the basics of 3-D modeling and animation. But note that because of the complexity of 3-D applications, there is a steep learning curve that makes coverage of application specifics impractical in an introductory text. So this chapter will contain fewer specific references to specific application tools and commands than previous chapters, and will focus on the general concepts and features you need to understand to create 3-D images and animations.

FIGURE 12-3
Toy Story

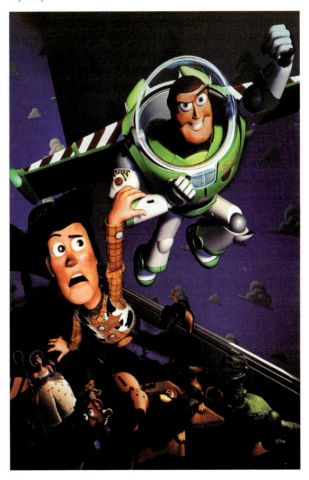

CINEMA 4D: AN OVERVIEW

What You'll Learn

In this lesson, you will learn about the major features of Cinema 4D.

Cinema 4D Tools

In the ten years since its introduction, Maxon Cinema 4D has evolved into a powerful yet easy-to-use modeling, rendering, and animation application. Cinema 4D is widely used in film, television, games, medical visualizations, and industrial and architectural design, and in graphics for print and the Web.

Because of the complexity of 3-D graphics, Maxon has made Cinema 4D's tools consistent in appearance and function, allowing you to learn one tool, then apply that knowledge to other, similar tools (see Figure 12-4). Cinema 4D has helper tools that let you perform repetitive modeling procedures quickly. Cinema 4D also has many classic modeling tools and primitives (basic 3-D shapes) that let you start constructing 3-D images almost immediately.

Cinema 4D Effects

Once you've created your 3-D models in Cinema 4D, you can apply a wide range of Cinema 4D animation effects and techniques. The application has a multilevel timeline that lets you organize and track every animation effect. You can also synchronize sound to your animation at any point on the timeline.

Two Cinema 4D features are important in creating realistic 3-D images: lighting and materials. Cinema 4D's lighting tools include nine lighting types, and dozens of ways to adjust each one. Cinema 4D can also work with 13 **channels** of material properties, which let you add multiple combinations of surface textures, surface materials (like skin, wood, or metal), shading of a surface to simulate light and shadow areas, and other properties such as color, reflectivity, and transparency. The different channel properties all work together. Because viewing your completed work is important, Cinema 4D's rendering engine can display complex images on your monitor quickly and accurately.

Cinema 4D can save and export to multiple formats, which means you can integrate your projects into many types of presentations. For Web design, you can create formats for Macromedia Flash, Macromedia Director, and VRML (Virtual Reality Modeling Language). If your models are going out to architects or scene designers, Cinema 4D can create files for all of the popular CAD applications.

FIGURE 12-4

Maxon Cinema 4D

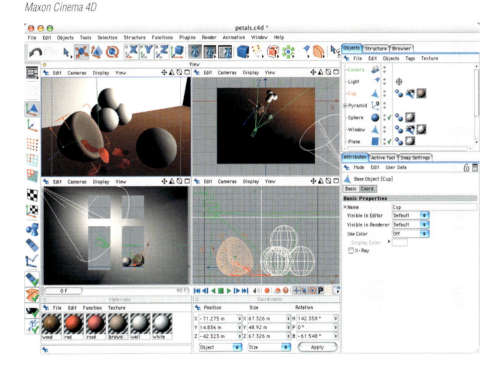

CREATE A NEW WORKSPACE

What You'll Learn

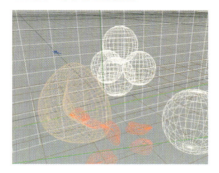

▶ *In this lesson, you will learn about creating and saving a new project.*

Viewing the 3-D Space

Three-dimensional design applications let you replicate images of the world around you. To do this, the computer must attempt to re-create this world by using the three dimensions discussed in Chapter 7. This 3-D space is defined by its **width**, **height**, and **depth**, or on the computer as the **x-, y-, and z-axes**. Viewing your work in multiple views lets you track image changes in all three dimensions. When you are working in a file in Cinema 4D, you can activate different **viewing modes** (ways of viewing your models), called **viewports**, that let you see your project in different viewing modes at the same time. Figure 12-5 shows four different viewports of the same image; each viewport is showing a different viewing mode.

FIGURE 12-5
Viewports

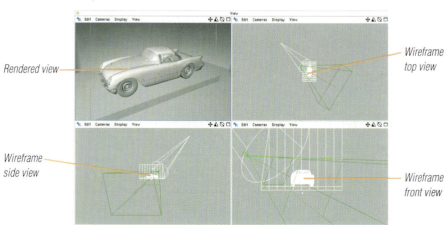

Rendered view

Wireframe top view

Wireframe side view

Wireframe front view

Viewing modes are also necessary when you are rendering complex images. Three-dimensional animation programs place heavy demands on a computer's processor; the more complex your image or animation, the longer it will take for your computer to redraw changes. Viewing modes can let you preview your changes using views that require less memory, speeding the design process. As shown in Figure 12-6, the viewing modes range from a simple box view to a wireframe view to an advanced shading view.

Saving the 3-D Work Area

You can launch Cinema 4D the same way you launch the other programs in this book: by using the Dock or Applications folder (Macintosh) or the Programs or All Programs menu (Windows). To save your project click **File** and then click **Save** to save your project as a Cinema 4D file. The Cinema 4D work area is shown in Figure 12-7. Here you can see how the three-dimensional space contains grids that go off in each of the three axes. You create and manipulate 3-D objects within this space. You can move objects in any of the three axes and rotate them in any direction you choose.

FIGURE 12-6
Viewing modes

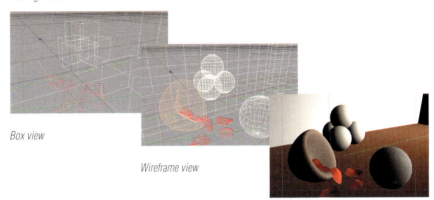

Box view

Wireframe view

Shading view

FIGURE 12-7
3-D workspace

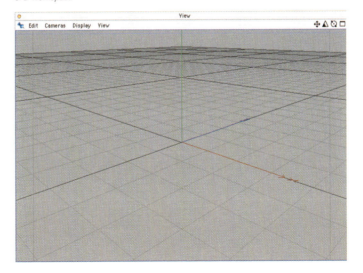

MODEL 3-D FORMS

What You'll Learn

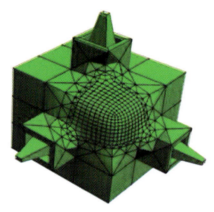

In this lesson, you will learn about creating and manipulating basic 3-D forms.

Get Down to Basics

In any 3-D project, you begin by constructing **models**, which are the objects you will use in your project. Because model construction can be time-consuming, understanding three-dimensional design will save you time. (Creating animations for your models, by contrast, takes less time.) You need to analyze and break down every form into its most basic shapes. Then you create, manipulate, and store each of these component shapes until all of the pieces have been constructed. Then you put the pieces together to create complex 3-D models.

Draw your images out first

Three-dimensional modeling and animation requires a great deal of technical and creative skill. Moreover, the applications themselves will at times seem overwhelming. Sketching your ideas on paper before you get on the computer will simplify your production process. One of the best examples of this is when Disney decided to start work on *The Lion King*: The studio brought in several live lions and other animals that were to appear in the movie. The lead animators gathered around with their pencils and drawing pads and spent hours drawing the animals from every possible angle. These sketches allowed the animators to work quickly and with greater accuracy once they got on the computer.

Develop Primitives

Every object in a 3-D application is created by connecting a series of polygons together. **Polygons** are multisided shapes, such as a triangle or octagon. Connected polygons are called a **polygon mesh**, and can be as simple as a cube (six connected 4-sided polygons) up to complex models made up of thousands of polygons. The 3-D artist can then push, pull, add, subtract, twist, and bend the object into whatever shape is necessary.

Primitives are pre-made polygons, including basic three-dimensional geometric shapes or other useful models, such as pyramids and doughnuts, supplied with a 3-D application. Primitives can be cubes, cones, spheres, cylinders, and so forth (see Figure 12-8). Cinema 4D provides 16 primitives, as shown in Figure 12-9. Designers who use 3-D applications use primitives as building blocks for their models; they can distort or combine primitives to make additional unique or complex shapes.

FIGURE 12-8
Primitive shapes

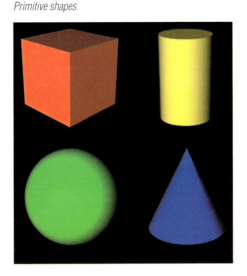

FIGURE 12-9
Primitives in Cinema 4D

Boolean Operations Create Complex Forms

A popular way to create more complex forms is to use **Boolean operations**, which let you combine simple forms into more complex forms and unique form combinations. Some of these operations include **union**, where two forms are combined into a more complex form; **intersection**, where two forms are combined and the overlap is saved, and the rest of the forms are deleted; and **subtraction**, where two forms are combined and the area where the two forms overlap, plus one of the forms, are subtracted (deleted) from the combined form. Cinema 4D has a tool that allows you to select and apply these operations with a couple of easy mouse clicks (see Figure 12-10).

Freeform Modeling Techniques

You will be able to work with basic geometric forms and Boolean operations up to a certain level. For even more complex forms, you will need to use one of the **freeform modeling** methods (see Figure 12-11). Most 3-D applications use techniques that let you mold a form's polygons into the three-dimensional shapes you need. The first technique is called **spline-based modeling**, which is a similar technique to the Bezier curves used in vector-draw software discussed in Chapter 2. **Splines** are the wires that make up a three-dimensional wireframe of an object. Each spline has control points that you can modify and adjust to create the required shape. These control points use handles (also called

FIGURE 12-10
Boolean operations

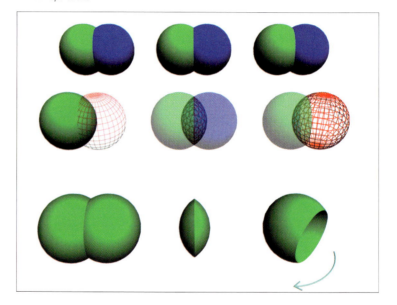

tangents) that are similar to the handles that control vector paths. By manually dragging these handles, you can adjust and "model" the surface of your form. Like vector art, these spline-based techniques are also resolution independent, giving you a smooth surface no matter how close you view your form. Another spline-based system used by several 3-D applications is Non-Uniform Rational B-Splines, or **NURBS.**

The second freeform modeling technique is **subdivision surface modeling**. This technique is becoming more popular in several 3-D applications because it combines the best of polygon and spline-based modeling. You build a model using polygon-based segments, which act as the boundary for each area. Within the boundary is a spline-based surface that you can adjust at low surface detail, but you can adjust your detail as desired to create higher resolution surfaces. This technique can produce more detailed results in less time than with a spline-based modeling system.

Recreating Nature

Another technique that is used in 3-D modeling applications is called **procedural modeling**. This technique uses very complex formulas to take into account such processes as how nature creates a forest of trees, or how tornadoes develop from a storm. Using the principles of **fractal geometry**, applications take a small amount of information (like how waves roll up to a beach with a palm tree) and

FIGURE 12-11
Freeform modeling

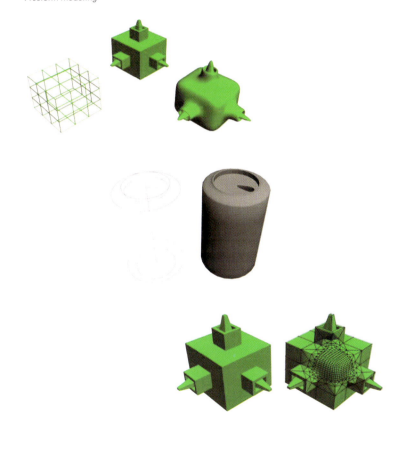

re-create an entire scene (such as a beach with a grove of palm trees and waves splashing on the beach). A common 3-D technique often used for modeling nature is called **particle systems**, in which a program can re-create smoke, rain, or dust from a small amount of random information, instead of having to use thousands of objects and having to keep track of all of them at once (see Figure 12-12).

Adding Realism to Forms

Creating an accurate form is just part of the modeling process. The next step is to apply a surface to the model, a technique known as **shading**, which adds color, texture, patterns, or the effect of materials on the surface of a three-dimensional object. Many shading techniques are built into 3-D applications, allowing the designer to apply different looks quickly to the same form. Shading surfaces include wood, metal, glass, plastic, grass, and many more.

The 3-D designer can also import a bitmapped image of a material or texture and literally wrap it around a three-dimensional form. This technique, known as **texture shading**, saves production time when creating a unique form (see Figure 12-13). For example, if you were creating an image of a sand castle on a beach, you could find a picture of sand and apply it to your model to produce a realistic representation of a sand castle, without having to spend the time creating the sand grain by grain. You can even use a digital camera to take a picture of a

FIGURE 12-12
Particle systems

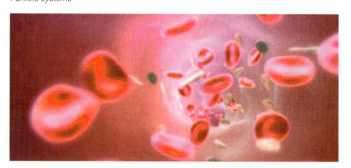

FIGURE 12-13
Texture shading

texture, download the picture to your computer, and use the image to create texture shading.

Previewing Your Work

As you work with different modeling and shading techniques, you will want to preview your work. 3-D applications use **realtime renderings**, in which the software creates a low-resolution preview that shows some basic details. Realtime renderings are not as detailed as the advanced rendering techniques discussed later in this chapter, but they are acceptable for viewing the progress of your project.

Wireframe is the fastest and most basic preview method, because it doesn't display the surface modeling or any textures or colors. It shows the basic structure of each form within a scene, so it's mainly used to preview the shapes and sizes of each model and the position of the models within the scene. **Flat shading** is the second preview method; it applies a color and tone to each polygon on your model's surface. This technique is slower to render than wireframe but is the fastest method that provides an image of a model's surface. **Gouraud shading** (developed by Henri Gouraud in 1971) is a mathematical technique in which the edges of the polygons are **interpolated** (averaged together) so the colors and textures blend together. This preview method creates a more accurate and detailed rendering, but also takes much longer to preview (see Figure 12-14).

FIGURE 12-14

From wireframe to Gourard shading

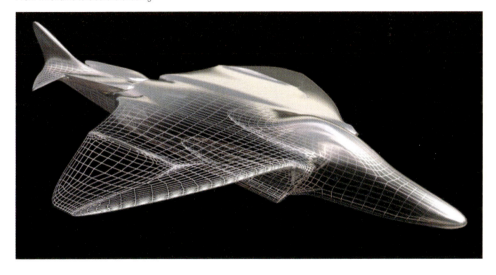

WORK WITH LIGHT AND SPACE

What You'll Learn

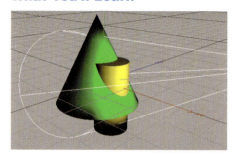

 In this lesson, you will learn about lighting your animation to create realistic space.

Lighting Brings It All Together

Using lighting is a specialized skill in the 3-D process. Lighting can directly affect how your audience perceives a form or group of forms within a scene. Lighting can be dramatic, subtle, or expressive, and can enhance both the object and the over-all space being lit.

Most 3-D applications feature three types of lighting: ambient light, spot light, and fill light. **Ambient light** is light that spreads over an entire scene without focusing on any particular object. It tends to make objects easily recognizable but doesn't emphasize any part of the scene. **Spot lighting** does the opposite of ambient lighting: It creates a focus on one form or area within a scene, and can create more dramatic lighting effects, including distinct highlights and shadows. Changing the angle of a spot light can change how the viewer perceives three-dimensional space, by drawing the viewer's eye to a specific spot in the scene, or changing the emphasis on various forms within the

scene (see Figure 12-15). **Fill lighting** is more directional than ambient lighting, but unlike spot lighting it doesn't create strong highlights or shadows.

You can also adjust lighting by changing the light's color. Light has a different color depending on the time of day being por-trayed; morning light tends to be warmer in color, whereas evening light looks cooler. The light inside a room can vary depending on the light source: Light from a group of candles will appear to have a different color than light from a bright electrical lamp. And light will change color depending on the color of the object that is reflecting the light.

Different Viewpoints

Another aspect of 3-D design is the position of the **camera** (the tool that determines how the audience views a scene) in relation to the user or audience that is going to view the project. Like a photographer, you have to choose the **frame of reference**, which means that you decide from what angle the audience will view the space making up the scene (see Figure 12-16). You also need to determine the **cropping** of the scene, which refers to how much or how little of the scene the audience will see. The camera position defines the **viewing plane**, which acts like a rectangular viewing window that defines the cropping of the scene. By adjusting the **target** (the area the camera is focused on) and the viewing plane, you determine what your audience will see in your scene.

Another way to influence your audience's perception of a scene is to adjust the scene's focus. **Focus** is how clearly the images appear within a scene. Focus can be sharp, so that all images can be seen clearly, or you can soften or blur an object or an entire scene. As with a camera, you can adjust two aspects of focus. **Depth of field** determines how much of a scene's background and foreground are in focus. **Field of view** determines how wide or narrow the view of the scene is, affecting the focus of images to the left and right of the audience's view of the scene.

FIGURE 12-15
Ambient versus spot lighting

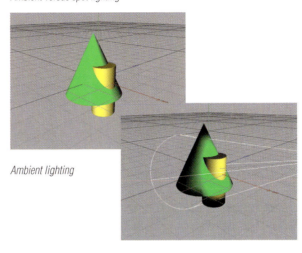

Ambient lighting

Spot lighting

FIGURE 12-16
Changing frame of reference

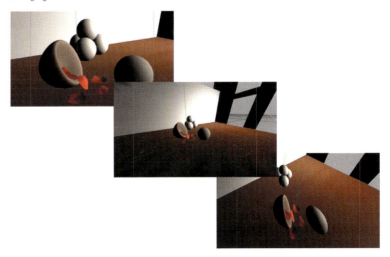

BASIC ANIMATION CONCEPTS

What You'll Learn

▶ *In this lesson, you will learn about how an animated project is developed.*

Animation Techniques

In Chapters 9 and 11, you learned about 2-D animation techniques. Although many of these concepts are similar in 3-D animation, the big difference is the addition of the z-axis, which gives your animation a higher degree of realism. In the most powerful 3-D applications, the images you create can become even more realistic, to the point where you may not be able to tell what's real and what's animation. The addition of time, which is the fourth dimension of design, adds a new set of parameters and possibilities to your work.

Like 2-D animation, 3-D applications use a timeline to keep track of the animation movements. You can set keyframes along the timeline to designate changes within the animation. All of these changes (such as the movement of your model) are tracked on three axes (x, y, and z) instead of the two axes used in 2-D animation. You can also

set tweens between keyframes, which lets the application automatically redraw the model as it changes between the keyframes. So as your model changes its position within the scene, the appearance of movement will be added by the tweens.

You can also add motion paths to your model; a **motion path** is a three-dimensional path that your model will follow through your scene. Motion paths create more realistic movement than two-dimensional paths. You can also apply motion paths to models, the camera, and lighting, which lets you bring the viewer "into" any part of your scene. Camera motion techniques include **tracking**, which follows your model as it moves through a scene; **panning**, which follows a curved path like your head turning to view a scene; and **fly-through**, which moves you through a scene as if you were moving in a car or plane (see Figure 12-17).

Working with Advanced Effects

Each 3-D application you use has its own range of animation effects. Many also work with third-party software developers to develop **plug-ins**, small software programs that add additional capabilities to an application. One important animation technique calculates and displays the effects of nature on your model, such as animating the effects of gravity, animating how a model will start to run or stop running, or what happens when your model jumps up and down. To accomplish these effects, 3-D applications let you add a variety of **attributes** to your model, such as height and weight. The application uses these attributes to calculate how your model will be affected by the forces of nature, as shown in Figure 12-18.

FIGURE 12-17
Camera movement

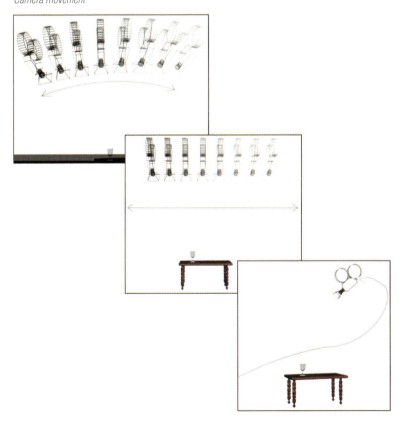

Creating motion is another complex area of 3-D animation. As you develop more complex models, you have to **link** (connect) their component pieces together so the application can calculate how to add movement. You have to tell the application which pieces are connected and how; these connections are called **chains** (which act like the joints in your body), and will also affect the motion of your model. 3-D applications work with **kinematics**, the science of motion, to make these complex motions work (see Figure 12-19). **Forward kinematics** is a mechanical motion process in which you describe the required motion for each piece of the model to make the movement work. But 3-D applications also use **inverse kinematics**, in which you start a movement at one end of the chain, and the rest of the chain reacts to it and creates the necessary motion without having to be told what to do. Motion created using this technique is much more realistic than other techniques.

The ability to create complex motion is difficult even in the most powerful 3-D application. Recreating human motion is especially challenging, so in many

FIGURE 12-18
Natural attributes

instances designers use the technique of **motion-capture**. A human subject will be filmed, and the film is then brought into the animation where the animator can use it as a guide to create more accurate motion. Today this can be done electronically: The subject wears a body suit with small white lights at important parts of the body. As the subject moves, a strobe-light system flashes light at high speed; this is captured and recorded by a computer, which can translate the movement into the 3-D application. An excellent example of this process is the character Gollum in the *Lord of the Rings* trilogy. Actor Andy Serkis was filmed throughout the process as a live character in all of Gollum's scenes. Then he would go back into the motion capture studio and recreate his scenes for the computer. The animators would composite the Gollum character over Andy, creating an impressively realistic virtual character.

FIGURE 12-19
Kinematics

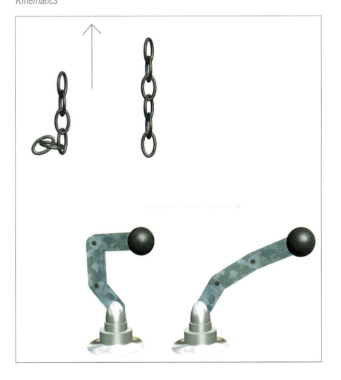

RENDER AND EXPORT FILES

What You'll Learn

▶ *In this lesson, you will learn about rendering and exporting 3-D files for a variety of presentations.*

Creating the Final Rendering

After you complete your model or animation, you need to do a final rendering. This is a separate process from the preview renderings you did to check your design's progress earlier in the project. The final rendering is like taking a final picture or series of pictures of your project, and displays your final model or animation as your viewers will see it. First, you need to decide what quality the rendering needs to be. How detailed do you want your models to appear? How accurately do you want your animations to run? Many of these decisions will be based on whether your project is going out to the Web, to CD-ROM, or to a video or movie-based presentation. Figure 12-20 shows an object in its final rendered form.

There are a number of techniques for performing a final rendering. **Phong shading** (developed by Bui Tuong Phong in 1975) is a more detailed rendering technique that can achieve a high level of accuracy and

detail. An even more powerful rendering technique is **Ray tracing.** This is one of the most realistic methods of rendering, because it has the ability to re-create color and light as you see it in the real world. Ray tracing has the ability to calculate how light will reflect off a form based on its shape and the materials that make up the form.

The final method of rendering is **Radiosity**, which is based on the Ray tracing method. This technique is even more complex, taking into account not only light reflection and surface materials but the transfer of energy as light bounces between different forms within a scene. Radiosity is the most accurate rendering method available today, but it takes large amounts of computer power (and time) to render. It's important to remember that the more detailed and complex a rendering technique is, the more time it will take for the computer to perform.

A Variety of Formats

Once you render a completed file, applications like Cinema 4D let you export the file to a wide variety of 2-D and 3-D file formats. This includes popular 3-D formats including DXF (used by 3-D StudioMax) and OBJ (used by Maya). You can also export to the Web using formats like ShockWave 3-D (the Director Web player), SWF (the Flash Web player), and VRML (a 3-D file format for the Web). Cinema 4D can also export to video formats, including the Apple Quicktime format and the Microsoft AVI format. In addition, you can export to many popular architectural and drafting electronic formats, including AutoCad, AllPlan, VectorWorks, and ArchiCAD.

FIGURE 12-20
Final rendering

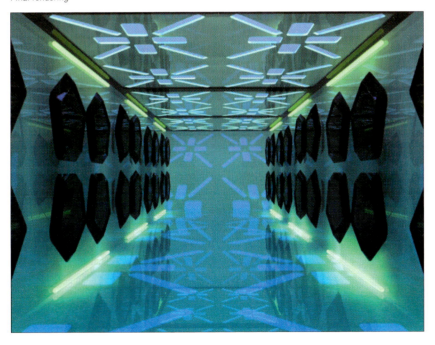

3-D modeling and animation is a broad segment of the digital media industry, and comes from a rich history of traditional animation for movies and television. Working within the three dimensions of space and the fourth dimension of time, you can create an infinite array of shapes, images, and animation effects. 3-D applications let you create your own models from scratch, or you can start with a variety of primitive shapes that you can combine and reshape any way you choose. You can add textures and surfaces to your models, and use lighting and shading to bring even the simplest form life. Once you have completed your models, you can animate them, using keyframes and motion paths to start moving your models through a virtual space. Cameras and lighting can add more depth and realism, as can natural attributes, forward and inverse kinematics, and motion capture. Your final files can be rendered to several levels of visual quality, then exported to many popular file formats for 3-D and Web presentations.

ambient light
attributes
Boolean operations
camera
chains
channel
cropping
depth
depth of field
field of view
fill light
flat shading
fly-through
focus
forward kinematics
fractal geometry
frame of reference
freeform modeling
Gouraud shading
height
interpolate
intersection
inverse kinematics
kinematics
link
model
motion-capture
motion paths
NURBS
panning

particle systems
Phong shading
plug-ins
polygon
polygon mesh
primitives
procedural modeling
Radiosity
Ray tracing
realtime renderings
shading
spline
spline-based modeling
spot light
subdivision surface modeling
subtraction
tangent
target
texture shading
tracking
union
viewing plane
viewing mode
viewport
width
wireframe
x-axis
y-axis
z-axis

1. Who created *The Enchanted Drawing* in 1900?

_____

_____

_____

2. What is considered the first true animated cartoon, and who produced it?

_____

_____

3. Who produced the first computer-animated piece nominated for an Academy Award?

_____

4. What are the axes that make up three-dimensional space?

_____

5. What is a polygon?

_____

_____

6. What is a primitive?

_____

_____

7. Name three Boolean operations:

_____

_____

_____

8. Briefly describe spline-based modeling:

_____

_____

_____

9. What are particle systems?

_____

_____

10. What is mapping?

_____

_____

_____

11. What is the difference between ambient light and spot light?

_____

_____

_____

12. How can the camera be used to affect the audience's view of a scene?

_____

_____

_____

13. What is the difference between depth of field and field of view?

_____

_____

_____

14. What is Gouraud shading?

_____

_____

_____

15. What are motion paths?

_____

_____

_____

16. What is a chain?

_____

_____

_____

17. What is the difference between forward and inverse kinematics?

_____

_____

_____

18. What is motion-capture?

_____

_____

_____

Cinema 4D is one of the most popular 3-D modeling and animation applications in the industry. Use your favorite search engine to locate the Maxon Web site. Explore the site and review Cinema 4D's 3-D modeling and animation capabilities. Write a one- to two-page report that includes answers to these questions:

- What is the number of the current release?
- Name at least five fields in which the application is used.
- What platform(s) is it available on, and what are the recommended system requirements?
- Name three of the additional modules that are available for use with Cinema 4D.
- What packaging options are available?

One Step Beyond

Three more applications that are used in the industry are Discreet 3D StudioMax, NewTek Lightwave 3-D, and Alias Products Maya. Use your favorite search engine to research each of these products and create a table with each product in a column and each piece of information down the left side, and fill in the blanks for each product.

Two Steps Beyond

Use the information you obtain from the Web to write a three- to four-page paper comparing and contrasting the capabilities of the four products, noting any areas or uses in which one application differs from the others.

Although this chapter does not contain specific steps, you may have access to another reference that does. If so, use it as a reference in completing this exercise.

You're working at Awesome Animations Studio when you're asked to create an image for Chess Masters Game Shop. The owner wants you to create a highly detailed, three-dimensional model of a classical king chess piece. Research the shape of this chess piece, then in whatever 3-D application use a combination of primitive shapes to build a realistic king chess piece. Experiment with color, texture, and shading. When you are finished save your file as **chess_king_1**.

One Step Beyond

The client called and said they now want a queen chess piece. Create this new model and save it as **chess_queen_1**.

Two Steps Beyond

Well, looks like a typical day at work: The client now wants a knight chess piece. This piece will require a little more modeling work beyond just using primitive shapes. Create this new model and save it as **chess_knight_1**.

Each of the four applications discussed in Project Builder 1, Maxon Cinema 4D, Discreet 3D StudioMax, NewTek Lightwave 3-D, and Alias Products' Maya, have been used in various movies and other projects, such as games and on the Web. Using your favorite search engine, research each product and write a two- to four-page report on how each application has been used out in different types of industries. Include what companies use each application and give examples for each use of the application. Also, note if one application seems to be used more in a particular area of the industry then the other applications. You can start by examining the Gallery section of each product's Web site.

FIGURE 12-21
Professional 3-D project

Figure 12-22 shows two examples of actual 3-D projects. Look carefully at each one and write a 1- to 2-page critique of how you think each project might have used the concepts and application features discussed in this chapter.

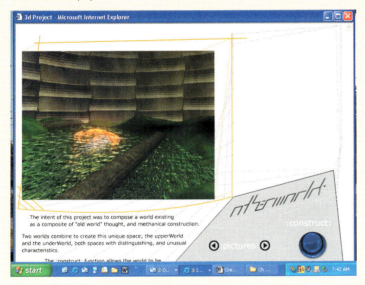

Shaun Tinney
3-D imaging project
AIGA Web site
www.shauntinney.com

Chris Hallbeck
Room 2
Swift Insight self-promotional
www.stratacafe.com

.eps
The file extension for a specialized Postscript file used to store both bitmapped and vector graphics; .eps files can output at any resolution and can be grayscale or color.

.fla
The Flash movie file extension.

.gif
The file extension for a bitmapped graphics format used specifically for the Web.

.htm
The file extension for an HTML document. See also **HTML**.

.jpg
The file extension for a compressed bitmapped image format used in both grayscale and color, and which works best with complex photographic images.

.psd
The file extension for Photoshop's native file format that lets you preserve layers and, in the RGB color mode, lets you access all the tools and commands available in Photoshop.

.swf
The native Flash file extension.

.tif
A file format used for printed graphics; the original bitmapped file format developed by Aldus and Microsoft Corporations, this format can be any resolution, in grayscale or color, and is widely supported on both Macintosh and Windows computers.

3-D modeling and animation
A form of digital media that lets designers create 3-dimensional images that move and use sound.

A/B editing
In digital video editing, a method in which video clips and transitions are on separate tracks.

Absolute link
On a Web page, a link that connects to an exact location on the Web.

Actions
In Web animation, behaviors you can apply to animated objects, such as Play or Stop.

ActionScript
The programming language of Macromedia Flash.

Additive primary colors
In the RGB color model, the three colors, red, green, and blue, that make up white light.

Adobe Acrobat
Software that lets you read and modify documents in PDF format, a format that allows documents to appear and print the same on any computer, regardless of platform.

Adobe Reader
Software that lets you read documents in PDF format.

Alignment
In graphic design, a method of creating organization and movement in a design by lining up elements to create columns or visual lines.

Alignment
In word processing and page layout, the horizontal location of text between the margins; left, right, center, and justified.

Alpha
In Flash, the adjustment of transparency of an instance.

Alternating rhythm
See **Rhythm**.

Alternative solutions
In the design process, the designer creates several possible solutions to a client's design "problem," selecting one of the alternatives as the final solution.

Ambient light
Light that spreads over an entire scene without focusing on any particular object.

Analog proofs
Proofs made from the films that will be used to eventually print the job on a printing press.

Anchor points
In Illustrator and FreeHand, the location that connects two vector paths. See also **Beziér curves**.

Artboard
In a mechanical, the board on which text and graphics were pasted, a process largely replaced by electronic page layout software.

Assets folder
The usual name for the default images folder in Web design software.

Asymmetrical balance
In a design, a structure in which forms on one part of the design are different from the forms in another part of the design, yet the overall design still achieves visual balance.

Attributes
In 3-D applications, characteristics such as height and weight.

Audio
Sound.

Background layer
In a Photoshop document, the one layer that is always present.

Balance
The equal distribution of forms in a design. See also **Symmetrical balance** and **Asymmetrical balance**.

Banner
The area at the top of a Web page with the company name and/or logo; also called a masthead.

Baseline
On a line of type, the location where the bottoms of most letters line up horizontally with each other.

Behavior
In Flash, an action by an object. In Director, actions that you can apply to a sprite, such as moving or changing color.

Berners-Lee, Tim
A programmer who developed the foundation for Hypertext Markup Language (HTML), the programming language that is the foundation of the World Wide Web.

Beziér curves
In vector-draw software, a path made up of **anchor points** and **direction lines**.

Bins
In digital video editing, folders that group content items, such as audio, graphics, and video.

Bitmapped art
Artwork that made up of a series of dots, which vary in value and in color, arranged in a grid; also called **Raster art**.

Bitmapped text
In Director, text you can create that is treated as a graphic so you can add special effects to it, such as warp and distort.

Black-and-white laser prints
Printouts of a document made on a laser printer; the most common digital proofing method available because of its speed and low cost.

Blackletter type
A heavy type style based on Gutenberg's original printing typefaces.

Boolean operations
In 3-D software, operations in which you combine simple forms into more complex forms and unique form combinations, such as union, subtraction, or intersection.

Border thickness
The width of a table border in Web design software.

Brightness
In Flash, one characteristic of an instance.

Browser
See **Web browser**.

Calibrate
To set up a scanning device, monitor, or printer so that it will accurately read color profiles; usually performed by a color management specialist (CMS).

Camera obscura
An ancient camera; a box that used light to project images on the wall of a darkened room.

Camera
In 3-D software, a tool that sets the frame of reference in a view.

Camera-ready art
See **pasteups**.

Cast

In Director, a collection of images, videos, or text you can use in a movie.

Cast member

In Director, a text, video, or graphic in a cast.

CCD

A component of flatbed scanners that are like electronic eyes that capture light in flatbed scanners; stands for **charged coupled devices**.

Cell padding

In Web design software, the space in a table cell between the cell border and the text it contains.

Cell spacing

In Web design software, the space between each cell in a table.

Cell

In Web design software, the intersection of a row and column in a table; in gravure printing, the recessed etched areas on a plate cylinder that takes ink.

CERN

The European Laboratory for Particle Physics, where Tim Berners-Lee, a programmer, developed the foundation for Hypertext Markup Language (HTML), the programming language that is the basis for the World Wide Web.

Chains

In 3-D software, ways of linking different components in 3-D animation to create a working figure or other structured form.

Channel

In Director, an individual timeline for a movie element; in Cinema 4D, levels that let you add multiple levels of material properties.

Character palette

In Illustrator, Photoshop, and InDesign, the palette containing tools that let you change the type style, size, leading, and other type properties.

Chronology

The sequencing of events in time.

Clip

In digital video, a video, still photo, audio, or graphics file that becomes part of your video.

CMYK

See **Process color**.

Collage

A work of art featuring a combination of various objects and materials pasted onto a flat surface.

Collect for output

A QuarkXPress command that assembles all the necessary components of a file for output.

Color (Mixer and Tints palette)

In FreeHand, the palette that lets you create colors and screen tints.

Color laser prints

Printouts that are used to proof color files.

Color management

A process that standardizes color from input devices such as scanners and graphics software using RGB to output devices that use CMYK.

Color mode

In Photoshop, the designation for a color model. See also **Color model**.

Cropping

To hide or delete portions of an image by reducing the size of the frame that contains it.

Color model

How color is described within a system of color reproduction.

Color profile

A setting attached to a file that designates the type of device to which it will be printed. This profile follows the file to every computer system that it may be viewed on, so monitors will display it correctly and printers will print it accurately.

Color

An important design element that helps viewers distinguish or identify objects.

Columns

In page layout software, divisions of the space between margins into a series of vertical spaces to organize type and graphics in the professional manner you often see in newspapers and magazines.

Commenting tools
In Adobe Acrobat, tools that let readers annotate a document, including the tools on the Commenting and Advanced Commenting toolbars.

Comments
In Adobe Acrobat, text that you can embed in a PDF document to communicate with another reader of that document.

Composite output
Printer or imagesetter output that shows all of the page elements in the correct colors and position. See also **Separations**.

Compositing
In digital video, assembling images into the final video.

Composition
An arrangement of forms in space.

Comprehensive
In the design process, an accurate reproduction of potential solutions to a client's problems. If produced manually with markers, these are called "marker comps"; computer-generated comprehensives are called "comps."

Compression
An electronic process used by Adobe Acrobat that "squeezes" all the file information into the smallest digital space possible.

Content
All of the graphics, images, text, video, sound, and animation required to complete a digital media project, including copy, illustrations, and photography.

Contone proofs
Continuous tone proofs that simulate the spi dots used in many newer direct-to-platesetting systems.

Contrast
In a design, the principle that makes one element appear different from the other elements in the design.

Copyright
Laws intended to limit unauthorized use of intellectual property.

Copywriting
The creation of words used in any visual project, such as headlines.

Creativity
The ability to create original solutions, particularly in the field of art.

CSS (Cascading style sheets)
Named collections of formatting characteristics that let Web designers apply consistent formatting to their Web pages.

CSS-based sizings
In Dreamweaver, the sizing of type in pixels, rather than named sizes.

Curved paths
In Illustrator and FreeHand, curved lines composed of anchor points and direction lines.

Define the problem
In the design process, the stage in which the designer or account executive determines what the client needs, such as a brochure or a Web site, as well as the budget and time frame required.

Defined text box
In Flash, a box that exactly matches the size of the text it encloses.

Depth of field
In 3-D media, the variable that determines which images will be in focus and which will not.

Depth
In 3-D design, the third dimension, represented by the z-axis.

Desaturate
To mute a color, such as the effect you can achieve using the Sponge tool in Photoshop.

Descender
In typography, the parts of some letters, such as g, y, and j, that drop below the baseline. See also **Baseline**.

Design elements
The building blocks of any design; they include line, shape, value, color, texture, and space.

Design principles
The rules designers use to organize elements in space; they include balance, proximity, alignment, unity, emphasis, and rhythm.

Design process
The structured methodology that designers follow in creating solutions; the steps include Define the problem, Research the

Project, Create Thumbnails and Roughs, Prepare Comprehensives, and Review and Refine the Design.

Device independent

A characteristic of a file format, such as PDF, that can be opened on any computer running almost any operating system.

Digital camera

A camera that captures photographic images as electronic data rather than on film.

Digital color proof

High-quality color proofs that come in two types, halftone and continuous tone (contone).

Digital proofs

Proofs made from electronic files; includes black-and-white laser, inkjet, color laser, large-format inkjet, and direct color proofs.

Digital video

The use of motion picture-based moving pictures on the computer and on the Web.

Direction lines
See **Beziér curves**.

Document layout

The structure of a document, which you can change in a PDF file using Adobe Acrobat, such as changing the page order, renumbering the pages, and inserting, replacing, or deleting pages.

Download

To get a document or other object from a remote location, such as an FTP site.

dpi (dots per inch)

A method of describing the resolution of digital output from printing devices.

Drum scanner

An electronic image capturing device that uses a drum and PMTs (photo multiplier tubes) to capture images.

Duration

The amount of time it takes to tell the events of the story and the amount of time the story covers.

Dynamic range

The amount of information in a film or video, at a given quality.

Editing

In analog or digital media, cutting and pasting segments in a desired order to create a chronological sequence.

Electronic documents

Documents that are saved as digital information on a disk or other storage device, to preserve the documents and reduce the amount of storage space that paper documents occupy.

Electronic forms

Forms, such as tax forms, that are available over the Internet; people can fill them out either online or on a printed copy of the form.

Electronic publishing

A new area of graphic communications targeted by Adobe Acrobat that lets publishers create magazines, books, and other publications in 100 percent digital form as PDF files. PDF publications save paper and can be distributed anywhere to anyone who owns a computer.

Electronic scanner

A device designed to capture illustrations and photographs electronically. See also **Drum scanner** and **Flatbed scanner**.

Electrostatic printing

A printing process similar to xerography that uses a liquid-based toner made up of superfine particles that create a highly detailed and accurate image.

E-mail

The technology that permits the sending and receiving of electronic messages over the Internet.

E-mail attachments

A document attached to an e-mail message in order to send that document to another person.

Embed

A way of including a graphic in a page layout document that includes the entire image, not just a reference to it; usually increases the size of the page layout document significantly. See also **Link**.

Emphasis

A design principle in which one element of a design is made to look more important that the rest of the elements in that design.

End frame
In Director, the last frame in a sprite's timeline.

Environment
In sound design, the location where a piece of music is played.

Etching
In gravure printing, the process of creating a recessed area on a plate cylinder.

External cast
In Director, separate casts for items, usually grouped by type, such as sounds or a type of graphic; external casts are separate files available to other movies.

External link
On a Web page, links to other Web sites.

Fidelity
In sound design, the connection between sound and story.

Field of view
In 3-D media, the viewing width and height of a scene.

Field text
In Director, a type of low-resolution text that can be downloaded rapidly and viewed on older computers without loss of speed.

File format
The way in which a file is stored on disk, such as .eps, which determines how the file can be used. Page layout software lets you import many different file formats, such as .eps, .tif, and .bmp.

Fill light
In 3-D media, lighting that doesn't create strong shadows.

Fill
The interior area of a shape.

Film
Also called graphic arts film, the material used in photographing artwork; it is used to produce realistic representations of images both in grayscale and in full color.

Firewire
A computer connection that allows for rapid data transfer, it is a name for IEEE 1394; other company names for this technolgy are ilink and Lynx.

Flat shading
In 3-D software, a preview method that applies a color and tone to each polygon on a model's surface.

Flatbed scanner
A scanning device that uses CCDs (charged coupled devices), which are like electronic eyes, to capture the light that is reflected from or shone through an image.

Flexography
A letterpress process that uses plastic or hard rubber printing plates.

Fly-through
In 3-D software, a motion path that moves you through a scene as if you were moving in a car or plane.

Focal point
In a design, the location or element that draws the viewer's eye because it stands out from the rest of the design.

Focoltone system
A color system that lets you select spot colors for printing. See also **Pantone system**, **Toyo system**, and **Trumatch system**.

Focus
In photography, how clearly you can see the images in a scene.

Fonts
Files that a computer accesses to create a type style on a monitor or for printing. There are three major font file formats: Postscript Type 1, TrueType, and OpenType.

Format
In graphics software, the boundaries of a composition; in computer terminology, a file type, such as .eps, .tif, and .gif.

Forward kinematics
In 3-D design, a mechanical motion process in which you describe the required motion for each piece of the model to make the movement work.

Fps (Frames per second)
The speed at which Flash plays back a timeline or Director plays back a score.

Fractal geometry
A procedure in 3-D modeling that samples a small amount of information and creates larger scenes, using geometric principles.

Frame of reference

In photography and design, the angle from which the audience will view a scene's space and how much of the scene they will see.

Frame rate

In Web animation software, the rate at which your animation will run; measured in frames per second (fps).

Frame

In page layout software, a bounding box that encloses an object, usually a graphic; in Web animation software, areas that contain consecutive images; on a Director timeline, a unit representing a small segment of time.

Freeform modeling

In 3-D software, a way of creating complex 3-D forms and molding them into different shapes.

FTP (File Transfer Protocol)

A system that allows computer users to send out (upload to a site) and bring in (download from a site) documents stored on a remote computer, called an FTP site; used for documents that are too large to send as e-mail attachments.

Fundamentals of design

The design principles and elements that designers must know to create effective design solutions.

GIF animations

A series of graphic images that are displayed one right after the other, like a simple cartoon

Gouraud shading

In 3-D modeling, a mathematical technique in which the edges of polygons are averaged together so the colors and textures blend together.

Gradient

A type of fill in which colors or grades of colors flow from one to another.

Graphics link

On a Web page, graphics that Web page users click to display another site.

Gravure

A type of printing press that uses a large metal cylinder and an etched, recessed image area.

Grayscale

The combination of black and white, creating shades of gray. See also **Value**.

Grid

A formalized division of a page into a set pattern of square and rectangular spaces to help visually organize a design.

Guides

Nonprinting lines you can drag onto a page from a ruler that help you align objects on a page.

Gutter

In page layout, the space between columns; also the white space between two facing pages in a book.

Halftone proofs

A type of digital color proof intended to match the dots used on the printing press to provide a highly accurate match to the final printed piece.

Halides

In traditional film, small silver particles that darken upon exposure to light.

Handles

On a path, the end point of a direction line that you can drag to create curved paths.

Hardware RIP

Computer systems that contain all the software necessary to RIP a file. See also **Raster Image Processor**.

Height

The second dimension in 3-D space, represented by the y-axis.

Hexidecimal system

A way of designating Web-safe colors that uses three pairs of letters and/or numbers in a six-character name to represent the makeup of that color.

Highlight

In many types of software, to select text or an object before applying a characteristic to it, usually by dragging across it with the mouse pointer.

Homepage

The main navigational page of a Web site and usually the first page that appears when users link to a Web site.

HTML
Short for Hypertext Markup Language, the programming language used to create pages for the World Wide Web.

HTML-based sizings
In Dreamweaver, seven type sizes, ranging from xx-small to xx-large.

HTTP (hypertext-transfer protocol)
A network protocol developed by Tim Berners-Lee that connected collections of hyperlinked pages at different locations on the Internet.

HyperCard
The first application with multimedia capabilities.

HyperTalk
The programming language used by the HyperCard application.

I

Illustrators
Artists who create drawings, paintings, or other types of hand-drawn or electronically generated art specifically for design projects.

Image assembly
In traditional printing, the process printers used to combine large amounts of film for the printing press.

Imagesetter
Machines that output graphic arts film that is then used to expose printing plates.

Import
To bring a document created in a source program into the current program, such as importing a Photoshop image into a QuarkXPress document.

index.htm
The filename Web page designers usually assign to a site's home page.

Inkjet printing
A printing process that uses small nozzles to spray ink onto a page; can produce highly accurate results.

Insertion point
In many software types, the blinking cursor that indicates where typed text will be inserted next.

Instance
In Flash, one use of a symbol (a representation of a graphic) in an animation.

Intensity
In time design, the amount of perceived or actual energy in a particular scene.

Interactivity
Where the viewer interacts with an on-screen presentation.

Interface
The design or look of software, including its menus, commands, and dialog boxes.

Internal cast
In Director, a cast that is part of the current file. See also **External cast**.

Internal link
On a Web page, links that link to the same page or site.

Internet Explorer
The most popular Web browser program on Windows computers.

Interpolate
To average together. See also **Gouraud shading**.

Intersection
In 3-D modeling, a Boolean operation in which two forms are combined and the overlap is saved, and the rest of the forms are deleted.

Inverse kinematics
In 3-D design, a mechanical motion process in which you start a movement at one end of a chain, and the rest of the chain reacts to it and creates the necessary motion without having to be told what to do.

Italic
A type style in which letters are slanted to the right.

J

Java
A programming language used to create compact applications that users can run in conjunction with a Web browser.

Keyframe
In Flash and Director, a specific frame along the timeline in which you designate an event to occur.

Kinematics
The science of motion. See also **Forward kinematics** and **Inverse kinematics**.

Kiosk
A computer in a free-standing information center, usually at a public location, such as a trade show or store.

Kodak camera
The camera first developed in 1888 that allowed non-photographers to photograph the world around them.

Landscape
See **Orientation**.

Large-format inkjet prints
Output created on machines that use highly accurate ink systems and can print to large formats, usually 24" to 48" wide; they can also print rolls many feet in length.

Layer effects
In Photoshop, effects achieved by manipulating a graphic's layers.

Layering order
In Photoshop, the stacking order of layers on the Layers palette.

Layers palette
In Photoshop, the area that lets you add, delete, or duplicate layers.

Layers
In Photoshop, Flash, and other programs, multiple "levels" on which you can place parts of a drawing so you can more easily manage the image parts.

Leading
The vertical space between lines of type.

Letterpress printing
An output method that uses a raised image area on a plate called the image area; the recessed part was the nonimage area.

Library
In Flash, the location where you store your symbols.

Light
Illumination that either defines, adds to, or subtracts from a viewed object's volume or mass; can also add to a form's emotional quality.

Line length
The horizontal dimension of lines of type on a page.

Line
The most basic design element, it has four properties: length, width, style, and color.

Lingo
A Director programming language that lets advanced users program interactive effects.

Link
In page layout software, a connection that exists between the page layout document and the original graphic, (sometimes called the source graphic); also, the connection between text boxes that allows type to flow from one text box to another when one box is resized; in 3-D animation, linking component pieces so an application can calculate how to add movement.

Lithographic printing
An output process that uses chemicals and the process of water and ink not mixing to create an image on a printing plate

Local root folder
In a Web site, the folder that the application searches to find and display all site content.

Lossy
A characteristic of an image whereby it loses quality when you open and resave it.

lpi (lines per inch)
A method of describing the resolution of an image for printing; the number of rows (lines) of dots measured left-to-right and top-to-bottom.

Macromedia Flash Player
A free program that lets users view a Flash animation.

Margins
The border of white space around the edge of a page.

Marker
In Director, indicators that target a specific frame.

Marking engine
On an imagesetter or platesetter, the exposure and processing unit that contains a laser that exposes either film or plate material under the control of the RIP computer.

Mass
The amount of matter in a 3-D form, generally one made of a substance, such as stone, wood, or clay.

Masthead
On a Web page, another name for a banner.

Mechanicals
See **Pasteups**.

Media
In printing, the type of material on which a project is printed, such as envelopes or letter-sized paper.

Modes
In Flash, variations of a tool.

Monitor proofing
Proofing files on a computer monitor instead of on expensive output devices.

Motion paths
In 3-D modeling, a three-dimensional path that a model follows through a scene.

Motion tween
In Flash, an animated effect you apply to create motion.

Motion
Movement, an aspect of time, the fourth dimension of design.

Motion-capture
A technique used to create complex motion in 3-D animation, in which a human subject is filmed, and then the animator uses it as a guide to create more accurate motion.

Movie properties
In Director, the characteristics of a movie that you can set, such as the stage size or color model.

Multimedia
The use of two or more media on the computer, including designs, images, video, and sound.

Navigation buttons
On a Web page, the buttons users click to activate hyperlinks that display other Web pages or other portions of the current page.

Negative space
The area around a form where no forms reside.

Netscape
A popular Web browser for both Windows and Macintosh computers.

Network
A group of connected computers that can communicate with each other.

Nondestructive
A characteristic of video editing software, meaning that you don't destroy your original videos when editing them.

Nonimage area
In letterpress printing, the recessed part of a printing plate that is not inked.

Nonlinear
In video editing, the ability to edit clips in any order you wish.

Nonplate-based (nonimpact) printing
Printing technologies that do not rely on plates or impact, including xerography, electrostatic, and inkjet technologies.

Nonproportional
A method of resizing an image that distorts the image.

NTSC (National Television System Committee)
The broadcast standard for the United States and North America.

NURBS (Non-Uniform Rational B-Splines)
In 3-D modeling, a spline-based system used by several 3-D applications.

Objects
Forms created by vector-draw software, in contrast to pixels, which comprise bit-mapped images; vector-draw objects can be easily reshaped to create other forms.

Oblique
A letter posture similar to italic but referring to sans serif fonts.

Offset lithography
A printing technology that features several cylinders that use ink and water to offset an inked image from one cylinder to another.

OpenType
Font files that can be used on either operating system, which makes moving and reading graphics files between the two operating systems much easier and more accurate; developed by Adobe and Microsoft in 1999.

Optimize
In Web design, to prepare images to be displayed quickly and correctly on the Web.

Ordered list
In Web design software, a numbered list.

Orientation
The layout of a document, either Portrait, with the longer page dimension on the sides, or Landscape, with the longer dimension along the top and bottom of the document.

Orthographic projection
A technique that accurately represents a form's structure: the six sides of an object (top, bottom, front, back, left side, and right side) are projected around the object on an imaginary cube, creating a three-dimensional representation of the form.

Output mode
A printing specification that determines how your document will print; see **Composite output** and **Separations**.

Page layout software
Software, such as QuarkXPress and InDesign, that lets you assemble text and graphics easily on a page.

PAL (Phase Alternating Line)
The broadcast standard for Europe and many other parts of the world.

Palette
In Director, the color model you will use in your movie.

Panning
In 3-D media, a camera motion that follows a model through a scene.

Pantone system
Also called the Pantone Matching System (PMS), a color system that lets you select spot colors. See also **Focoltone system**, **Toyo system**, and **Trumatch system**.

Paragraph Composer
A feature of Adobe InDesign that uses a technology that attempts to re-create a visually pleasing texture in large blocks of type.

Paragraph formatting
A feature of word processing and page layout software that lets you modify paragraph settings such as left indent, right indent, first line indent, space before, and space after for entire paragraphs.

Particle systems
A 3-D technique in which a program can recreate smoke, rain, or dust from a small amount of random information.

Pasteups
Pieces of illustration board with graphics and type manually pasted on them. A printer photographs them to produce film; also called **mechanicals** and **camera-ready art**.

Paths
See **Vector paths**.

Perspective drawing
A drawing that is an accurate representation of a form in space.

Phong shading
In 3-D graphics, a rendering technique that achieves a high level of accuracy and detail.

Photography
Creating visual imagery through the use of a camera.

Pitch
How high or low a sound is.

Pixels
Also called picture elements, a series of dots that compose bitmapped graphic images.

Place
The process of importing various raster and vector images into a file.

Plate burner
In lithographic printing, a device that shoots high intensity light at a piece of film and an unexposed plate. The clear image areas of the film would allow the light to expose the plate coating (hardening it).

Plate-based (impact) printing
A printing technology that uses a printing plate to transfer an image to paper; the plate impacts, or presses against, the paper to make the transfer. Includes letterpress, off-set lithography, gravure, and screen printing.

Platesetter
A device that outputs printing plates directly from electronic files without the need for film.

Playhead
In Flash and video editing, marks the location from which an animation or video will play.

Plug-ins
Small software programs that add additional capabilities to an application.

PMT (Photomultiplier tubes)
In drum scanners, a stationary tube that scans an image and collects image information in electronic form.

Point
A measurement unit for type, strokes, and leading that equals 1/72 of an inch.

Polygon mesh
Polygons that are connected in a 3-D modeling application.

Polygon
Multisided shapes that are connected in a 3-D modeling application.

Portable Document Format (PDF)
The format used by the Adobe Acrobat software, this format creates documents that can be opened and read on any computer using almost any operating system.

Portrait
See **Orientation**.

Positive images
A form that appears in a space; the area with no forms is called negative space.

PostScript Type 1
A type of font developed by Adobe in 1984; used on both Windows and Macintosh computers.

PostScript
The page description language that tells a computer or an output device how an electronic file is suppose to look and output.

PowerPoint
Part of the Microsoft Office Suite, a program that has some multimedia capabilities.

ppi (pixels per inch)
A measurement unit of resolution for electronic dots on computer screens and electronic devices such as a scanner or printer.

Preferred 3-D Renderer
In Director, a movie property that lets you choose the best 3-D rendering method for your computer hardware.

Preflight
The process of checking a file, usually performed by a printer, to make sure all linked graphics and fonts have been included.

Preview
To view a Web page in several browsers.

Primitives
Basic three-dimensional geometric shapes, such as pyramids and donuts, supplied with a 3-D application.

Print dialog box
In most software, the area that lets you select a printer, the number of copies, media choices, scaled outputs, and output modes.

Print film
A technology for capturing and printing images.

Printed proof
A printout of a document, used to check its content and layout; see also **Monitor proofing**.

Printer selection
In a Print dialog box, the section that lets you choose the printer you want to use.

Printing plates
A metal, rubber, or plastic material on which an image or group of images are exposed; the plate is then used to print the project on a printing press.

Procedural modeling
A 3-D modeling technique that uses complex formulas to take into account such processes as how nature creates a forest of trees or how tornadoes develop from a storm.

Process cameras
Specialized cameras that printers use to photograph artwork for reproduction on a printing press.

Process color
A color model in which four colors—cyan, magenta, yellow, and black—are printed one on top of the other to produce other colors; also called **CMYK color model**.

Production team
A group of artists, programmers, and other specialists working together to produce a project.

Production
Before computers, the process of converting hand-drawn comprehensives into film for printing; now, the process of preparing electronic files for printing.

Programmers
Members of a production team who use the programming languages used on the Web and in other digital media applications.

Progressive rhythm
See **Rhythm**.

Project Settings
In video editing software, settings that match up the input device and output file specifications based on broadcast industry standards for video.

Project
In digital video editing, a collection of files.

Projector file
A self-contained, self-running version of a Director movie that shows all the elements and actions you have created on the stage.

Proof
A laser or inkjet output copy, created by a designer or production person.

Proofing process
A process, starting during the design phase, of printing test copies to check the document; most proofs today are digitally produced.

Properties palette
In FreeHand, the tool collection that lets you change type properties, including the type style, size, and leading.

Proportional
A method of resizing an image that does not distort the image.

Prototype
A working version of a digital media project.

Proximity
In a design, the grouping of elements according to criteria such as content, shape, or color.

Proxy
In a page layout document, a placeholder image that represents a linked graphic that resides outside of the page layout file.

Quicktime
A movie file format commonly used for CD presentations as well as on the Web.

Raster artwork
See **Bitmapped art**.

Raster Image Processor (RIP)
A software application that translates a graphics file into dots so that it can be output to film or to printing plates, or printed on a digital printing device.

Ray tracing
In 3-D modeling, a rendering technique that can recreate color and light as you see it in the real world by calculating how light will reflect off of a form based on its shape and the materials from which the form is made.

Realtime renderings
In 3-D applications, a type of preview in which the software creates a low resolution preview that shows some basic details.

Regular text
In Director, text like that you would create using a word processor.

Relative link
A link to a location in the current Web site.

Render the Timeline
In digital video software, a procedure that lets you view your video with transitions.

Render

The final process after you have completed a model or animation, like taking a final picture of a project.

Research the project

In the design process, the stage in which the designers explore the subject area for which they are designing to learn as much as possible, which will markedly improve the quality of possible solutions they create.

Resolution dependent

A characteristic of bitmapped images in which the quality of the image depends on the number of pixels per inch; the more pixels per square inch, the higher the image quality.

Resolution independent

A characteristic of images based on vector paths, in which the quality of the image depends on mathematically calculated vector paths, allowing them to be enlarged without loss of quality.

Resolution

The number of dots that make up an image. See also **lpi**, **spi**, **dpi**, and **ppi**.

Review tools

Adobe Acrobat tools you can use to mark up a document in PDF format, such as the Text Edits tool, the Highlighter tool, as well as the Show, Shape, and Text Box tools.

Review

In Adobe Acrobat, to go through a PDF document and mark it using Reviewing tools, such as the Text Edits tool and the Highlighter tool.

RGB

A color model that uses the three primary additive colors: red, green, and blue.

Rhythm

In a graphic design, the use of repeating elements to create visual movement. Rhythm is called **progressive rhythm** if the repetitions are in equal amounts; it is called **alternating rhythm** if the repetitions are in unequal amounts. In sound design, the cadence of a sound.

Rough cuts

Prototypes of videos and animations, that show the project as it would appear in the final presentation.

Rough

In the design process, a tighter, more visually refined representation of a single thumbnail concept.

Rubber banding

In digital video editing, fine-tuning the volume of a sound clip by dragging controls.

Rule

A line, like one drawn with a pen or with a Line tool.

Ruler guide

See **Guide**.

Rulers

Measurement tools on the top and the left side of a graphics application window that help you position objects and from which you can drag ruler guides onto the page.

Safari

A popular Web browser for the Macintosh computer.

Sans serif typefaces

Typefaces in which the letter strokes have a consistent width and do not have serifs (small tick marks) on the letters.

Saturate

To heighten the color of an image, such as with the Sponge tool in Photoshop.

Save

To transfer a document from a computer's random access memory to a permanent storage device.

Scale

To enlarge or reduce an object.

Scan files

An Adobe Acrobat option that lets you scan documents into PDF file.

Scope

In time design, the overall breadth of ideas and events being presented.

Score panel

In Director, another name for the score.

Score

In Director, the working area where you add cast members to make them part of the movie as sprites.

Screen printing

A plate-based printing process that uses a fine mesh plastic, metal, or silk screen and a light-sensitive stencil to print images.

Screen tints
A printer technique that takes a solid color and breaks it into a series of dots of uniform size and spacing.

Select/selection
In many types of software, to highlight text or an object before applying a characteristic to it, usually by dragging across it with the mouse pointer.

Separations
In print media software, an output mode in which each color is printed on a separate page, simulating how the file will output to film or printing plates.

Serif typefaces
Typefaces in which the letter strokes have varying widths and serifs (small tick marks) are present on the letters.

Setting
A project's physical location and all its visual and other physical aspects, including the wardrobe, props, and historical references.

Shading
In 3-D modeling, a technique that adds color, texture, patterns, or the effect of materials on the surface of a three-dimensional object.

Shapes
The visual forms that designers use to build designs; the most basic shapes are the circle, the square, and the triangle.

Shockwave Player
A plug-in that allows a browser to play Director movies over the Internet.

Single-track editing
In digital video editing, an editing method in which the video clips and the transitions are laid out in one continuous line on one track.

Site folder
A folder that contains all the content for a Web site.

Site layout
In Web page design, a sketch of each page arranged in a tree diagram.

Software RIP
See **Raster Image Processor**.

Source code
The HTML code that underlies a Web page.

Source graphic
In a page layout document, the original graphic that is linked.

Space
The area or void into which designers place forms.

Special effects
In graphics software, effects that can be applied to objects, such as shadow, feathered edges, and transparency.

spi (spots per inch)
A measurement of resolution for electronic dots on computer screens and electronic devices such as a scanner or a printer.

Spline
In 3-D modeling, the wires that make up a three-dimensional wireframe of an object with control points that you can adjust to create the required shape.

Spline-based modeling
A 3-D modeling technique in which a spline's control points are dragged to change an object's shape.

Spot colors
Ink colors that have been mixed to a specific hue. The most common type of spot color is the Pantone Matching System.

Spot light
In 3-D photography and design, light that creates a strong focus on one form or area within a scene, often creating strong shadows.

Sprite
On the Director stage, a reference to a cast member.

Square serif type
A type style that features blocky, square corners; also called slab serif.

Stack
In HyperCard, a collection of electronic cards with fields containing text, graphics, and navigation buttons.

Stage
The Flash and Director work area.

Static text
In Flash, text with no specific behavior applied

Stencil
In screen printing, a light-sensitive material applied to a screen; when exposed to light, the image area remains soft and is washed away, allowing ink to go through it during printing.

Stock photography and video
Prerecorded photography and video files on various subjects that can be purchased.

Stop action
In Flash, a feature that causes an animation to stop after the first play-through.

Storyboard
A scene-by-scene presentation of how a motion graphics project will progress.

Storytelling
Communicating the story in a project.

Straight paths
A stroke with no curves between anchor points.

Stroke
A line's thickness, color, line style, or texture.

Style sheets
A feature of word processing and page layout software that lets you define type styles for any document element, such as headlines, subheads, body copy, bulleted type, and photo taglines, and that help you define, organize, and apply almost any combination of text formatting attributes, including size, leading, color, formatting, and alignment.

Subdivision surface modeling
In 3-D modeling, a freeform modeling technique that combines polygon-based and spline-based techniques.

Subscript
Text that is smaller and slightly below the baseline.

Subtraction
A 3-D modeling technique where two forms are combined and the area where the two forms overlap plus one of the forms are subtracted (deleted) from the other form.

Superscript
Text that is smaller and slightly above the baseline.

Surface modeling
See **Subdivision surface modeling**.

Swatches palette
In Illustrator and InDesign, the palette that allows you to create colors and screen tints.

Symbol
In Flash, a representation of a graphic that can be used over and over again.

Symmetrical balance
A design structure in which the position of forms on one side of the design matches the position of forms on the other side.

Table
On a Web page, a way of organizing content in columns and rows.

Tangents
In spline-based modeling, handles that are dragged to change a form's shape.

Target
In 3-D software, the location on which the camera is focused.

Tempo
In a digital media presentation, the speed at which time passes; controlled by both the events being recorded and the individual recording the event. In Director, the speed at which the score plays back.

Test Movie
A temporary Flash movie file that previews your animation in a separate window.

Text box
In QuarkXPress and InDesign documents, a placeholder for text on a page.

Text indent
In Web design software, increasing the distance of text from the margin.

Text link
Text on a Web page that user clicks to display another Web page or another location on the same page.

Text outdent
In Web design software, decreasing the distance of text from the margin.

Texture shading
A 3-D modeling technique in which you import a bitmapped image of a material or texture and wrap it around a three-dimensional form.

Texture
A surface pattern that gives the impression that an object has a particular tactile feel.

Three-dimensional space
Space defined by its width (the x-axis), height (the y-axis), and depth (the z-axis).

Thumbnails
Small, fast sketches that the designer uses to explore a number of potential solution to a client's design problem. A designer typically creates many thumbnails and then discards all but the few best ones.

Tile
A method of printing a document in which different parts of the file print at actual size on separate sheets of paper.

Time design
The design of the duration, tempo, intensity, scope, setting, and chronology of events in a digital presentation.

Timeline
In Flash, the area of the screen that shows the structure of your project; in Director, an area of the screen where you manipulate the frames of your movie.

Tint
Color, one of the four instance variables you can change.

Toolbar
In graphics software, the palette that contains the tools you use to create, modify, and move graphics and type in your project.

Toolbox
In Photoshop, the screen area that is divided into four main areas: selection tools, modification tools, vector/type tools, and miscellaneous tools. QuarkXPress and InDesign have similar tools.

Toyo system
A color system that lets you select spot colors. See also **Focoltone system**, **Pantone system**, and **Trumatch system**

Tracking
In 3-D applications, following a model as it moves through a scene.

Transform
In vector-draw software, to modify an object using a tool such as the Scale tool or the Rotate tool.

Transitions
In video editing, effects that allow for a visual change from one video clip to another video clip in your project.

Transparency
A characteristic you can apply to layers that allows the viewer to see through whatever is on the layer.

Transparency film
In film-based photography, the type of film used to create slides.

TrueType
A font type developed to run on both Macintosh and Windows operating systems; Postscript and TrueType font files on a Macintosh cannot be used on a Windows computer, and vice versa.

Trumatch system
A color system that lets you select spot colors. See also **Focoltone system**, **Toyo system**, and **Pantone system**.

Tweening
In a Flash animation, the ability of the software to fill in intermediate frames in an animation.

Type posture
A characteristic of type, including italic and oblique.

Type size
The height of type, measured in points.

Type style
The design and shape of letterforms.

Type tool cursor
Also called the insertion point, the blinking bar that indicates where typed text will appear.

Type
In a document, letters, numbers, or symbols.

U

Union
In creating complex 3-D forms with Boolean operations, combining two forms into a more complex form.

Unity
A design principle in which similar elements in a design "work together" visually.

Unordered list
In Web design, a bulleted list.

Upload speed
The time it takes for a file to transmit from your computer to another location, such as an FTP site.

Upload
To send out over the Internet, such as to place a file on an FTP site.

Value
The use of various shades of gray; also called **grayscale**.

Vector paths
In vector-draw software, mathematical points connected by paths that plot out the edge of an image.

Vector-draw software
Software, such as Adobe Illustrator and Macromedia FreeHand, that create drawings through the use of vector paths.

Video tape
A digital recording medium which was a lower-quality, lower-cost alternative to high-quality movie film.

Viewing plane
In using the 3-D software camera tool, a rectangular viewing window that defines the cropping of a scene.

Viewport
In 3-D software, a way of reviewing your project that lets you work in different viewing modes at the same time.

Volume
An enclosed area of space, such as a cone or a sphere.

Warp Text effect
In Photoshop and Illustrator, a type effect you can use to distort text in various shapes.

Web animation
The creation, design, and production of graphics that incorporate motion on a Web page.

Web browser
Software that allowed computers to display the content of an HTML-programmed Web page with text and pictures instead of lines of code.

Web design
The creation, design, and production of pages that are intended for display on the World Wide Web.

Web pages
An option in Adobe Acrobat that lets you download Web pages in PDF format.

Web-safe colors
A series of RGB-based colors that appears the same on any computer using any browser.

Wire frame
In 3-D modeling, a preview method that doesn't show surface modeling, textures, or colors.

WYSIWYG
Acronym for "What You See Is What You Get," a concept that indicates that what viewers see on the screen is reasonably close to the printed version of the same document.

x-, y-, and z-axes
On a computer, the representations of width, height, and depth in a 3-D design.

x-coordinate
In graphics software, the measurement that indicates the horizontal location of an object in a space.

Xerography
A photocopier system.

y-coordinate
In graphics software, the measurement that indicates the vertical location of an object in a space.

Zoom
In many types of software, the ability to "move in" to get a closer look at a document.